Visual Basic .NET
Threading Handbook

Kourosh Ardestani
Fabio Claudio Ferracchiati
Sandra Gopikrishna
Tejaswi Redkar
Srinivasa Sivakumar
Tobin Titus

Wrox Press Ltd. ®

Visual Basic .NET Threading Handbook

© 2002 Wrox Press

First published June 2002

Published by Wrox Press Ltd,
Arden House, 1102 Warwick Road, Acocks Green,
Birmingham, B27 6BH
United Kingdom
Printed in the United States
ISBN 1-861007-13-2

Trademark Acknowledgments

Credits

Authors
Kourosh Ardestani
Fabio Claudio Ferracchiati
Sandra Gopikrishna
Tejaswi Redkar
Srinivasa Sivakumar
Tobin Titus

Additional Material
Andrew Polshaw

Technical Reviewers
Richard Bonneau
Mark Horner
Craig McQueen
Erick Sgarbi
David Whitney

Technical Editors
Nick Manning
Daniel Maharry

Commissioning Editor
Andrew Polshaw

Managing Editor
Jan Kolasinski

Project Manager
Beckie Stones

Production & Layout
Abbie Forletta
Sarah Hall

Index
Michael Brinkman

Proof Reader
Chris Smith

Cover
Natalie O'Donnell

About the Authors

Kourosh Ardestani

Kourosh specializes in building effective data-driven internet solutions based on the .NET platform. He has been working with ASP.NET and other .NET technologies since the very first release of the .NET runtime. He has a B.Sc. in information and computer science with a minor in business management in addition to being an MCSD, MCSE, MCDBA, MCSA along with various other prominent IT certifications. He's also the three-time winner of the ACM programming challenge. When not working with computers, he enjoys reading, playing music, and watching nature shows.

I want to thank Andrew Polshaw whose persistence and concerted effort made this book a reality.

I would like to acknowledge and express my sincere gratitude to all the great minds that lived before us who strived and persevered through countless impediments to make this world of ours a better place through their positive contributions. We are all forever indebted to your efforts.

Fabio Claudio Ferracchiati

Fabio Claudio Ferracchiati is a software developer and technical writer. In the early years of his ten-year career he worked with classical languages and 'old' Microsoft tools like Visual Basic and Visual C++. After five years he decided to dedicate his attention to the Internet and all the related technologies. In 1998 he started a parallel career writing technical articles for Italian and international magazines. He works in Rome for CPI Progetti Spa (http://www.cpiprogetti.it), where he develops Internet/Intranet solutions using Microsoft technologies. Fabio would like to thank Wrox for the chance to write this book.

> *Dedication to Danila: As in every book I write and will write, a special thank you goes to my unique love. You can't imagine how is important to have a woman like her near me in the happy and sad moments that life gives to us. I love you so much...*

Sandra Gopikrishna

Sandra Gopikrishna is a Technical Specialist with Infosys Technologies Limited, Chennai. He has a strong passion for Microsoft.NET technologies and enjoys sharing his knowledge through MSDN forums and various web sites like ASPToday.com, CSharpToday.com, dotnet101.com and pinpub.com. He has been awarded the Microsoft Asia Most Valuable Professional for his contribution towards .NET technologies. He spends his free time reading, listening to music, and making friends. Gopikrishna can be reached at s_gopikrishna@hotmail.com.

> *I would like to thank my family members for their continuous encouragement and support. My special thanks to Balaji Venkatesan (Project Manager, Infosys, Chennai), Kunal Sikka (Community Specialist, Microsoft, India) and Srinivasa Sivakumar, who introduced me to Wrox. Last but not least, I would like to thank Beckie Stones and Andrew Polshaw of Wrox Press for giving me a chance to share my knowledge.*

Tejaswi Redkar

Tejaswi Redkar is a software evangelist. He holds a Master's degree in Engineering from San Jose State University, California. His areas of interest include designing scalable multi-tiered distributed applications and new generation embedded devices. Recently he filed a patent for his innovations in managing telemetry gateways. When he is not working he can be found eating exotic food.

I would like to thank Wrox Press for giving me the opportunity to express my ideas through articles. I would also like to thank my dear wife Arohi for continuing to motivate me.

Srinivasa Sivakumar

Srinivasa Sivakumar is a software consultant, developer and writer. He specializes in web and mobile technologies using Microsoft solutions. He currently works at Chicago for TransTech, LLC. He has co-authored various books, including *Professional ASP.NET Web Services, ASP.NET Mobile Controls – Tutorial Guide*, .NET Compact Framework, *Beginning ASP.NET 1.0 with VB.NET, Professional ASP.NET Security, The Complete Visual C# Programmer's Reference Guide*, and *.NET Compact Framework*. He has also written technical articles for ASPToday.com, CSharpToday.com, .NET Developer, and more. In his free time he likes to watch Tamil movies and listen to Tamil sound tracks (especially one's sung by Mr. S.P Balasubramaniyam).

Tobin Titus

Tobin has several years of experience in software development and in the consulting industry. He started working with BASIC in the 5th grade on an Atari 800XL computer. With the release of Visual Basic, Tobin moved to Windows programming and has been developing Windows and web-based solutions ever since. Tobin specializes in internet applications solutions with Visual Basic, Java, and now Microsoft .NET tools – VB.NET, C#, and ASP.NET. He is also authoring the BrainBench certification exam on Visual Basic .NET (www.brainbench.com). Currently, Tobin does work for some of the best companies in the world including his own – Dax Software and Consulting, LLC (www.daxsoftware.com).

Thanks go to everyone who has supported me in my career. To the staff at Bethel Christian High School in Pennsylvania and Bob Jones University in South Carolina, thank you for your unfailing faith and uncompromising positions. Thanks go to Carol, for putting up with my never-ending work schedule. Special thanks to my parents who sacrificed so much for our family. And a special loving memory to my Grandmother Helm who was always able to encourage me to do better with just a simple hug – and maybe a little taste of fudge!

VB.NET

Threading

Handbook

Table of
Contents

Table of Contents

VB.NET

Threading

Handbook

Introduction

Introduction

Multithreaded applications are those that appear to be performing numerous tasks at the same time. Rather than going from start to finish in a `Main()` method, and the methods fired from within this method, the application will execute code in a completely different order, and that order is mostly defined by the operating system. Concurrent applications are written in different ways depending on the platform and the operating system, giving varying control over this process. VB 6, for instance, gave you no control, and it would implement threading behind the scenes, so that when an event occurred, such as a button click, it would run the relevant method in an apartment thread, which essentially provided a copy of the resources available to the application. The .NET Framework has made available, to Visual Basic programmers, a full and powerful threading model, that allows you to control exactly what runs in a thread, when the thread exits, and how much data it should have access to.

This book will teach you how to take advantage of the threading capabilities provided by the .NET Framework, guiding you through the various features made available to you, while pointing out pitfalls for you to avoid. The .NET Framework provides a completely different threading model, Free Threading, which may take some getting used to if you are only familiar with the apartment model of VB 6.

As a developer, perhaps you need to create an application that never or rarely waits while processing some data, and is permanently available to respond to users and events. This can only happen if you build a multithreaded application. You can find many articles on the Web, and chapters in other books that tell you how to create a thread with the .NET Framework and how to perform some rudimentary operations; however, implementing the code is only half of the story. When you are using a multithreaded application, the type of operations that would normally block your application, such as file system operations, and so are ideal candidates for threading, are the kinds of operations that could produce synchronization or scalability issues, as more than one thread could be operating on the same file at the same time. This book, apart from teaching you how to create and manipulate threads, teaches you how to design your application so that you can avoid many of these issues; applying the appropriate kind of lock, and not blocking a thread while it waits for some other operation to complete.

Book Outline

Below is a detailed outline of what this book covers chapter by chapter.

Chapter 1 – Defining Threads

In this chapter, we go back to first principles and define what a thread is and what happens in a multitasking operation. By clarifying the terms used in this book, it will give you a better understanding of what is going on under the hood when you create a multithreaded application. We also define **AppDomains** – a concept introduced with the .NET Framework, which helps to provide some basic security and protection for your threads and applications, by allowing data to be shared easily only within the same AppDomain.

Chapter 2 – Threading in .NET

In this chapter, we show how to create a thread in .NET, using the ThreadStart delegate, and setting the priority of a thread. We also cover a straightforward way of performing a threaded task by using Timers to schedule a thread to execute at some regular interval. After this, we cover the traps behind threads, and so describe when you should consider using a thread, as inappropriate use could cause your system resources to deplete, or your application to block.

Chapter 3 – Working with Threads

Here is where we actually get to the finer details of implementing threads in your application, describing how to perform locking, implement monitors, and generally make your application thread safe. This topic is known as **synchronization**, and it can be implemented in many different ways. We cover such topics as **mutexes**, synchronization using events, and thread synchronization with shared fields. At the end of this chapter, we walk you through the creation of a database connection pool and thread safe wrapper, which use threads and the synchronization techniques described earlier in this chapter.

Chapter 4 – Design Patterns

This chapter ties together the practice with the theory, explaining the models in which the .NET Framework operates, and the kinds of theoretical models your threaded application can fit into, along with how to implement them, and the traps of which you should be aware. This is by no means an exhaustive chapter on this topic, as large academic tomes have been written on this topic, but it provides you a good grounding in the design issues involved.

Chapter 5 – Scaling Threaded Applications

This chapter covers two main topics. First, we cover the `ThreadPool` class, which contains a fixed number of threads that your application can make use of to save the overhead of the creation and destruction of threads. We cover how and when to make use of this pool, before mentioning the benefits of SMP. The second part of the chapter describes the creation of a thread management class, that will allow you to manage the number of threads you create in your application, and handle the queuing of threads when you hit the maximum number of threads specified in its constructor. This will shield much of the work involved in managing threads, and allow you to concentrate on the application.

Chapter 6 – Debugging and Tracing Threads

Because you can have numerous threads, all of them operating concurrently, using what should be the same data, it can prove very difficult to debug a multithreaded application when something goes wrong. Visual Studio .NET, and the `System.Diagnostics` namespace, provide various features to allow you to follow the execution of your threads. In this chapter, we describe how to make use of these features, and how to monitor the performance of your application.

Chapter 7 – Networking and Threading

In this final chapter, we bring everything together to show the creation of a threaded application that makes use of asynchronous method calls. This chapter demonstrates asynchronous operations in action within threads and walks you through the creation of a client server application that is always available for requests from the user, and the network.

What You Need to Know

This is not a beginner's guide. The authors expect you to already be a proficient .NET Framework programmer. Knowledge of Visual Basic .NET would be useful, as the code used is entirely in this language. You may already have some knowledge of threading, and we refer to the older VB 6 apartment-threaded model, but prior knowledge of threading in .NET or otherwise is not a prerequisite for this book.

This book should enable you to be confident in creating multithreaded, concurrent applications that make effective use of the available resources. Knowledge of threading within .NET is essential for you to create worthwhile and scalable enterprise applications.

Andrew Polshaw
Editor – Visual Basic .NET Handbook Series

VB.NET

Threading

Handbook

1

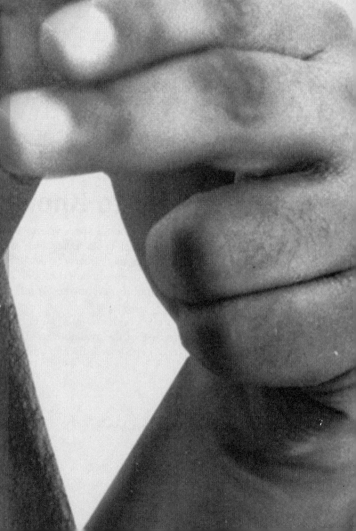

Defining Threads

Threading describes the ability of a development framework to spin off parts of an application into 'threads', which run out of step with the rest of the program. In most programming languages, you have the equivalent of a Sub Main(), and each line is executed in sequence, with the next line executing only after the previous has completed. A thread is a special object that is part of the general multitasking abilities of an operating system, which allows parts of the application to run independently of the execution of others, and so out of the general **execution sequence** of the application. We later discuss the different types of multitasking as well.

A new concept is that of **free threading**, which is completely new for most Visual Basic developers; we will define this term and further explain the support provided in Visual Basic .NET. We will briefly compare this free-threading model to Visual Basic 6.0's apartment-threading model. We won't dwell on the differences for too long since this isn't a history lesson. However, understanding what sets these models apart will help you to understand why free-threading was one of the most requested and most anticipated features in Visual Basic .NET. This chapter's concepts are essential to your understanding of the remainder of this book, as you will learn:

- ❑ What a thread is, conceptually
- ❑ Some comparisons between various multitasking and threading models
- ❑ Where threads exist and how they are allocated processor time
- ❑ How threads are controlled and managed using interrupts and priorities
- ❑ The concept of application domains, and how they provide finer grained control on the security of your application than that provided in a simple process environment

By understanding many of the concepts of threading and how they are structured in .NET, you will be better placed to make programming decisions on how to implement these features in your applications, before learning the details of implementation as provided in the rest of the book.

Threading Defined

By the end of this section, you will understand the following:

❑   What multitasking is and what the different types of multitasking are

❑   What a process is

❑   What a thread is

❑   What a primary thread is

❑   What a secondary thread is

Multitasking

As you probably know, the term **multitasking** refers to an operating system's ability to run more than one application at a time. For instance, while this chapter is being written, Microsoft Outlook is open as well as two Microsoft Word windows. Additionally, the system tray shows additional applications running in the background. When clicking back and forth between applications, it would appear that all of them are executing at the same time. The word "application" is a little vague here, though; what we really are referring to are processes. We will define the word "process" a little more clearly later in this chapter.

Classically speaking, multitasking actually exists in two different flavors. These days Windows uses only one style in threading, which we will discuss at length in this book. However, we will also look at the previous type of multitasking so we can understand the differences and advantages of the current method.

In earlier versions of Windows, and in some other operating systems, a program was allowed to execute until it **cooperates** by releasing its use of the processor to the other applications that are running. Because it is up to the application to cooperate with all other running programs, this type of multitasking is called cooperative multitasking. The downside to this type of multitasking is that if one program does not release execution, the other applications will be locked up. What is actually happening is that the running application hangs and the other applications are waiting in line. This is quite like a line at a bank. A teller takes one customer at a time. The customer more than likely will not move from the teller window until all their transactions are complete. Once finished, the teller can take the next person in line. It doesn't really matter how much time each person is going to spend at the window. Even if one person only wants to deposit a check, they must wait until the person in front of them who has five transactions has finished.

Thankfully, we shouldn't encounter this problem with current versions of Windows (2000 and XP). The current method of multitasking used by the operating system is very different. An application is now allowed to execute for a short period before it is involuntarily interrupted by the operating system and another application is allowed to execute. This interrupted style of multitasking is called **pre-emptive multitasking.** Pre-emption is simply defined as interrupting an application to allow another application to execute. It's important to note that an application may not have finished its task, but the operating system is going to allow another application to have its time on the processor. The bank teller example above does not fit here. In the real world, this would be like the bank teller pausing one customer in the middle of their transaction to allow another customer to start working on their business. This doesn't mean that the next customer would finish their transaction either. The teller could continue to interrupt one customer after another – eventually resuming with the first customer. This is very much like how the human brain deals with social interaction and various other tasks. While pre-emption solves the problem of the processor becoming locked, it does have its own share of problems as well. As you know, some applications may share resources such as database connections and files. What happens if two applications are accessing the same resource at the same time? One program may change the data, become interrupted, and then allow the other program to again change the data. Now two applications have changed the same data. Both applications assumed that they had exclusive access to the data. Let's look at the simple scenario illustrated in Figure 1.

Figure 1

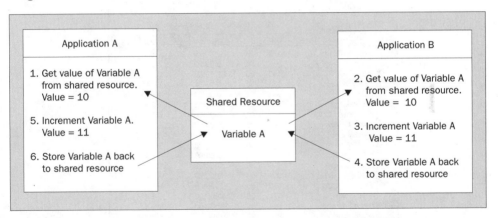

In Step 1, Application 1 obtains an integer value from a data store and places it in memory. That integer variable is set to 10. Application A is then pre-empted and forced to wait on Application B. Step 2 begins and Application B then obtains that same integer value of 10. In Step 3, Application B increments the value to 11. The variable is then stored to memory by Application B in Step 4. In Step 5, Application A increments this value as well. However, because they both obtained a reference to this value at 10, this value will still be 11 after Application A completes its increment routine. The desired result was for the value to be set to 12. Both applications had no idea that another application was accessing this resource, and now the value they were both attempting to increment has an incorrect value. What would happen if this were a reference counter or a ticket agency booking plane tickets?

The problems associated with pre-emptive multitasking are solved by synchronization, covered in Chapter 3 of this handbook.

Processes

When an application is launched, memory, and any other resource for that application, is allocated. This physical separation of this memory and resources is called a **process**. Of course, the application may launch more than one process. It's important to note that the words "application" and "process" are not synonymous. The memory allocated to the process is isolated from that of other processes and only that process is allowed to access it.

In Windows, you can see the currently running processes by accessing the task manager. Load up the task manager and it will contain three tabs: Applications, Processes, and Performance. The Processes tab shows the name of the process, the process ID (PID), CPU usage, the processor time used by the process so far, and the memory being used by the application. Applications and the processes appear on separate tabs, for a good reason. Applications may have one or more processes involved. Each process has its own separation of data, execution code, and system resources.

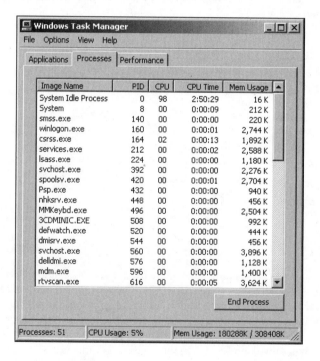

Threads

You will also notice that the task manager has summary information about process CPU utilization. This is because the process also has an execution sequence that is used by the computer's processor. This execution sequence is known as a **thread**. This thread is defined by the registers in use on the CPU, the stack used by the thread, and a container that keeps track of the thread's current state. The container mentioned in the last sentence is known as **Thread Local Storage**. The concepts of registers and stacks should be familiar to any of you used to dealing with low-level issues like memory allocation; however, all you need to know here is that a stack in the .NET Framework is an area of memory that can be used for fast access and either stores value types, or pointers to objects, method arguments, and other data that is local to each method call.

Single-Threaded Processes

As noted above, each process has at least one of these sequential execution orders, or threads. Creating a process includes starting the process running at a point in the instructions. This initial thread is known as the **primary** or **main thread**. The thread's actual execution sequence is determined by what you code in your application's functions and subroutines. For instance, in a simple Visual Basic 6.0 application, the primary thread is defined in your application's property dialog, where you choose a form, or Sub Main(), as your startup object.

Now that we have an idea of what a process is and that it has at least one thread, let's look at a visual model of this relationship in Figure 2:

Figure 2

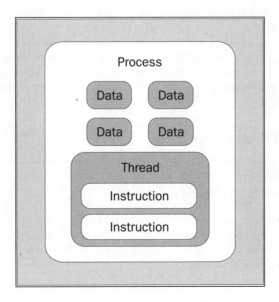

Looking at the diagram above, you'll notice that the thread is in the same isolation as the data. This is to demonstrate that the data that you declare in this process can be accessed by the thread. The thread executes on the processor and uses the data within the process, as required. This all seems simple; we have a physically separated process that is isolated so no other process can modify the data. As far as this process knows, it is the only process running on the system. We don't need to know the details of other processes and their associated threads to make our process work.

> **To be more precise, the thread is really a pointer into the instruction stream portion of a process. The thread does not actually contain the instructions, but rather it indicates the current and future possible paths through the instructions determined by data and branching decisions.**

Time Slices

When we discussed multitasking, we stated that the operating system grants each application a period to execute before interrupting that application and allowing another one to execute. This is not entirely accurate. The processor actually grants time to the process. The period that the process can execute is known as a **time slice** or a **quantum**. The period of this time slice is also unknown to the programmer and unpredictable to anything besides the operating system. Programmers should not consider this time slice as a constant in their applications. Each operating system and each processor may have a different time allocated.

Nevertheless, we did mention a potential problem with concurrency earlier, and we should consider how that would come into play if each process were physically isolated. This is where the challenge starts, and is really the focus of the remainder of this book. We mentioned that a process has to have at least one thread of execution – at least one. Our process may have more than one task that it needs to be doing at any one point in time. For instance, it may need to access a SQL Server database over a network, while also drawing the user interface.

Multithreaded Processes

As you probably already know, we can split up our process to share the time slice allotted to it. This happens by spawning additional threads of execution within the process. You may spawn an additional thread in order to do some background work, such as accessing a network or querying a database. Because these secondary threads are usually created to do some work, they are commonly known as **worker threads**. These threads share the process's memory space that is isolated from all the other processes on the system. The concept of spawning new threads within the same process is known as **free threading**.

10

As some of you may already understand by now, the concept of free threading is very different from the apartment-threading model we were used to using in Visual Basic 6.0. With apartment threading, each process was granted its own copy of the global data needed to execute. Each thread spawned was spawned within its own process, so that threads could not share data in the process's memory. Let's look at these models side by side for comparison. The diagram in Figure 3 demonstrates the apartment threading concept, while that in Figure 4 demonstrates the free threading concept. We won't spend a much time on this, but it's important to describe these differences:

Figure 3

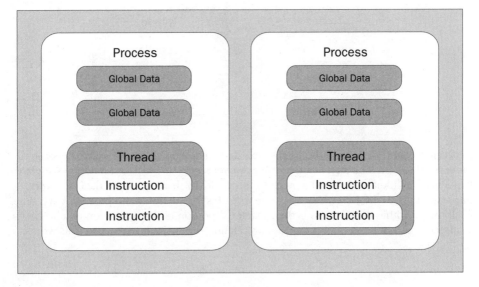

As you can see, each time you want to do some background work, it happens in its own process. This is therefore called running **out-of-process**. This model is vastly different from the free-threading model shown in Figure 4.

Figure 4

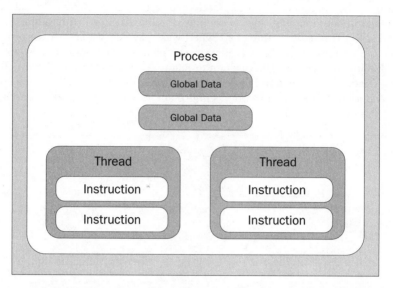

You can see that we can get the CPU to execute an additional thread using the same process's data. This is a significant advantage over single threaded apartments. We get the benefits of an additional thread as well as the ability to share the same data. It is very important to note, however, that only one thread is executing on the processor at a time. Each thread within that process is then granted a portion of that execution time to do its work. Let's go one more time to a diagram (Figure 5) to help illustrate how this works.

Figure 5

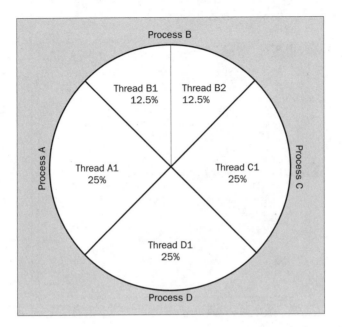

For the sake of this book, the examples and diagrams assume a single processor. However, there is an even greater benefit to multi-threading your applications if the computer has more than one processor. The operating system now has two places to send execution of the thread. In our bank example we spoke of earlier, this would be similar to opening up another line with another teller. The operating system is responsible for assigning which threads are executed on which processor. However, the .NET platform does provide the ability to control which CPU a process uses if the programmer so chooses. This is made possible with the `ProcessorAffinity` property of the `Process` class in the `System.Diagnostics` namespace. Bear in mind, however, that this is set at the process level and so all threads in that particular process will execute on the same processor.

The scheduling of these threads is vastly more complicated than demonstrated in the last diagram, but for our purposes, this model is sufficient for now. Since each thread is taking its turn to execute, we might be reminded of that frustrating wait in line at the bank teller. However, remember that these threads are interrupted after a brief period. At that point, another thread, perhaps one in the same process, or perhaps a thread in another process, is granted execution. Before we move on, let's look at the task manager again.

Launch Task Manager and return to the Processes tab. Once open, go to the View | Select Columns menu. You will see a list of columns that you can display in the Task Manager. We are only concerned with one additional column at this point – the Thread Count option. Select this checkbox and click OK. You should see something like this:

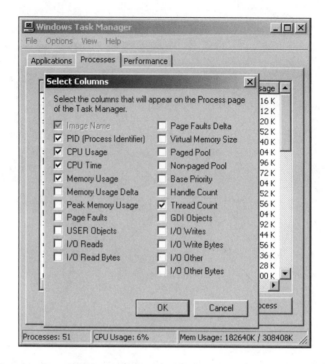

You will notice that several of your processes have more than one thread. This reinforces the idea that your program may have many threads for one just one process.

How Interrupts and Thread Local Storage Work

When one thread runs out of time in its allocated time slice, it doesn't just stop and wait its turn again. Each processor can only handle one task at a time, so the current thread has to get out of the way. However, before it jumps out of line again, it has to store the state information that will allow its execution again. If you remember, this is a function of Thread Local Storage (**TLS**). The TLS for this thread, as you may remember, contains the registers, stack pointers, scheduling information, address spaces in memory, and information about other resources in use. One of the registers stored in the TLS is a program counter, which tells the thread which instruction to execute next.

Interrupts

Remember that we said that processes don't necessarily need to know about other processes on the same computer. If that were the case, how would the thread know that it's supposed to give way to anther process? This scheduling decision nightmare is handled by the operating system for the most part. Windows itself (which after all is just another program running on the processor) has a main thread, known as the system thread, which is responsible for the scheduling of all other threads. Windows knows when it needs to make a decision about thread scheduling by using **interrupts**. We've used this word already, but now we are going to define exactly what an interrupt is. An interrupt is a mechanism that causes the normally sequential execution of CPU instructions to branch elsewhere in the computer memory without the knowledge of the execution program. Windows determines how long a thread has to execute and places an instruction in the current thread's execution sequence. This period can differ from system to system and even from thread to thread on the same system. Since this interrupt is obviously placed in the instruction set, it is known as a software interrupt. This should not be confused with hardware interrupts, which occur outside the specific instructions being executed. Once the interrupt is placed, Windows then allows the thread to execute. When the thread comes to the interrupt, Windows uses a special function known as an interrupt handler to store the thread's state in the TLS. The current program counter for that thread, which was stored before the interrupt was received, is then stored in that TLS. As you may remember, this program counter is simply the address of the currently executing instruction. Once the thread's execution has timed out, it is moved to the end of the thread queue for its given priority to wait its turn again. Look at Figure 6 for a diagram of this interruption process:

Figure 6

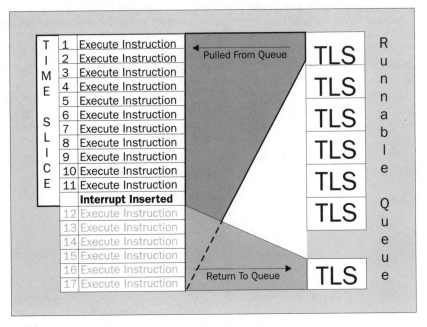

> **The TLS is not actually saved to the queue; it is stored in the memory of the process that contains the thread. A pointer to that memory is what is actually saved to the queue.**

This is, of course, fine if the thread isn't done yet or if the thread needs to continue executing. However, what happens if the thread decides that it doesn't need to use all of its execution time? The process in context switching is slightly different initially, but the results are the same. A thread may decide that it needs to wait on a resource before it can execute again. Therefore, it may yield its execution time to another thread. This is the responsibility of the programmer as well as the operating system. The programmer signals the thread to yield. The thread then clears any interrupts that Windows may have already placed in its stack. A software interrupt is then simulated. The thread is stored in TLS and moved to the end of the queue just as before. I will not diagram this concept as it's quite easy to understand and very similar to the diagram above. The only thing to remember is that Windows may have already placed an interrupt on the thread's stack. This must be cleared before the thread is packed up otherwise, when the thread is again executed, it may be interrupted prematurely. Of course, the details of this are abstracted from us. Programmers do not have to worry about clearing these interrupts themselves.

Thread Sleep and Clock Interrupts

As we stated, the program may have yielded execution to another thread so it can wait on some outside resource. However, the resources may not be available the next time the thread is brought back to execute. In fact, it may not be available the next 10 or 20 times a thread is executed. The programmer may wish to take this thread out of the execution queue for a long period so that the processor doesn't waste time switching from one thread to another just to realize it has to yield execution again. When a thread voluntarily takes itself out of the execution queue for a period, it is said to **sleep**. When a thread is put to sleep, it is again packed up into TLS, but this time, the TLS is not placed at the end of the running queue; it is placed on a separate sleep queue. In order for threads on a sleep queue to run again, they are marked to do so with a different kind of interrupt called a **clock interrupt**. When a thread is put into the sleep queue, a clock interrupt is scheduled for the time when this thread should be awakened. When a clock interrupt occurs that matches the time for a thread on the sleep queue, it is moved back to the runnable queue where it will again be scheduled for execution. An illustration of this can be found in Figure 7:

Figure 7

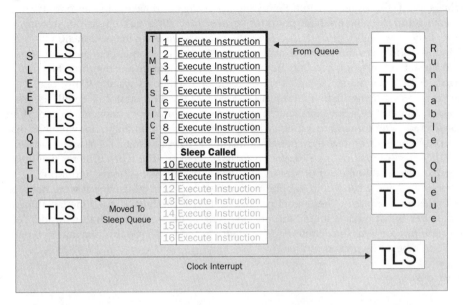

Thread Abort

We've seen a thread interrupted, and we've seen a thread sleep. However, like all other good things in life, threads must end. Threads can be stopped explicitly as a request during the execution of another thread. When a thread is ended in this way, it is called an **abort**. Threads also stop when they come to the end of their execution sequence. In any case, when a thread is ended, the TLS for that thread is de-allocated. The data in the process used by that thread does not go away, however, unless the process also ends. This is important because the process may have more than one thread accessing that data. Threads cannot be aborted from within themselves; a thread abort must be called from another thread.

Thread Priorities

We've seen how a thread can be interrupted so that another thread can execute. We have also seen how a thread may yield its execution time by either yielding that execution once, or by putting itself to sleep. We have also seen that thread just end. The last thing we need to cover for the basic concept of threading is how threads prioritize themselves. Using the analogy of our own lives, we understand that some tasks we need to do take priority over other tasks. For instance, while there is a grueling deadline to meet with this book, the author also needs to eat. Eating may take priority over writing this book because of the need to eat. In addition, if this author stays up too late working on this book, rest deprivation may elevate the body's priority to sleep. Additional tasks may also be given by other people. However, those people cannot make that task the highest priority. Someone can emphasize that a task may be important, but it's ultimately up to the recipient of the task to determine what should be of extremely high importance, and what can wait.

The information above contains much theory and analogy; however, this very closely relates to our threading concept. Some threads just need to have a higher priority. Just as eating and sleeping are high priorities because they allow us to function, system tasks may have higher priorities because the computer needs them to function. Windows prioritizes threads on a scale of 0 to 31, with larger numbers meaning higher priorities. A priority of 0 can only be set by the system and means the thread is idle. Priorities between 1 and 15 can be set by users of a Windows system. If a priority needs to be set higher than 15, it must be done by the administrator. We will discuss how an administrator does this later. Threads running in priority between 16 and 31 are considered to be running real-time. When we refer to the term real-time, we mean that the priority is so high that they pre-empt threads in lower priorities. This pre-emption has the effect of making their execution more immediate. The types of items that might need to run in real-time are processes like device drivers, file systems, and input devices. Imagine what would happen if your keyboard and mouse input were not high priorities to the system. The default priority for user-level threads is 8. One last thing to remember is that threads inherit the priority of the processes in which they reside. Let's diagram this for your future reference in Figure 8. We'll also use this diagram to break these numbers down even further.

Figure 8

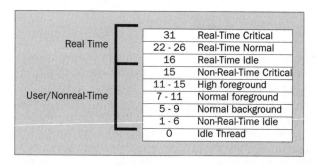

Real Time	31	Real-Time Critical
	22 - 26	Real-Time Normal
	16	Real-Time Idle
	15	Non-Real-Time Critical
	11 - 15	High foreground
User/Nonreal-Time	7 - 11	Normal foreground
	5 - 9	Normal background
	1 - 6	Non-Real-Time Idle
	0	Idle Thread

In some operating systems, such as Windows, as long as threads of a higher priority exist, threads in lower priority are not scheduled for execution. The processor will schedule all threads at the highest priority first. Each thread of that same priority level will take turns executing in a round-robin fashion. After all threads in the highest priority have completed, then the threads in the next highest level will be scheduled for execution. If a thread of a higher priority is available again, all threads in a lower priority are pre-empted and use of the processor is given to the higher priority thread.

Administrating Priorities

Based on what we know about priorities, it may be desirable to set certain process priorities higher so that any threads spawned from those processes will have a higher likelihood of being scheduled for execution. Windows provides several ways to set priorities of tasks administratively and programmatically. Right now, we will focus on setting priorities administratively. This can be done with tools such as the task manager (which we have already seen), and two other tools called pview and pviewer. You can also view the current priorities using the Window's performance monitor. We won't concentrate on all of these tools right now. We will briefly look at how to set the general priority of processes. If you remember, back when we first introduced processes, we launched the task manager to view all of the processes currently running on the system. What we didn't cover is the fact that we can elevate the priority of a particular process in that very same window.

Let's try changing a process's priority. First, open up an instance of an application such as Microsoft Excel. Now launch the task manager and go to the Processes tab again. Look at an instance of Excel running as a process. Right-click on EXCEL.EXE in the list and choose Set Priority from the menu. As you can see, you can change the priority class as you wish. It wouldn't make much sense to set the priority of Excel high, but the point is you could if you wanted to. Every process has a priority and the operating system isn't going to tell you what priorities you should and should not have. However, it will warn you that you may be about to do something with undesirable consequences; but that choice is still left up to you.

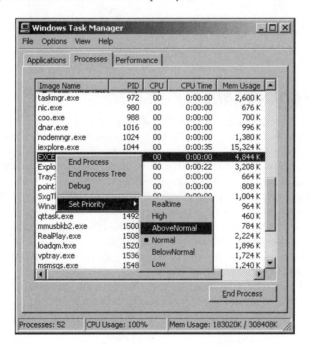

19

In the previous screenshot, you can see that one of the priorities has a mark next to it. This mark represents the current priority of the process. It should be noted that when you set a priority for one process, you are setting it for that one instance only. This means that all other currently running instances of that same application will retain its default process level. Additionally, any future instances of the process that are launched will also retain its default process level.

Thread Support in Visual Basic .NET

As we have already mentioned, the idea of free threading is a very new concept to the Visual Basic developer. Many developers have found ways to manipulate the API to attempt spawning new threads, but this often can result in undesirable consequences. The other option that Visual Basic developers had in the past was to create an out-of-process component, which would indeed spawn a new thread – but within a new process and therefore with its own set of data. However, when Microsoft adapted Visual Basic to fit the .NET Framework, it came up with a major set of upgrades including the ability to free-thread an application. In this next section, we will look at how that support is provided and more of how threading is done as opposed to what it is. We will also cover some of the additional support provided to help further separate processes

By the end of this section, you will understand:

❑ What the System.AppDomain class is and what it can do for you

❑ How the .NET runtime monitors threads

System.AppDomain

When we explained processes earlier in this chapter, we established that they are a physical isolation of the memory and resources needed to maintain themselves. We later mentioned that a process has at least one thread. When Microsoft designed the .NET Framework, it added one more layer of isolation called an **application domain** or **AppDomain**. This application domain is not a physical isolation as a process is; it is a further logical isolation within the process. Since more than one application domain can exist within a single process, we receive some major advantages. In general, it is impossible for standard processes to access each other's data without using a proxy. Using a proxy causes much overhead and coding can be complex. However, with the introduction of the application domain concept, we can now launch several applications within the same process. The same isolation provided by a process is also available with the application domain. Threads can execute across application domains without the overhead associated with inter-process communication. Another benefit of these additional in-process boundaries is that they provide type checking of the data they contain.

Microsoft encapsulated all of the functionality for these application domains into a class called System.AppDomain. Microsoft .NET namespaces have a very tight relationship with these application domains. Any time that a namespace is loaded in an application, it is loaded into an AppDomain. Unless otherwise specified, the namespace is loaded into the calling code's AppDomain. Application domains also have a direct relationship with threads; they can hold one or many threads, just like a process. However, the difference is that an application domain may be created within the process and without a new thread. This relationship could be modeled as shown in Figure 9:

Figure 9

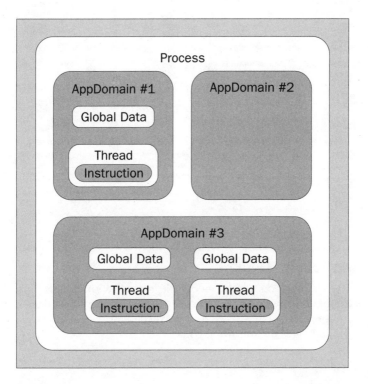

In .NET, the **AppDomain** and **Thread** classes cannot be inherited for security reasons.

Each application contains one or more AppDomains. Each AppDomain can create and execute multiple threads. If you look at Figure 10, in machine X there are two OS processes Y and Z running. The OS process X has four running AppDomains A, B, C, and D. The OS process Y has two AppDomains A and B.

Figure 10

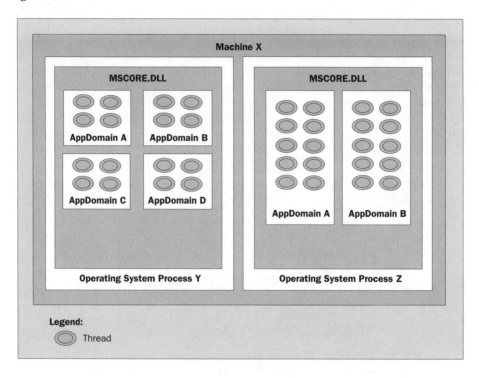

Setting AppDomain Data

You've heard the theory and seen the models; let's now get our hands on some real code. In the example below, we will be using the AppDomain to set data, retrieve data, and identify the thread that the AppDomain is executing. Create a new class file called appdomain.vb and enter the following code:

```
Imports System
Imports System.AppDomain

Public Class MyAppDomain
  Public Domain As System.AppDomain

  Public Sub SetDomainData(ByVal name As String, _
                      ByVal value As String)
    Domain.SetData(name, CType(value, Object))
  End Sub

  Public Function GetDomainData(ByVal name As String) As String
    Return Domain.GetData(name)
  End Function
```

```
Public Shared Sub Main()
    Console.WriteLine("Retrieving current domain")
    Dim Obj as New MyAppDomain()
    Obj.Domain = System.AppDomain.CurrentDomain()

    Dim DataName As String
    DataName = "MyData"

    Dim DataValue As String
    DataValue = "Some Data to be stored"

    Console.WriteLine("Setting domain data")
    Obj.SetDomainData(DataName, DataValue)

    Console.WriteLine("Getting domain data")
    Console.WriteLine("The Data found for key '" + DataName + _
                "' is '" + Obj.GetDomainData(DataName) _
                + "' running on thread id: " _
                + Obj.Domain.GetCurrentThreadId.ToString())
    Console.ReadLine()
    End Sub
End Class
```

Your output should look something like this:

```
Retrieving current domain
Setting domain data
Getting domain data
The Data found for key 'MyData' is 'Some Data to be stored' running on thread id: 1372
```

This is straightforward for the experienced VB.NET developer. However, let's look at the code and determine exactly what is happening here. On the first line we find:

```
Imports System.Appdomain
```

This line simply allows us to access the AppDomain objects. Now let's look at the next important piece of this class:

```
Public Sub SetDomainData(ByVal name As String, _
                        ByVal value As String)
    Domain.SetData(name, CType(value, Object))
    End Sub
```

This method takes parameters for the name of the data to be set, and the value. You'll notice that the SetData() method has done something a little different when it passes the parameters in. Here we cast the String value to an Object data type as the SetData() function takes an object as its second parameter. Since we are only using a String, and a String inherits from System.Object, we could just use the variable without casting it to an object. However, other data that you might want to store would not be as easy to store. We have done this conversion as a simple reminder of this fact. Let's move on to the next function:

```
Public Function GetDomainData(ByVal name As String) As String
   Return Domain.GetData(name)
End Function
```

This function is very straightforward. We use the `GetData()` method of the
`AppDomain` to obtain data based on a key value. In this case, we are just passing the
parameter from our `GetDomainData()` method to the `GetData()` method. Then we
return the result of that method to our calling subroutine.

Finally, let's look at `Sub Main()`:

```
Public Shared Sub Main()
   Console.WriteLine("Retrieving current domain")
   Dim Obj as New MyAppDomain()
   Obj.Domain = System.AppDomain.CurrentDomain()

   Dim DataName As String
   DataName = "MyData"

   Dim DataValue As String
   DataValue = "Some Data to be stored"

   Console.WriteLine("Setting domain data")
   Obj.SetDomainData(DataName, DataValue)

   Console.WriteLine("Getting domain data")
   Console.WriteLine("The Data found for key '" + DataName + _
                     "' is '" + Obj.GetDomainData(DataName) _
                     + "' running on thread id: " _
                     + Obj.Domain.GetCurrentThreadId.ToString())
   Console.ReadLine()
End Sub
```

We start by setting the `Domain` variable with a reference to the current `AppDomain`
object. Then we set the two strings that will make up our parameters when calling our
previously explained methods. Next we call our methods – passing both parameters to
the `SetDomainData()` method and passing one parameter when calling the
`GetDomainData()` method. Finally, you will notice that we can obtain the currently
executing `ThreadID` with a simple call to the `GetCurrentThreadId` property of our
`AppDomain` object. However, we have to use the `ToString()` method to write it to
the console as this function returns a `Double`.

Executing Code within a Specified AppDomain

Now let's look at how to create a new application domain and make some important
observations about the behavior when creating threads within the newly created
`AppDomain`. The following code is contained within `create_appdomains.vb`:

```
Imports System

Public Class CreateAppDomains
  Public Shared Sub Main()

      Dim DomainA As AppDomain
      Dim DomainB As AppDomain

      DomainA = AppDomain.CreateDomain("MyDomainA")
      DomainB = AppDomain.CreateDomain("MyDomainB")

      Dim StringA = "DomainA Value"
      Dim StringB = "DomainB Value"

      DomainA.SetData("DomainKey", StringA)
      DomainB.SetData("DomainKey", StringB)

      CommonCallBack()
      DomainA.DoCallBack(AddressOf CommonCallBack)
      DomainB.DoCallBack(AddressOf CommonCallBack)

      Console.ReadLine()
  End Sub

  Shared Sub CommonCallBack()
    Dim Domain As AppDomain
    Domain = AppDomain.CurrentDomain

    Console.WriteLine("The Value '" + Domain.GetData("DomainKey") + _
                      "' was found in " + _
                      Domain.FriendlyName.ToString() + _
                      " running on thread id: " + _
                      Domain.GetCurrentThreadId().ToString())
  End Sub
End Class
```

The output of this compiled class should look similar to this:

```
The Value " was found in create_appdomain.exe running on thread id: 1372
The Value 'DomainA Value' was found in MyDomainA running on thread id: 1372
The Value 'DomainB Value' was found in MyDomainB running on thread id: 1372
```

You'll notice in this example we have created two application domains. To do this, we call the shared method CreateDomain(). The parameter that the constructor takes is a friendly name for the AppDomain instance that we are creating. We will see that we can access the friendly name later by way of a read-only property. Here is the code that creates the AppDomain instances:

```
Dim DomainA As AppDomain
Dim DomainB As AppDomain

DomainA = AppDomain.CreateDomain("MyDomainA")
DomainB = AppDomain.CreateDomain("MyDomainB")
```

Next we call the SetData() method again. We won't redisplay the code here because we have explained its use in the last example. However, what we need to explain next is how we get code to execute in a given AppDomain. We do this with the DoCallBack() method. This method takes a CrossAppDomainDelegate as its parameter. In this instance, using the AddressOf operator along with the method that we want to execute will work in the same way:

```
CommonCallBack()
DomainA.DoCallBack(AddressOf CommonCallBack)
DomainB.DoCallBack(AddressOf CommonCallBack)
```

You'll notice that we call CommonCallBack() first. This is to execute our CommonCallBack() method within the context of the main AppDomain. You'll also notice from the output that the FriendlyName property of the main AppDomain is the executable's name.

Lastly, let's look at the CommonCallBack() method itself:

```
Shared Sub CommonCallBack()
   Dim Domain As AppDomain
   Domain = AppDomain.CurrentDomain

   Console.WriteLine("The Value '" + Domain.GetData("DomainKey") + _
                     "' was found in " + _
                     Domain.FriendlyName.ToString() + _
                     " running on thread id: " + _
                     Domain.GetCurrentThreadId().ToString())
End Sub
```

You'll notice that this is rather generic so it will work in no matter what instance we run it. We use the CurrentDomain property once again to obtain a reference to the domain that is executing the code. We then use the FriendlyName property again to identify the AppDomain we are using.

Lastly, we call the GetCurrentThreadId() method here. When we look at our output, you can see that we get the same thread ID no matter what AppDomain we are executing in. This is important to note because this not only means that an AppDomain can have zero or many threads, but also that a thread can execute across different domains.

Thread Management and the .NET Runtime

The .NET Framework provides more than just the ability for free-threaded processes and logical application domains. In fact, the Framework supplies an object representation of processor threads. These object representations are instances of the System.Threading.Thread class. We will go more in depth into this in the next chapter. However, before we move on to the next chapter, we must understand how **unmanaged threads** work in relation to **managed threads**. That is to say, how unmanaged threads created outside of the .NET world relate to instances of the managed Thread class, which represent threads running inside of the .NET CLR.

The .NET runtime monitors all threads that are created by .NET code. It also monitors all unmanaged threads, which may execute managed code. Since managed code can be exposed by COM-callable wrappers, it is possible for unmanaged threads to wander into the .NET runtime.

When unmanaged code does execute in a managed thread, the runtime will check the TLS for the existence of a managed Thread object. If a managed thread is found, the runtime will use that thread. If a managed thread isn't found, it will create one and use it. It's very simple, but is necessary to note. We would still want to get an object representation of our thread no matter where it came from. If the runtime didn't manage and create the threads for these types of inbound calls, we wouldn't be able to identify the thread, or even control it, within the managed environment.

The last important note to make about thread management is that once an unmanaged call returns back to unmanaged code, the thread is no longer monitored by the runtime.

Summary

We have covered a wide range of topics in this chapter. We covered the basics of what multitasking is and how it is accomplished by the use of threads. We established that multitasking and free threading are not the same thing. We described processes and how they isolate data from other applications. We also described the function of threads in an operating system like Windows. You now know that Windows interrupts threads to grant execution time to other threads for a brief period. That brief period is called a time slice or a quantum. We described the function of thread priorities and the different levels of these priorities, and that threads will inherit their parent process's priority by default.

In this chapter, we also described how the .NET runtime monitors threads created in the .NET environment and additionally any unmanaged threads that execute managed code. We described the support for threading in the .NET Framework. The System.AppDomain class provides an additional layer of logical data isolation on top of the physical process data isolation. We described how threads could cross easily from one AppDomain to another. Additionally, we described how an AppDomain doesn't necessarily have its own thread as all processes do.

VB.NET

Threading

Handbook

2

2

Threading in .NET

In Chapter 1 we described *what* threading is. We covered a lot of the common ground that many may be familiar with already. Knowing the *what* portion of threading is important. In this chapter, you will see how to implement some basic threading; however, it is of equal, if not greater importance, to understand **when** to use threading.

By the end of this chapter, you will understand:

- ❑ The System.Threading namespace
- ❑ What design issues there are in the use of threads
- ❑ What resources are used by threads
- ❑ What are good opportunities for threading
- ❑ What mistakes to avoid when using threads

System.Threading Namespace

We have already mentioned that threads in the managed code are represented by a System.Threading.Thread class instance. In this section, we will discuss the System.Threading namespace in depth, as well as its contents. The classes available in the System.Threading namespace are listed in the following table.

Class	Description
AutoResetEvent	This class, which cannot be inherited, notifies one or more waiting threads that an event has occurred.
Interlocked	This class protects against errors by providing atomic operations for variables that are shared by multiple threads.
ManualResetEvent	This class cannot be inherited and occurs when notifying one or more waiting threads that an event has occurred.
Monitor	This class provides a mechanism that synchronizes access to objects.
Mutex	A synchronization primitive that grants exclusive access to a shared resource to only one thread. It can also be used for inter-process synchronization.
ReaderWriterLock	This class defines the lock that implements single-writer and multiple-reader semantics.
RegisteredWaitHandle	This class, which cannot be inherited, represents a handle that has been registered when calling the RegisterWaitForSingleObject() method.
SynchronizationLockException	This exception is thrown when a synchronized method is invoked from an unsynchronized block of code.
Thread	This class creates and controls a thread, sets its priority, and gets its status.
ThreadAbortException	This class, which cannot be inherited, is the exception that is thrown when a call is made to the Abort() method.
ThreadExceptionEventArgs	This class provides data for the ThreadException event.
ThreadInterruptedException	This exception is thrown when a thread is interrupted while it is in a waiting state.

Class	Description
ThreadPool	This class provides a pool of threads that can be used to post work items, process asynchronous I/O, wait on behalf of other threads, and process timers.
ThreadStateException	This is the exception that is thrown when a Thread is in an invalid ThreadState for the method call.
Timeout	This class, which cannot be inherited, contains a constant used to specify an infinite amount of time.
Timer	This class, which cannot be inherited, provides a mechanism for executing methods at specified intervals.
WaitHandle	This class encapsulates operating system-specific objects that wait for exclusive access to shared resources.

We won't use all of these classes in this section, but it's useful to understand what this namespace makes available to us.

Thread Class

Right now, we are going to focus on the Thread class, since this class represents our processor threads. This class allows us to do everything, from managing a thread's priority, to reading its status.

Let's start by looking at a table of this class's Public methods.

Public Method Name	Description
Abort()	This overloaded method raises a ThreadAbortException in the thread on which it is invoked, to begin the process of terminating the thread. Calling this method usually terminates the thread.
AllocateDataSlot()	This Shared method allocates an unnamed data slot on all the threads.
AllocateNamedDataSlot()	This Shared method allocates a named data slot on all threads.

Table continued on following page

Public Method Name	Description
Equals()	This overloaded method determines whether two object instances are equal.
FreeNamedDataSlot()	This Shared method frees a previously allocated named data slot.
GetData()	This Shared method retrieves the value from the specified slot on the current thread, within the current thread's current domain.
GetDomain()	This Shared method returns the current domain in which the current thread is running.
GetDomainID()	This Shared method returns a unique application domain identifier.
GetHashCode()	This method serves as a hash function for a particular type, suitable for use in hashing algorithms and data structures like a hash table.
GetNamedDataSlot()	This Shared method looks up a named data slot.
GetType()	This method gets the Type of the current instance.
Interrupt()	This method interrupts a thread that is in the WaitSleepJoin thread state.
Join()	This overloaded method blocks the calling thread until a thread terminates.
ResetAbort()	This Shared method cancels an Abort() requested for the current thread.
Resume()	This method resumes a thread that has been suspended.
SetData()	This Shared method sets the data in the specified slot on the currently running thread, for that thread's current domain.
Sleep()	This Shared and overloaded method blocks the current thread for the specified number of milliseconds.
SpinWait()	This Shared method causes a thread to wait the number of times defined by the iterations parameter.

Public Method Name	Description
Start()	This method causes the operating system to change the state of the current instance to ThreadState.Running.
Suspend()	This method will either suspend the thread, or if the thread is already suspended, has no effect.
ToString()	This method returns a String that represents the current object

Now let's look at another table, this time containing its Public properties.

Public Property Name	Description
ApartmentState	Sets or gets the apartment state of this thread.
CurrentContext	This Shared property gets the current context in which the thread is executing.
CurrentCulture	Sets or gets the culture for the current thread.
CurrentPrincipal	This Shared property sets or gets the thread's current principal. It is used for role-based security.
CurrentThread	This Shared property gets the currently running thread.
CurrentUICulture	Used at runtime, this property sets or gets the current culture used by the Resource Manager to look up culture-specific resources.
IsAlive	Gets a value that indicates the execution status of the current thread.
IsBackground	Sets or gets a value that indicates whether a thread is a background thread or not.
IsThreadPoolThread	Gets a value indicating whether a thread is part of a thread pool.
Name	Sets or gets the name of the thread.
Priority	Sets or gets a value that indicates the scheduling priority of a thread.
ThreadState	Gets a value that contains the states of the current thread.

Again, we won't use all of these properties and methods in this chapter, but it was important to list these as a reference. We've seen these class members, but it does us little good until we can at least create a thread – or a reference to one. So let's get our feet wet with a simple VB .NET threading example.

Creating a Thread

We are going to use a simple example here. This isn't a good example of why you should use a new thread but it strips off all of the complexities that will be covered later. Create a new console application with a file called `simple_thread.vb` and place the following code in it:

```
Imports System
Imports System.Threading

Public Class SimpleThread

  Public Sub SimpleMethod()
    Dim I as Integer = 5
    Dim X as Integer = 10
    Dim iResult as Integer = I * X
    Console.WriteLine("This code calculated the value " & _
                      iResult.ToString() & " from thread ID: " & _
                      AppDomain.GetCurrentThreadId().ToString())
  End Sub

  Public Shared Sub Main()
    Dim obj as New SimpleThread
    obj.SimpleMethod()
    Dim t As New Thread(AddressOf obj.SimpleMethod)
    t.Start()
    Console.ReadLine()
  End Sub
End Class
```

Now save, compile, and execute the file. Your output should look something like this:

```
This code calculated the value 50 from thread id: 1400
This code calculated the value 50 from thread id: 1040
```

Let's walk through this simple example and make sure we understand what is happening here. As we have already established, the threading functionality is encapsulated in the `System.Threading` namespace. As such, we must first import this namespace into our project. Once the namespace is imported, we want to create a method that can be executed on the main (primary) thread and one on our new worker thread. We use `SimpleMethod()` in our example:

```
Public Sub SimpleMethod()
  Dim I as Integer =  5
  Dim X as Integer = 10
  Dim iResult as Integer = I * X
  Console.WriteLine("This code calculated the value " & _
                    iResult.ToString() & " from thread id: " & _
                    AppDomain.GetCurrentThreadId().ToString())
End Sub
```

As you can see, we are using the `AppDomain` class that we introduced in Chapter 1 to find out what thread we are running on.

Our program's entry point is the `Main()` method. The first thing we do inside this method is execute our `SimpleMethod()` subroutine. The next part is important. We get our first look at creating a thread and it may seem a bit confusing at first glance:

```
Dim t As New Thread(AddressOf SimpleMethod)
```

We are declaring a variable called `t` as a new `Thread`. The `Thread` class constructor takes a method name as its sole parameter. In front of that method name, we use the `AddressOf` operator. This parameter is actually a `ThreadStart` delegate, which is a member of the `System.Threading` namespace as well. One last thing to notice is that the method name is not accompanied by parentheses; it simply takes the method's name prefixed with an `AddressOf` operator.

Alternatively, we could have used the following code:

```
Dim ts As New ThreadStart(AddressOf SimpleMethod)
Dim t As New Thread(ts)
```

This would seem superfluous at first glance, but we can find a good use for this method in the future.

On our next line we call the `Start()` method of the `Thread` object. We follow this up with `Console.ReadLine()` so the program will wait on your key input before exiting our main thread:

```
t.Start()
Console.ReadLine()
```

OK, so we've created a thread that doesn't really do anything. The fact that we are displaying different Thread IDs doesn't really do much as far as describing what is happening here. We are going to create another program that simulates a long process executing in the background while another process executes in the foreground. Create a new console application and place this code in a new file called `do_something_thread.vb`:

```
Imports System
Imports System.Threading

Public Class DoSomethingThread

    Shared Sub WorkerMethod()
        Dim i As Integer
        For i = 1 To 1000
            Console.WriteLine("Worker Thread: " & i.ToString())
        Next
    End Sub
```

```
Shared Sub Main()
    Dim ts As New ThreadStart(AddressOf WorkerMethod)
    Dim t As New Thread(ts)
    t.Start()

    Dim i As Integer
    For i = 1 To 1000
        Console.WriteLine("Primary Thread: " & i.ToString())
    Next

    Console.ReadLine()
End Sub
End Class
```

Your output may be somewhat different every time. The thread execution will be switched at different points in the loop every time. But your concatenated results will look something like this:

```
Primary Thread: 1
Primary Thread: 2
Primary Thread: 3
...
Worker Thread: 743
Worker Thread: 744
Worker Thread: 745
...
Primary Thread: 1000
```

We won't walk through this code because it doesn't introduce any new coding techniques. However, this was important to show you because it demonstrates that the execution of one thread is interrupted to allow the other thread to execute.

ThreadStart and Execution Branching

Let's now come back to our ThreadStart delegate. Remember that we said that we could use a ThreadStart instance as our Thread constructor's parameter. Let's take a quick look at why you might want to use these objects instead of just passing in the function name with an AddressOf operator.

Let's examine a quick example in a real-world scenario. Suppose that you want to perform some background routine when a user launches an application. Depending on who is launching the application, you want to perform different routines. For instance, let's say that when an administrator logs into an application, you want to run a background process that will gather report data and format it. That background process will alert the administrator when the report is available. You probably wouldn't want to perform the same reporting function for an ordinary user as you would for an administrator. This is where ThreadStart is useful.

Let's look at some example code. We aren't going to code the exact scenario described above, but we will show you how you can branch based on a certain criteria defined in a `ThreadStart`. Create a new console application and place the following code in a file called `ThreadStartBranching.vb`:

```vb
Imports System
Imports System.Threading

Public Class ThreadStartBranching
    Enum UserClass
        ClassAdmin
        ClassUser
    End Enum

    Shared Sub AdminMethod()
        Console.WriteLine("Admin Method")
    End Sub

    Shared Sub UserMethod()
        Console.WriteLine("User Method")
    End Sub

    Shared Sub ExecuteFor(ByVal uc As UserClass)
        Dim ts As ThreadStart
        Dim tsAdmin As New ThreadStart(AddressOf AdminMethod)
        Dim tsUser As New ThreadStart(AddressOf UserMethod)

        If uc = UserClass.ClassAdmin Then
            ts = tsAdmin
        Else
            ts = tsUser
        End If

        Dim t As New Thread(ts)
        t.Start()
    End Sub

    Shared Sub Main()
        ExecuteFor(UserClass.ClassAdmin)
        ExecuteFor(UserClass.ClassUser)
        Console.ReadLine()
    End Sub
End Class
```

The output from the code is quite simple:

```
Admin Method
User Method
```

We will detail some of the important points to observe here. First, you will notice that we created an enumeration of the types of user that may be executing code:

```
Enum UserClass
  ClassAdmin
  ClassUser
End Enum
```

The next thing you'll notice is that we created two methods: `AdminMethod()` and `UserMethod()`. These would theoretically execute a long series of instructions that would be completely different for the two different user types. In our case, we just want to identify that they have run so we write them out to the console:

```
Shared Sub AdminMethod()
  Console.WriteLine("Admin Method")
End Sub

Shared Sub UserMethod()
  Console.WriteLine("User Method")
End Sub
```

The next thing you'll notice is that within the `ExecuteFor()` method we declared a variable called `ts` as a `ThreadStart` class, but didn't create an instance with the `New` keyword. We then created two new `ThreadStart` objects that point to the different methods created above:

```
Dim ts As ThreadStart
Dim tsAdmin As New ThreadStart(AddressOf AdminMethod)
Dim tsUser As New ThreadStart(AddressOf UserMethod)
```

OK, so now we have two new `ThreadStart` objects and a variable that can hold an instance of a `ThreadStart`. Then we branch our code with an `If` statement and set our empty `ts` variable to the instance of the `ThreadStart` that coincides with our business rule:

```
If uc = UserClass.ClassAdmin Then
  ts = tsAdmin
Else
  ts = tsUser
End If
```

Lastly, as usual, we create a thread and execute it using the formerly empty variable:

```
Dim t As New Thread(ts)
t.Start()
```

Thread Properties and Methods

As we showed in the beginning of this chapter, there are many properties and methods of the `Thread` class. We promised that controlling the execution of threads was made much simpler with the `System.Threading` namespace. So far, all we have done is create threads and start them.

Let's look at two more members of the Thread class; the Sleep() method and the IsAlive property. In Chapter 1 we said that a thread may go to sleep for a time until it is clock-interrupted. Putting a thread to sleep is as simple as calling an instance member's Sleep() method. We also stated that we could determine a thread's state. In the following example we are going to use the IsAlive property to determine if a thread has completed its executions and the Sleep() method to pause the execution of a thread. Look at the following code, thread_sleep.vb, where we will make use of both of these members:

```vb
Imports System
Imports System.Threading

Public Class ThreadState

    Shared Sub WorkerFunction()
        Dim i As Integer
        Dim ThreadState As String

        For i = 1 To 50000
            If i Mod 5000 = 0 Then
                ThreadState = Thread.CurrentThread.ThreadState.ToString()
                Console.WriteLine("Worker: " + ThreadState)
            End If
        Next
        Console.WriteLine("Worker Function Complete")
    End Sub

    Shared Sub Main()
        Dim ThreadState As String
        Dim t As New Thread(AddressOf WorkerFunction)
        t.Start()

        While t.IsAlive
            Console.WriteLine("Still waiting. I'm going back to sleep.")
            Thread.CurrentThread.Sleep(200)
        End While

        ThreadState = t.ThreadState.ToString()
        Console.WriteLine("He's finally done! Thread state is: " + _
                        ThreadState)
        Console.ReadLine()
    End Sub
End Class
```

Your output should look similar to the following (try experimenting with the values in the For loop and passed to the sleep() method to see different results):

```
Still waiting. I'm going back to sleep.
Worker: Running
Worker: Running
Worker: Running
Worker: Running
Worker: Running
Worker: Running
Worker: Running
Worker: Running
Worker: Running
Worker: Running
Worker Function Complete
He's finally done! Thread state is: Stopped
```

Let's look at the `Main()` method where we have used our new concepts First, we create a thread and pass it the method we want to execute as a delegate:

```
Dim t As New Thread(AddressOf WorkerFunction)
t.Start()
```

This was nothing new. As usual, our `Main()` method continues to execute alongside our new thread as the processor switches between them. Then we use the `IsAlive` property of our newly created thread to see if it is still executing. We will continue to test this variable. While the thread is alive, we will continue to sleep for 200 milliseconds, wake up the thread, and test if our other thread is still alive:

```
While t.IsAlive
    Console.WriteLine("Still waiting. I'm going back to sleep.")
    Thread.CurrentThread.Sleep(200)
End While
```

Next we want to look at the `ThreadState` property that we have used twice in our code. The `ThreadState` property is actually a property that returns an enumerated type. The enumeration tells you exactly in what state the thread is in. We can either test this property with an `If` statement as we did in our last example or use the `ToString()` method on the property and write out its state in text form:

```
ThreadState = t.ThreadState.ToString()
Console.WriteLine("He's finally done! Thread state is: " + _
                  ThreadState)
```

The rest of this code is standard and doesn't need to be reviewed. There are some important things to note. The first is that we tell one thread to sleep for a specified period so that we yield execution to our other threads. We do that with the `Thread` object's `Sleep()` method – passing in the length of time in milliseconds that we want to the thread to sleep. In addition, we can test our threads to see if they have finished executing by using the `IsAlive` property. Lastly, we can use the `ThreadState` property of our thread instances to determine their exact thread state.

Thread Priorities

The thread priority determines the relative priority of the threads between one another. The `ThreadPriority` enumeration defines the possible values for setting a thread's priority. The available values are:

- ❏ Highest

- ❏ AboveNormal

- ❏ Normal

- ❏ BelowNormal

- ❏ Lowest

When a thread is created by the runtime and it has not been assigned any priority then it will initially have the `Normal` priority. However, this can be changed using the `ThreadPriority` enumeration. Before seeing an example for the thread priority, let's see what a thread priority looks like. Let's create a simple threading example that just displays the name, state, and the priority information about the current thread, `thread_priority.vb`:

```vb
Imports System
Imports System.Threading

Public Class ThreadPriority

   Public Shared worker As Thread

   Shared Sub Main()

      Console.WriteLine("Entering Sub Main()")

      worker = New Thread(AddressOf FindPriority)

      'Let's give a name to the thread
      worker.Name = "FindPriority() Thread"

      worker.Start()

      Console.WriteLine("Exiting Sub Main()")
   End Sub

   Shared Public Sub FindPriority()
      Console.WriteLine("Name: " & worker.Name())
      Console.WriteLine("State: " & worker.ThreadState.ToString())
      Console.WriteLine("Priority: " & worker.Priority.ToString())
   End Sub

End Class
```

There is a simple method called FindPriority() that displays the name, state and priority information of the current thread, which produces output like the following:

```
Entering the Sub Main()
Exiting the Sub Main()
Name: FindPriority() Thread
State: Running
Priority: Normal
```

We know the worker thread is running with a Normal priority. Let's add a new method called FindPriority2() and call it with a different priority, thread_priority2.vb:

```
Imports System
Imports System.Threading

Public Class ThreadPriority

  Public Shared worker As Thread
  Public Shared worker2 As Thread

  Shared Sub Main()

    Console.WriteLine("Entering Sub Main()")

    worker = New Thread(AddressOf FindPriority)
    worker2 = New Thread(AddressOf FindPriority2)

    'Let's give a name to the thread
    worker.Name = "FindPriority() Thread"
    worker2.Name = "FindPriority2() Thread"

    ' Give the new thread object the highest priority
    worker2.Priority = Threading.ThreadPriority.Highest

    worker.Start()
    worker2.Start()

    Console.WriteLine("Exiting Sub Main()")
  End Sub

  Shared Public Sub FindPriority()
    Console.WriteLine("Name: " & worker.Name())
    Console.WriteLine("State: " & worker.ThreadState.ToString())
    Console.WriteLine("Priority: " & worker.Priority.ToString())
  End Sub

  Shared Public Sub FindPriority2()
    Console.WriteLine("Name(2): " & worker2.Name())
    Console.WriteLine("State(2): " & worker2.ThreadState.ToString())
    Console.WriteLine("Priority(2): " & worker2.Priority.ToString())
  End Sub

End Class
```

The output from `thread_priority2.vb` will be something like the following:

```
Entering Sub Main()
Name(2): FindPriority2() Thread
State(2): Running
Priority(2): Highest
Exiting Sub Main()
Name: FindPriority() Thread
State: Running
Priority: Normal
```

Threads are scheduled for execution based on the priority set using the `Priority` property. Every operating system will execute a thread priority differently and the operating system could change the priority of the thread.

There is no way to our application can restrict the operating system from changing the priority of the thread that was assigned by the developer, since the OS is the master of all threads and it knows when and how to schedule them. For example, the priority of the thread could be dynamically changed by the OS due to several factors, such as system events like user input that has higher priority, or lack of memory that will trigger the garbage collection process.

Timers and Callbacks

We've seen some simple examples of threading. What we haven't covered at all is the issue of synchronization, although we will cover that in much greater detail in the next chapter. As threads run out of sequence from the rest of the application code, we cannot be certain that actions affecting a particular shared resource that occur in one thread will be completed before code in another thread wants to access that same shared resource. There are various methods of dealing with these issues, but here we will cover one simple way; the use of timers. Using a timer, we can specify that a method is executed at a specific regular interval, and this method could check that the required actions have been completed before continuing. This is a very simple model, but can apply to a variety of situations.

Timers are made up of two objects, a `TimerCallback` and a `Timer`. The `TimerCallback` defines the action to be performed at a specified interval, whereas the `Timer` is the timer itself. The `TimerCallback` associates a specific method with the timer. The `Timer`'s constructor (which is overloaded) requires four arguments. The first is the `TimerCallback` specified earlier. The second is an object that can be used to transmit state across to the method specified. The latter two arguments are the period after which to start counting, and the period with which it will fire the `TimerCallback` method call. They can be entered as integers or longs, but as you will see below, an alternative is to use the `System.TimeSpan` object with which you can specify the intervals in ticks, milliseconds, seconds, minutes, hours, or days.

The easiest way to show how this works is by demonstration, so below we will detail an application that fires two threads. The second thread will not perform its operations until the first has completed its operations; thread_timer.vb:

```
Imports System
Imports System.Threading
Imports System.Text
Imports Microsoft.VisualBasic

Public Class TimerExample

    Private message As String
    Private Shared tmr As Timer
    Private Shared complete As Boolean
```

Everything is straightforward above. We declare tmr as shared and class-wide as it will be defined in the Main() method:

```
Public Shared Sub Main()
    Dim obj As New TimerExample()
    Dim t As New Thread(AddressOf obj.GenerateText)
    t.Start()

    Dim tmrCallBack As New TimerCallback(AddressOf obj.GetText)
    tmr = New Timer(tmrCallBack, Nothing, TimeSpan.Zero, _
                    TimeSpan.FromSeconds(2))
```

Here we fire up a new thread that will execute on the GenerateText() method, which iterates through a For loop to generate a string and store it in the class-wide message field:

```
    Do
        If (complete) Then Exit Do
    Loop
    Console.WriteLine("Exiting Main...")
    Console.ReadLine()
End Sub
```

The above loop just freezes the Main() loop until the complete field is True. In a GUI different methods could be used, as the Application.Run() method puts the application in a perpetual loop anyway:

```
Public Sub GenerateText()
    Dim i As Integer
    Dim sb As StringBuilder = New StringBuilder()

    For i = 1 To 200
        sb.Insert(sb.Length, "This is Line ")
        sb.Insert(sb.Length, i.ToString())
        sb.Insert(sb.Length, ControlChars.CrLf)
    Next

    message = sb.ToString()
End Sub
```

Above is the first method used, which just generates 200 lines using a `StringBuilder` object, and then stores them in the `message` field.

```
Public Sub GetText(ByVal state As Object)
    If message Is Nothing Then Exit Sub
    Console.WriteLine("Message is :")
    Console.WriteLine(message)
    tmr.Dispose()
    complete = True
End Sub
End Class
```

The last method used in this class is fired every two seconds by the timer. If `message` hasn't been set yet, then it exits; otherwise it outputs a message and then disposes of the timer. This stops the timer from continuing to count. This should be performed as soon as the timer is no longer necessary.

The output from `thread_timer.vb` will be as follows:

```
Message is :
This is Line 1
This is Line 2

...

This is Line 199
This is Line 200

Exiting Main...
```

Spinning Threads with Threads

We've seen in code how to spawn a thread from the `Sub Main()`. In a similar way, we can also spawn multiple threads within a thread. For example, let's say we have a `Car` class that has a `Public` method called `StartTheEngine()`. The `StartTheEngine()` method calls another three `Private` methods called `CheckTheBattery()`, `CheckForFuel()`, and `CheckTheEngine()`. Since each of these tasks, checking the battery, fuel, and engine, can happen simultaneously, we can run each of these methods in a different thread. Here is how the `Car` class is implemented in `thread_spinning.vb`:

```
Imports System
Imports System.Threading

Class Car

    Public Sub StartTheEngine()
        Console.WriteLine("Starting the engine!")
```

```
      'Declare three new threads
      Dim batt As Thread = New Thread(AddressOf CheckTheBattery)
      Dim fuel As Thread = New Thread(AddressOf CheckForFuel)
      Dim eng As Thread = New Thread(AddressOf CheckTheEngine)

      batt.Start()
      fuel.Start()
      eng.Start()

      Dim i As Integer
      For i = 1 To 100000000
         '
      Next

      Console.WriteLine("Engine is ready!")
   End Sub

   Private Sub CheckTheBattery()
      Console.WriteLine("Checking the Battery!")

      Dim i As Integer
      For i = 1 To 100000000
         '
      Next

      Console.WriteLine("Finished checking the Battery!")
   End Sub

   Private Sub CheckForFuel()
      Console.WriteLine("Checking for Fuel!")

      Dim i As Integer
      For i = 1 To 100000000
         '
      Next

      Console.WriteLine("Fuel is available!")
   End Sub

   Private Sub CheckTheEngine()
      Console.WriteLine("Checking the engine!")

      Dim i As Integer
      For i = 1 To 100000000
         '
      Next

      Console.WriteLine("Finished checking the engine!")
   End Sub

End Class
```

In the StartTheEngine() method, we create three threads and then start each of them one by one.

```
Module Module1

    Sub Main()
        Console.WriteLine("Entering Sub Main!")

        Dim j As Integer
        Dim myCar As New Car()
        Dim worker As Thread = New Thread(AddressOf myCar.StartTheEngine)

        worker.Start()

        For j = 1 To 10000000
            '
        Next

        Console.WriteLine("Exiting Sub Main!")
    End Sub

End Module
```

In the Sub Main() method we simply create one more thread and execute the StartTheEngine() method in that thread, as illustrated in Figure 1.

Figure 1.

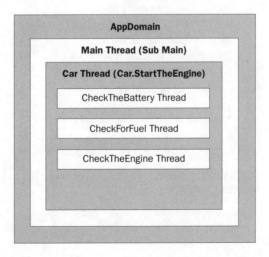

The output should look something like the following:

```
Entering Sub Main!
Exiting Sub Main!
Starting the engine!
Checking the Battery!
Checking for Fuel!
Checking the engine!
Finished checking the Battery!
Fuel is available!
Finished checking the engine!
Engine is ready!
```

As you can see, each of these methods works in it's own thread and is executed in its own time-sliced slot.

Spinning Threads with Threads with Threads

We can split the Car class into separate classes and we could build two more methods in a new Engine class called check1() and check2(). Then the Engine class will execute the check1() and check2() methods in its own thread as shown in Figure 2.

Figure 2.

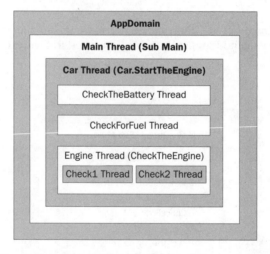

We'll remove the CheckTheEngine() method from the Car class and create one more class called Engine; see thread_spinning2.vb:

```
Class Engine

   Public Sub CheckTheEngine()
      Dim chck1 As Thread = New Thread(AddressOf Check1)
      Dim chck2 As Thread = New Thread(AddressOf Check2)

      check1.Start()
      check2.Start()
```

```
        Console.WriteLine("Checking the engine!")
        Dim count As Integer

        For count = 1 To 100000000
            '
        Next
        Console.WriteLine("Finished checking the engine!")
    End Sub

    Private Sub Check1()
        Console.WriteLine("Starting the engine check!!")

        Dim i As Integer
        For i = 1 To 100000000
            '
        Next

        Console.WriteLine("Finished engine check1!")
    End Sub

    Private Sub Check2()
        Console.WriteLine("Starting the engine check2!")

        Dim i As Integer
        For i = 1 To 100000000
            '
        Next

        Console.WriteLine("Finished engine check2!")
    End Sub

End Class
```

The Engine class has the public method CheckTheEngine() that creates two more threads and calls the check1() and check2() methods. Here is how the results may look:

```
Entering Sub Main!
Exiting Sub Main!
Starting the engine!
Checking the Battery!
Checking for Fuel!
Checking the engine!
Starting the engine check!!
Starting the engine check2!
Finished checking the Battery!
Fuel is available!
Engine is ready!
Finished engine check1!
Finished checking the engine!
Finished engine check2!
```

As you can see, spawning threads from within Threads is very easy. However, you may be interested in knowing the disadvantages; the performance degrades.

Performance Considerations

The more threads you create, the more work the system has to do to maintain the thread contexts and CPU instructions. The Processes tab of the Windows Task Manager will tell you how many processes and threads are currently running. However, these will be OS processes and they're not equivalent to the AppDomains.

If we want to know how many threads are running inside the CLR then you have to use the Windows Performance Monitor tool and add couple of CLR-specific performance categories. The CLR exposes a performance category called .NET CLR LocksAndThreads and we can use this category to get more information about the CLR-managed threads. Let's run the Performance Monitor and add the counters shown in the following table from the .NET CLR LocksAndThreads category.

Performance Counter	Description
# of current logical Threads	This counter displays the number of current managed threads in the application and includes both the running and stopped threads.
# of current physical Threads	This counter displays the number of OS threads created and owned by CLR. This counter may not map one to one with managed threads.
# of total recognized threads	This counter displays the number of current recognized threads by the CLR.
Current Queue Length	This counter displays number of threads that are waiting to acquire locks in the managed application.
Total # of Contentions	This counter displays the number of failures when the managed applications try to acquire locks.

Here is how the values looks like for our thread_spinning2 application:

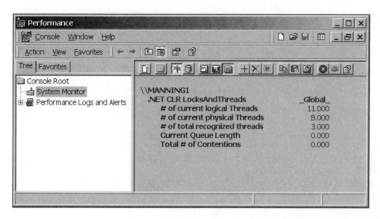

Here is a comprehensive overview of the ".NET CLR LocksAndThreads" performance counter information.

❑ The counter # of current local Threads specifies that 11 managed threads are created and owned by the CLR

> **Since we've added the counter instance "_Global_", we see all the threads created by the CLR.**

❑ The counter # of current physical Threads specifies that 8 OS threads are created and owned by the CLR

❑ The counter # of total recognized Threads specifies that 3 OS threads are recognized by the CLR and they're created by the Thread object

❑ The counter Total # of Contentions specifies that the runtime did not fail when it tried to acquirer managed locks. Managed lock fails are bad for the execution of code

Life Cycle of Threads

When a thread is scheduled for execution it can go through several states, including unstarted, alive, sleeping, etc. The Thread class contains methods that allow you to start, stop, resume, abort, suspend, and join (wait for) a thread. We can find the current state of the thread using its ThreadState property, which will be one of the values specified in the ThreadState enumeration:

❑ Aborted – The thread is in the Stopped state

❑ AbortRequested – The Abort() method has been called but the thread has not yet received the System.Threading.ThreadAbortexception that will try to terminate it

❑ Background – The thread is being executed in the background

❑ Running – The thread has started and is not blocked

❑ Stopped – The thread has stopped

❑ StopRequested – The thread is being requested to stop

❑ Suspended – The thread has been suspended

❑ SuspendRequested – The thread is being requested to suspend

❑ Unstarted – The Start() method has not yet been called on the thread

❑ WaitSleepJoin – The thread has been blocked by a call to Wait(), Sleep(), or Join()

Figure 3 shows the life cycle of a thread.

Figure 3.

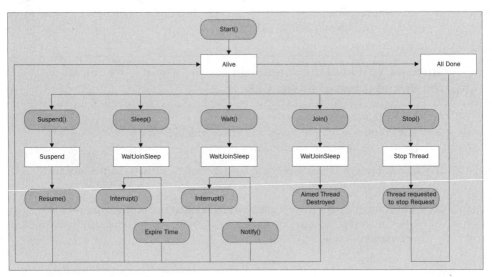

In this section, we'll explore the life cycle of threads.

Putting a Thread to Sleep

When we create a new thread we've to call the `Start()` method of the `Thread` object to schedule that thread. At this time, the CLR will allocate a time slice to the address of the method passed to the constructor of the `Thread` object. Once the thread is in the `Running` state, it can go back to either the `Sleep` or `Abort` states when the OS is processing the other threads. We can use the `Sleep()` method of the `Thread` class to put a thread to sleep. The `Sleep()` method is really useful if you are waiting for a resource and you want to retry for it. For example, let's say your application cannot proceed due to unavailability of a resource that it is trying to access. You may want your application to retry to access the resource after few milliseconds, in which case the `Sleep()` method is a good way to put the thread to sleep for a specified time before the application retries to access the resource.

The overloaded `Sleep()` method is available in two flavors. The first overload takes an integer as the parameter that will suspended the thread for number of milliseconds specified. For example, if you pass `100` to the parameter the thread will be suspended for 100 milliseconds. This will place the thread into the `WaitSleepJoin` state. Let's see an example for this, `thread_sleep2.vb`:

```
Imports System
Imports System.Threading

Public Class ThreadSleep

    Public Shared worker As Thread
    Public Shared worker2 As Thread

    Public Shared Sub Main()

        Console.WriteLine("Entering the Sub Main!")

        worker = New Thread(AddressOf Counter)
        worker2 = New Thread(AddressOf Counter2)

        'Make the worker2 object as highest priority
        worker2.Priority = ThreadPriority.Highest

        worker.Start()
        worker2.Start()

        Console.WriteLine("Exiting the Sub Main!")

    End Sub

    Public Shared Sub Counter()
        Dim i As Integer
        Console.WriteLine("Entering Counter")

        For i = 1 To 50
          Console.Write(i & " ")
          If i = 10 Then worker.Sleep(1000)
        Next
```

```
      Console.WriteLine()
      Console.WriteLine("Exiting Counter")
   End Sub

   Public Shared Sub Counter2()
      Dim i As Integer
      Console.WriteLine("Entering Counter2")

      For i = 51 To 100
        Console.Write(i & " ")
        If i = 70 Then worker.Sleep(5000)
      Next

      Console.WriteLine()
      Console.WriteLine("Exiting Counter2")
   End Sub
End Class
```

The Counter() method counts number from 1 to 50 and when it reaches 10 it sleeps for 1000 milliseconds. The Counter2() method counts from 51 to 100 and when it reaches 70 it sleeps for 5000 milliseconds. Here is how the output might look:

```
Entering the Sub Main!
Entering Counter2
51 52 53 54 55 56 57 58 59 60 61 62 63 64 65 66 67 68 69 70 Exiting
the Sub Main!
Entering Counter
1 2 3 4 5 6 7 8 9 10 11 12 13 14 15 16 17 18 19 20 21 22 23 24 25 26
27 28 29 30 31 32 33 34 35 36 37 38 39 40 41 42 43 44 45 46 47 48 49
50
Exiting Counter
71 72 73 74 75 76 77 78 79 80 81 82 83 84 85 86 87 88 89 90 91 92 93
94 95 96 97 98 99 100
Exiting Counter2
```

The second overload takes a TimeSpan as parameter and, based on the TimeSpan value, the current thread will be suspended. The TimeSpan is a structure defined in the System namespace. The TimeSpan structure has a few useful properties that return the time interval based on clock ticking. We can use Public methods such as FromSeconds() and FromMinutes() to specify the sleep duration. Here is an example, thread_sleep3.vb:

```
   Public Shared Sub Counter()
      ...
      For i = 1 To 50
        Console.Write(i & " ")
        If i = 10 Then worker.Sleep(System.TimeSpan.FromSeconds(1))
      Next
      ...
   End Sub
```

```
Public Shared Sub Counter2()
   ...
   For i = 51 To 100
      Console.Write(i & " ")
      If i = 70 Then worker.Sleep(System.TimeSpan.FromMinutes(0.1))
   Next
   ...
End Sub
```

The output will be similar to that of `thread_sleep2`.

Interrupting a Thread

When a thread is put to sleep, the thread goes to the `WaitSleepJoin` state. If the thread is in the sleeping state the only way to wake the thread is using the `Interrupt()` method. The `Interrupt()` method will place the thread back in the scheduling queue. Let's see an example for this, `thread_interrupt.vb`:

```
Imports System
Imports System.Threading

Public Class Interrupt

   Public Shared sleeper As Thread
   Public Shared worker As Thread

   Public Shared Sub Main()
      Console.WriteLine("Entering the Sub Main!")

      sleeper = New Thread(AddressOf SleepingThread)
      worker = New Thread(AddressOf AwakeTheThread)

      sleeper.Start()
      worker.Start()

      Console.WriteLine("Exiting the Sub Main!")
   End Sub

   Public Shared Sub SleepingThread()
      Dim i As Integer
      For i = 1 To 50
         Console.Write(i & " ")
         If i = 10 Or i = 20 Or i = 30 Then
            Console.WriteLine("Going to sleep at: " & i)
            sleeper.Sleep(20)
         End If
      Next
   End Sub
```

```
Public Shared Sub AwakeTheThread()
    Dim i As Integer
    For i = 51 To 100
        Console.Write(i & " ")
        If sleeper.ThreadState = _
            System.Threading.ThreadState.WaitSleepJoin Then
            Console.WriteLine("Interrupting the sleeping thread")
            sleeper.Interrupt()
        End If
    Next
End Sub
End Class
```

In the above example, the first thread (sleeper) is put to sleep when the counter reaches 10, 20, and 30. The second thread (worker) checks if the first thread is asleep. If so, it interrupts the first thread and places it back in the scheduler. The Interrupt() method is the best way to bring the sleeping thread back to life and you can use this functionality if the waiting for the resource is over and you want the thread to become alive. The output will look similar to the following:

```
Entering the Sub Main!
Exiting the Sub Main!
51 52 53 54 55 56 57 58 59 60 61 62 63 64 65 66 67 68 69 70 71 72 73
74 75 76 77 78 79 80 81 82 83 84 85 86 87 88 89 90 91 92 93 94 95 96
97 98 99 100 1 2 3 4 5 6 7 8 9 10 Going to sleep at: 10
11 12 13 14 15 16 17 18 19 20 Going to sleep at: 20
21 22 23 24 25 26 27 28 29 30 Going to sleep at: 30
31 32 33 34 35 36 37 38 39 40 41 42 43 44 45 46 47 48 49 50
```

Pausing and Resuming Threads

The Suspend() and Resume() methods of the Thread class can be used to suspend and resume the thread. The Suspend() method will suspend the current thread indefinitely until another thread wakes it up. When we call the Suspend() method, the thread will be place in the SuspendRequested or Suspended state.

Let's see an example for this. We'll create a new VB.NET application that generates prime numbers in a new thread. This application will also have options to pause and resume the prime number generation thread. To make this happen let's create a new VB.NET WinForms project called PrimeNumbers and build a UI like this in Form1.

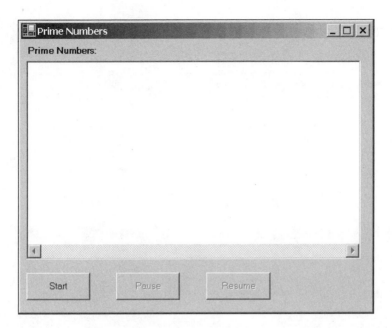

We've a `listbox` and three command buttons in the UI. The `listbox` is used to display the prime numbers and three command buttons are used to start, pause, and stop the thread. Initially we've disabled the pause and the resume buttons, since they can't be used till the thread is started. Let's see what the code is going to look like. We've declared a class level `Thread` object that is going to generated prime numbers.

```
Imports System
Imports System.Threading

Public Class Form1
  Inherits System.Windows.Forms.Form

  'Class level thread object
  Dim objWorkerThread As Thread
```

Double-click on the Start command button and add the following code.

```
Private Sub BtnStart_Click(ByVal sender As System.Object, _
            ByVal e As System.EventArgs) Handles BtnStart.Click

  'Let's create a new thread
  objWorkerThread = New Thread(AddressOf GeneratePrimeNumbers)

  'Let's give a name for the thread
  objWorkerThread.Name = "Prime Numbers Example"

  'Enable the Pause Button
  BtnPause.Enabled = True
```

```
        'Disable the Start button
        BtnStart.Enabled = False

        'Let's start the thread
        objWorkerThread.Start()
    End Sub
```

All the Start button does is create a new Thread object with the address of the
GeneratePrimeNumbers() method and assign the name Prime Number Example to
the thread. Then it enables the Pause button and disables the Start button. Then it starts
the Prime number generating thread using the Start method of the Thread class.

Let's double-click on the Pause button and add the following code.

```
    Private Sub BtnPause_Click(ByVal sender As System.Object, _
            ByVal e As System.EventArgs) Handles BtnPause.Click

        Try
            'If current state of thread is Running, then pause the Thread
            If (objWorkerThread.ThreadState = _
                System.Threading.ThreadState.Running) Then

                'Pause the Thread
                objWorkerThread.Suspend()

                'Disable the Pause button
                BtnPause.Enabled = False

                'Enable the resume button
                BtnResume.Enabled = True
            End If

        Catch Ex As ThreadStateException
            MessageBox.Show(Ex.ToString, "Exception", _
                        MessageBoxButtons.OK, MessageBoxIcon.Error, _
                        MessageBoxDefaultButton.Button1)
        End Try
    End Sub
```

The Pause button checks if the thread is in the Running state. If it is in the Running
state, it pauses the thread by calling the Suspend method of the Thread object. Then
it enables the Resume button and disables the Pause button. Since the Suspend method
can raise the ThreadStateException exception, we're wrapping the code with in a
Try...Catch block.

Double-click on the Resume button and add the following code.

```
    Private Sub BtnResume_Click(ByVal sender As System.Object, _
            ByVal e As System.EventArgs) Handles BtnResume.Click
```

```
'Check the thread state first
If objWorkerThread.ThreadState = _
   System.Threading.ThreadState.Suspended Or _
   objWorkerThread.ThreadState = _
   System.Threading.ThreadState.SuspendRequested Then

  Try
     'Resume the thread
     objWorkerThread.Resume()

     'Disable the resume button
     BtnResume.Enabled = False

     'Enable the Pause button
     BtnPause.Enabled = True

  Catch Ex As ThreadStateException
     MessageBox.Show(Ex.ToString, "Exception", _
                     MessageBoxButtons.OK, MessageBoxIcon.Error, _
                     MessageBoxDefaultButton.Button1)
  End Try
End If
End Sub
```

The **Resume** button checks if the state of the thread is Suspended or SuspendRequested before resuming the thread. If the state of the thread is either Suspended or SuspendRequested then it resumes the thread and disables the **Resume** button and enables the **Pause** button.

Well, so far our business logic is ready. Let's see the code that generates the prime numbers. Since our main aim is to use multithreading and not prime number generation, I'm not going to go deep into the code. The GeneratePrimeNumbers() method generates the first 255 prime numbers starting from 3. When the method finds a prime number it'll add the new prime number to an array as well as to the listbox. The first prime number, 2, will be automatically added to the listbox. Finally, the method will enable the **Start** button and disable the **Pause** button.

```
Public Sub GeneratePrimeNumbers()
   Dim lngCounter As Long
   Dim lngNumber As Long
   Dim lngDevideCounter As Long
   Dim bolIsPrime As Boolean
   Dim lngUpper As Long
   Dim PrimeArray(255) As Long

   'Init
   lngNumber = 3
   lngCounter = 2
   lngUpper = 1
```

```
      'We know that the first prime is 2. Therefore,
      'let's add it to the list and start from 3
      PrimeArray(1) = 2
      lstPrime.Items.Add(2)

      Do While lngCounter <= 255
         'Find the array index that contains the known prime
         'smaller than the root of the number.
         Do While PrimeArray(lngUpper + 1) < Math.Sqrt(lngNumber) _
                  And Not PrimeArray(lngUpper + 1) = 0

            lngUpper += 1
         Loop

         bolIsPrime = True

         'Try dividing this number by any already found prime
         'which is smaller then the root of this number.
         For lngDevideCounter = 1 To lngUpper
            If lngNumber Mod PrimeArray(lngDevideCounter) = 0 Then
               'This is not a prime number
               bolIsPrime = False

               'Exit the loop
               Exit For
            End If
         Next lngDevideCounter

         'If this is a prime number then display it
         If bolIsPrime Then
            'Guess we found a new prime.
            PrimeArray(lngCounter) = lngNumber
            'Increase prime found count.
            lngCounter += 1

            lstPrime.Items.Add(lngNumber)

            'Let's put the thread to sleep for 100 milliseconds.
            'This will simulate the time lag and we'll get time
            'to pause and resume the thread
                  objWorkerThread.Sleep(60)
         End If

         'Increment number by two
         lngNumber += 2
      Loop

      'Once the thread is finished execution enable the start
      'and disable the pause button
      BtnStart.Enabled = True
      BtnPause.Enabled = False
   End Sub
```

Well everything is ready now. Let's run the code and see how our application looks.

Well, everything looks good now and the code is working fine. But there is a huge flaw in our code. When the GeneratePrimeNumbers() method finds a prime number it adds the prime number back to the listbox control. It may not look like a problem for you if this code is running in a synchronized execution manner where both the prime number generation code and the user interface is running on the same thread. But in our example, the UI in running in a different thread from the GeneratePrimeNumbers() method. Therefore, when we go between threads to write data this could cause some unexpected behaviors in our application.

The best way to address this problem is using delegates. Simply, delegates are smart function pointers, and they provide starting points to functions. We can declare a delegate and we can use the delegate to inform the UI thread to update the listbox control itself. In this way, we're not crossing the threading boundaries and the application stability is not compromised.

Let's see how we can implement this operation. Let's add one more public delegate called UpdateData next to the objWorkerThread thread declaration:

```
Public Class Form1
    Inherits System.Windows.Forms.Form

    'Class level thread object
    Dim objWorkerThread As Thread
```

```
Public Delegate Sub UpdateData(ByVal RtnVal As String)
```

Let's modify the GeneratePrimeNumbers() method little bit to call the delegate from it. We've added a new string array with the initial value as 2, since the first prime number is 2. Then we've declared a new object of the type UpdateData as a delegate and we've passed the address of the UpdateUI method. Then we've used the Me.Invoke method with the delegate object and the string array to inform the user interface to update itself. We've done the same when we found a prime number.

Form1 is represented as Me in this context.

```
Public Sub GeneratePrimeNumbers()
    Dim lngCounter As Long
    Dim lngNumber As Long
    Dim lngDevideCounter As Long
    Dim bolIsPrime As Boolean
    Dim lngUpper As Long
    Dim PrimeArray(255) As Long
    Dim Args() As String = {"2"}
    Dim UIDel As New UpdateData(AddressOf UpdateUI)

    . . .

    'We know that the first prime is 2. Therefore,
    'let's add it to the list and start from 3
    PrimeArray(1) = 2
    Me.Invoke(UIDel, Args)

    . . .

    'If this is a prime number then display it
    If bolIsPrime Then
        'Guess we found a new prime.
        PrimeArray(lngCounter) = lngNumber
        'Increase prime found count.
        lngCounter += 1

        Args(0) = lngNumber
        Me.Invoke(UIDel, Args)

        'Let's put the thread to sleep for 100 milliseconds.
        'This will simulate the time lag and we'll get time
        'to pause and resume the thread
        objWorkerThread.Sleep(60)
    End If
    . . .
```

The UpdateUI() method simply accepts the value that needs to be added to the listbox in its parameter and adds the value to the listbox. Since the UpdateUI method runs in the UI thread there are no cross-boundary thread updates and the stability of our application is not compromised:

```
Sub UpdateUI(ByVal strResult As String)
    lstPrime.Items.Add(strResult)
End Sub
```

Destroying Threads

The `Abort()` method can be used to destroy the current thread. The `Abort()` method would be very useful, if you want to terminate the thread for whatsoever reason, such as the thread is taking too much time to execute. When this method is called against a thread, the `ThreadAbortException` exception will be raised. So it is always a good idea to watch for this exception in the code.

Let's see an example for this. We're going to create a new project called Destroying and we'll copy the code from the previous prime number generation code into the new `Form1.vb class`. Let's add one more Stop button to the UI like this.

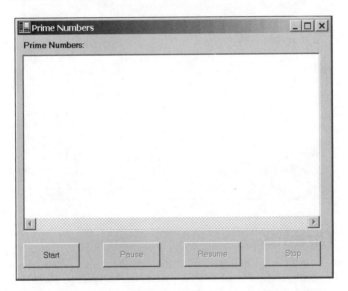

Let's add the following code into the Stop button.

```
Private Sub BtnStop_Click(ByVal sender As System.Object, _
            ByVal e As System.EventArgs) Handles BtnStop.Click
    Try
        'Enable the Start button and disable all others
        BtnStop.Enabled = False
        BtnPause.Enabled = False
        BtnResume.Enabled = False
        BtnStart.Enabled = True
```

```
      'Destroy the thread
      objWorkerThread.Abort()
   Catch Ex As ThreadAbortException
      MessageBox.Show(Ex.ToString, "Exception", _
                   MessageBoxButtons.OK, MessageBoxIcon.Error, _
                   MessageBoxDefaultButton.Button1)
   End Try
End Sub
```

This example is very similar to the previous example. The only difference is that we're using the `Abort()` method to destroy the thread when the user clicks on the **Stop** button. Then we're enabling the **Start** button and disabling all other buttons.

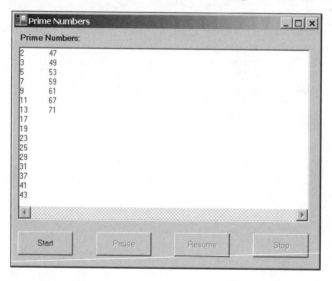

Joining Threads

The `Join()` method blocks the thread until the current thread is terminated. When we call the `Join()` method, the thread will be placed in the `WaitSleepJoin` state. This method is very useful, if one thread is dependent upon another thread. By simply joining two threads we are saying that the thread that is running when the `Join()` method is called will enter the `WaitSleepJoin` state and not return to the `Running` state until the method upon which the `Join()` method was called completes its tasks. Let's see an example for this, `thread_joining.vb`:

```
Imports System
Imports System.Threading

Public Class JoiningThread

    Public Shared SecondThread As Thread
    Public Shared FirstThread As Thread
```

```
Shared Sub First()
  Dim i As Integer
  For i = 1 To 250
    Console.Write(i & " ")
  Next
End Sub

Shared Sub Second()
  FirstThread.Join()
  Dim i As Integer
  For i = 251 To 500
    Console.Write(i & " ")
  Next
End Sub

Public Shared Sub Main()
  FirstThread = New Thread(AddressOf First)
  SecondThread = New Thread(AddressOf Second)

  FirstThread.Start()
  SecondThread.Start()

End Sub
End Class
```

In this simple example, the aim is to output numbers to the console sequentially, starting at 1 and finishing at 500. The First() method will output the first 250 numbers and the Second() method will produce those from 251 to 500. Without the FirstThread.Join() line in the Second() method, execution would switch back and forth between the two methods and our output would be scrambled (try commenting out the line and running the example again). By calling the FirstThread.Join() method within the Second() method, the execution of the Second() method is paused until the execution of whatever is in FirstThread (the First() method) has completed.

The Join() method is overloaded; it can accept either an integer or a TimeSpan as a single parameter and returns a Boolean. The effect of calling one of the overloaded versions of this method is that the thread will be blocked until either the other thread completes or the time period elapses, whichever occurs first. The return value will be True if the thread has completed and False if it has not.

Why Not Thread Everything?

We've seen several very useful benefits to threading; we can have several processes running at once, and several threads running within those processes. So, with all these benefits, why don't we just use new threads for all of our functions? Wouldn't that just make everything run fast? Not really. As a matter of fact, we will see in this section that quite the opposite can happen if we overuse threading.

Multithreaded applications require resources. Threads require memory to store the thread-local storage container. As you can imagine, the number of threads used is limited by the amount of memory available. Memory is fairly inexpensive these days so many computers have large amounts of memory. However, you should not assume that this is the case. If you are running your application on an unknown hardware configuration, you cannot assume that your application will have enough memory. Additionally, you cannot assume that your process will be the only one spawning threads and consuming system resources. Just because a machine has a lot of memory, doesn't mean its all for your application.

You will also discover that each thread also incurs additional processor overhead. Creating too many threads in your applications will limit the amount of time that your thread has to execute. Therefore, your processor could potentially spend more time switching between threads as opposed to actually executing the instructions that the threads contain. If your application is creating more threads, your application will gain more execution time than all the other processes with fewer threads.

To make this concept easier to understand, take the parallel example you'll find down at your local grocery store. Two cashiers are scanning groceries for their customers. However, there is only one bagger, who takes turns switching between the two cashiers. The bagger is rather efficient at jumping back and forth between the two registers and bagging the groceries because they don't pile up any faster than the bagger can bag the groceries. However, if two more cashiers open up lanes, it will become apparent that the bagger will spend more time jumping back and forth between the registers than they spend actually bagging groceries. Eventually, the store will need to get another bagger. In the case of threading, think of the cashiers as applications – or threads, and the bagger as a processor. The processor has to switch between threads. As the "threads" increase, the grocery store has to add another "processor" to be sure that the customers get the attention they need.

The phrase "too many threads" is a rather generic term – and rightly so. What constitutes "too many" on one system could be fine on another. Since hardware configurations largely dictate the number of threads available on a system, "too many" is an unquantifiable variable without specific configuration details and lots of testing.

It is for these reasons that Microsoft recommends that you use as few threads as possible in your applications. This limits the amount of resources required by the operating system.

Threading Opportunities

So, now I may have you wondering why you would thread at all if it could potentially have a negative impact on our application. The idea is that you will learn there is a time and place for threading. Learning which circumstances represent good opportunities to spawn a new thread is the key to making good design decisions. There are two distinct opportunities to consider spawning a new thread. In this section, we will discuss what those opportunities are.

Background Processes

The first opportunity to spawn a new thread occurs when your application needs to run a large process in the background while still keeping its user interface active and usable. We have all run into times when an application just didn't seem to respond because we had told it to query data or process a large piece of information. Take, for example, the case of professional graphics packages that are required to render graphics into a specific file format. In early versions of some products, asking the application to render a large graphic would result in the application becoming unresponsive until the rendering process had finished. This problem presents an ideal time to set a background thread to do your computer-intensive processing while leaving your user interface to run on the main application thread.

Let's take a look at an example of a background process that needs to spawn a new thread. This example demonstrates searching for files. When the search routine finds a file matching the pattern specified, it adds a new item to the listbox.

The code below will demonstrate that this function does indeed need its own thread:

```
Imports System.Threading
Imports System.IO

Public Class Form1
   Inherits System.Windows.Forms.Form

   Dim searchTerm as String
   Dim totalFiles As Int32
```

```
Private Sub Button1_Click(ByVal sender as System.Object, _
            ByVal e as System.EventArgs) Handles Button1.Click
    Search()
End Sub

Public Sub Search()
    searchTerm = TextBox1.Text
    ListBox1.Items.Clear()
    totalFiles = 0
    SearchDirectory("C:\winnt")
    MsgBox(totalFiles.ToString)
End Sub

Public Sub SearchDirectory(ByVal Path as String)

    ' Search the directory
    Dim di as New DirectoryInfo(Path)
    Dim f() as FileInfo = di.GetFiles(searchTerm)

    Dim myFile as FileInfo

    For Each myFile in f
        ListBox1.Items.Add(myFile.FullName)
    Next

    ' Search its sub directories
    Dim d() as DirectoryInfo = di.GetDirectories()
    Dim myDir as DirectoryInfo

    For Each myDir in d
        SearchDirectory(myDir.FullName)
    Next
End Sub

End Class
```

Go ahead and compile this example and run it. Type a search term in the search textbox, such as *.*, click the Single Thread Search button, and observe our problem. As you will see, we are searching for files and trying to update the user interface every time we find a file with our search criteria. However, because both the user interface and the search code are running on the same thread, we don't see the updates until the search code has completely finished its processing. Additionally, we cannot resize our form while the search is processing.

This rather long piece of code is actually a very simple demonstration. Most of the code listing is used to create and set up the form layout. Let's see if we can correct this problem with a simple change. In the Button_Click routine, add the following code to call the Search() function with the use of a new thread:

```
Private Sub Button2_Click(ByVal sender As System.Object, _
            ByVal e As System.EventArgs) Handles Button2.Click
    Dim t As New Thread(AddressOf Search)
    t.Start()
End Sub
```

Now recompile and run the program again. This time, type in the same search term and click the Multi Thread Search button. You can see that there is quite a difference. This time our results are displayed immediately. This is because Windows is now switching execution back and forth between the user interface and the search thread. The processor is now given a time slice to update the interface to reflect the changes in the listbox. You will also notice that we can now resize our form while it is searching.

There is one last thing to notice with this change. The search thread can access the data in the main thread. Data such as the searchTerm variable and the listbox can be accessed from within the search thread. This is one more demonstration of the fact that the global data of our process is available to all threads within the same process.

There are other background processes that may cause our interface to be unresponsive. We might want to do some intense processing, such as searching, sorting, formatting, parsing, and filtering a large number of records in a database. This would be another opportunity to consider using a new thread. You may also want to spawn a new thread if you want to run a routine that is constantly logging information. The user interface won't necessarily be unresponsive in this instance, but it may appear slow or sluggish if this type of routine isn't on its own thread.

Accessing External Resources

The second circumstance in which you might want to consider spawning a new thread occurs when you are accessing resources that are not local to your system. This might be a database process or a network file share somewhere on your network. In such cases, network performance could adversely affect your application performance.

Let's take the following example. We are going to connect to a database in this example. Let's assume that network performance is poor and may cause this application to be slow. Let's also assume that company policy dictates that no applications can be installed on the database server:

```
Imports System.Threading
Imports System.IO
Imports System.Data
Imports System.Data.SqlClient

Public Class Form1
  Inherits System.Windows.Forms.Form

  Public Sub Button1_Click(ByVal sender as System.Object, _
          ByVal e as System.EventArgs) Handles Button1.Click
    QueryData()
  End Sub

  Public Sub QueryData()
    Dim objReader as SqlDataReader
    Dim objConn as SqlConnection
    Dim objCommand as SqlCommand
```

```
      Dim intEmployeeID as Int32
      Dim strFirstName as String
      Dim strTitle as String
      Dim intReportsTo as Int32

      objConn = new SqlConnection("server=RemoteServer;" & _
                  "UID=RemoteUser;PWD=Password;database=northwind")
      objCommand = new SqlCommand("SELECT EmployeeID, FirstName, " & _
                  "Title, ReportsTo FROM Employees", objConn)
      objConn.Open()
      objReader = objCommand.ExecuteReader( _
                              CommandBehavior.CloseConnection)
      Do While (objReader.Read())
        intEmployeeID = objReader.GetInt32(0)
        strFirstName = objReader.GetString(1)
        strTitle = objReader.GetString(2)
        If (objReader.IsDBNull(3)) Then
          intReportsTo = 0
        Else
          intReportsTo = objReader.GetInt32(3)
        End If

        ListBox1.Items.Add(intEmployeeID.ToString() + " " + _
          strFirstName + " " + strTitle + " " + intReportsTo.ToString())
      Loop
      objReader.Close()
      objConn.Close()
    End Sub

  End Class
```

As you can see in this example, all we are doing is querying a remote database. The data returned will not be excessive, but you will notice that the user interface freezes while it takes time to get the data and update the listbox. We can again correct this by simply spawning a new thread and executing our database code within that thread. Let's add a second button and use the following code:

```
  Public Sub Button2_Click(ByVal sender as System.Object, _
        ByVal e as System.EventArgs) Handles Button1.Click
    Dim t as New Thread(AddressOf QueryData)
    t.Start()
  End Sub
```

Now when we run the code, we get a result similar to our last example. We can resize the form while the query runs. The interface is responsive throughout the entire query process.

Of course, I want to reiterate that this doesn't necessarily mean you should spawn a new thread every time you connect to a database. However, analyze your options to find out if you can move the database or the application so they reside on the same server. Also, make sure that this component isn't going to be continuously called from various client applications. Doing so would spawn additional threads for every call and consume more resources than you intended. There are ways to reuse objects and their threads without using a new thread every time your object is called. These issues will be covered in Chapters 3 and 5.

Threading Traps

We've seen the two main situations where it can be a good idea to use threading in your applications. However, there are some circumstances in which spawning a new thread would be a bad idea. Obviously, this isn't going to be a complete listing of inappropriate times to create new threads, but it is meant to give you an idea of what constitutes a bad threading decision. There are two main areas we'll look at here: the first is an instance where execution order is extremely important, and the second is a mistake seen quite often in code – creating new threads in a loop.

Execution Order Revisited

Recall the example do_something_thread.vb from earlier in the chapter where we created some code demonstrating the fact that execution randomly jumped from one thread to the other. It looked as if one thread would execute and show 10 lines in the console, then the next thread would show 15, and then return back to the original thread to execute 8. A common mistake in deciding whether to use threads or not is to assume that you know exactly how much code is going to execute in the thread's given time slice.

Here's an example that demonstrates this problem. It looks as if the thread t1 will finish first because it starts first, but that's a big mistake. Create a console application called ExecutionOrder and set its startup object to Sub Main. Build and run this example a few times – you'll get differing results:

```vb
Imports System
Imports System.Threading

Public Class ExecutionOrder
    Shared t1 as Thread
    Shared t2 as Thread

    Public Shared Sub WriteFinished(ByVal threadName as String)
        Select Case threadName
            Case "T1"
                Console.WriteLine()
                Console.WriteLine("T1 Finished")
            Case "T2"
                Console.WriteLine()
                Console.WriteLine("T2 Finished")
        End Select
    End Sub

    Public Shared Sub Main()
        t1 = New Thread(AddressOf Increment)
        t2 = New Thread(AddressOf Increment)
```

```
      t1.Name = "T1"
      t2.Name = "T2"

      t1.Start()
      t2.Start()
      Console.ReadLine()
   End Sub

   Public Shared Sub Increment()
      Dim I as Long

      For I = 1 to 1000000
         If I MOD 100000 = 0 Then
            Console.Write(" {" + Thread.CurrentThread.Name + "}")
         End If
      Next
      WriteFinished(Thread.CurrentThread.Name)
   End Sub
End Class
```

Sometimes t1 will finish then t2 will execute some more code and then finish. Sometimes t2 will finish completely and then t1 will execute to completion. The point is that you can't count on the threads completing in the order they were started. Later in this book we will discuss how you can synchronize threads to execute in a specified order. However, it's important to note synchronization doesn't happen by default.

This isn't the only problem associated with execution order. Take the next piece of example code where we show that data can be adversely affected by unsynchronized threads, ExecutionOrder2:

```
Imports System
Imports System.Threading

Public Class ExecutionOrder2
   Shared t1 As Thread
   Shared t2 As Thread
   Shared iIncr As Integer

   Public Shared Sub WriteFinished(ByVal threadName As String)

      Select Case threadName
        Case "T1"
          Console.WriteLine()
          Console.WriteLine("T1 Finished: iIncr = " + iIncr.ToString)
        Case "T2"
          Console.WriteLine()
          Console.WriteLine("T2 Finished: iIncr = " + iIncr.ToString)
      End Select
   End Sub
```

```
Public Shared Sub Main()
  iIncr = 0

  t1 = New Thread(AddressOf Increment)
  t2 = New Thread(AddressOf Increment)

  t1.Name = "T1"
  t2.Name = "T2"

  t1.Start()
  t2.Start()
  Console.Read()
End Sub

Public Shared Sub Increment()
  Dim I As Long

  For I = 1 To 1000000
    If I Mod 100000 = 0 Then
      Console.WriteLine(" {" + Thread.CurrentThread.Name + "} " + _
                        iIncr.ToString)
    End If
  Next

  iIncr += 1
  WriteFinished(Thread.CurrentThread.Name)
End Sub
End Class
```

This is a very similar class to ExecutionOrder. This time, however, we created a shared incrementing counter called iIncr. We tell the application to increment the variable before moving on to the WriteFinished() method. If we execute this application a few times, you will notice that the value of the incrementing counter will change at different times. Keep in mind again that we will show you how to synchronize these threads later on. These two examples should act as warnings that threads do not execute in the order that you want by default.

Threads in a Loop

One other common mistake made when someone discovers the joys of threading is that they create and use them within a loop. There follows a code example that demonstrates this, which is often implemented by programmers who are new to the threading concept. It is a common concept used by developers or system administrators to send notifications when an event occurs. The idea is not bad, but its implementation using a thread in the loop can cause many problems.

Please be aware that running this code may well disable your system. Don't run it unless you don't mind rebooting your machine to reclaim the resources the program will waste.

```vb
Imports System
Imports System.Threading
Imports System.Web.Mail
Imports System.Collections

Public Class LoopingThreads
   Delegate Sub SendMail(ByVal oMessageTo as String)

   Private Class MyMail
      Public EmailTo as String
      Public EmailFrom as String
      Public EmailSubject as String
      Public EmailBody as String
      Public SendThisEmail as SendMail   ' Delegate instance

      Public Sub Send()
         Dim oMail as New System.Web.Mail.MailMessage()
         oMail.To   = EmailTo
         oMail.From = EmailFrom
         oMail.Body = EmailBody
         oMail.Subject = EmailSubject
         oMail.BodyFormat = MailFormat.Text
         SmtpMail.Send(oMail)
         SendThisEmail(EmailTo)
      End Sub
   End Class

   Public Shared Function CreateEmail(ByVal oSendEmail as SendMail, _
      ByVal EmailTo as String, ByVal EmailFrom as String, _
      ByVal EmailBody as String, ByVal EmailSubject as String) as Thread

      Dim oMail as New MyMail()
      oMail.EmailFrom = EmailFrom
      oMail.EmailBody = EmailBody
      oMail.EmailSubject = EmailSubject
      oMail.EmailTo = EmailTo
      oMail.SendThisEmail = oSendEmail

      Dim t as New Thread(AddressOf oMail.Send)
      Return t
   End Function
End Class

Class Mailer
   Public Shared Sub MailMethod(ByVal oString as String)
      Console.WriteLine("Sending Email: " + oString)
   End Sub
```

```
End Class

Public Class DoMail
   Shared al as New ArrayList()

   Public Shared Sub Main()
      Dim I as Integer
      For I = 1 to 1000
         al.Add(i.ToString() + "@someplace.com")
      Next
      SendAllEmail()
   End Sub

   Public Shared Sub SendAllEmail()
      Dim I As Integer
      For I = 0 to al.Count - 1
         Dim t as thread = LoopingThreads.CreateEmail( _
                     AddressOf Mailer.MailMethod, Al(i), _
                     "johndoe@somewhere.com", _
                     "Threading in a loop", "Mail Example")
         t.Start()
         t.Join(Timeout.Infinite)
      Next
   End Sub
End Class
```

The code may be a little more complex than you thought because it also demonstrates how to use a delegate and a lengthy set of classes to call a thread with parameters. This is necessary because **threads can only create an entry on a subroutine that has no parameters.** As such, it is the duty of the programmer to create proxy methods that create the parameters for another function and return a thread object (we'll see more of this in later chapters). The calling method can then use the reference to the returned Thread to start execution.

Let's concentrate on the SendAllEmail method. This is where we loop through the ArrayList and send our parameters to the proxy method. We start a new thread for each and every email we want to send:

```
Public Shared Sub SendAllEmail()
   Dim I As Integer
   For I = 0 to al.Count - 1
      Dim t as Thread = LoopingThreads.CreateEmail( _
                  AddressOf Mailer.MailMethod, Al(i), _
                  "johndoe@somewhere.com", _
                  "Threading in a loop", "Mail Example")
      t.Start()
      t.Join(Timeout.Infinite)
   Next
End Sub
```

At first glance, this sounds like a good idea. Why not send email on another thread? It takes a long time to process sometimes doesn't it? This is true, but the problem is that we are now tying up the processor's execution time by switching between the threads. By the time this process is done, the time slice allocated to each thread is mainly spent unpacking and packing the thread local storage. Very little time is spent executing the instructions in the thread. The system may even lock up completely leaving poor John without any mail from us. What may make more sense is to create a single thread and execute the `SendAllEmail` method on that thread. Additionally, you could use a thread pool with a fixed number of threads. In this instance, when one thread in the pool has completed, it will spawn the next thread and send another email.

One common programming practice is to place work into a queue to be processed by a service. For instance, a bank may place an XML-based file in a network directory to be picked up by a service running on another server. The service would scan the directory for new files and process them one at a time. If more than one file is placed in the directory at a time, the service would process them one by one. In a typical environment, new files would be placed in this directory infrequently. Based on this information, at first glance, this might seem like a good time to start a new thread when a file is found. You would be right, but think about what would happen if the service that processes these files was stopped. What happens if a network problem prevents the service from accessing the directory for a long period of time? The files would pile up in the directory. When the service finally started again, or was allowed access to the directory once again, each file would essentially spawn a new thread on the service. Anyone who has used this model can tell you that this situation can bring a server to its knees.

The file model is just one example. Another similar model may be to use Microsoft BizTalk Server or Microsoft Message Queue with a service that processes items in a queue. All of these implementations have the same basic structure. The actual implementation isn't the important thing to note here. The point to walk away with is that if your work is being placed into a queue and you feel that multithreading is the answer; you might want to consider using thread pooling.

Summary

In this chapter we introduce the `System.Threading` namespace and examined the `Thread` class in detail. We also discussed some basic ideas to help you hone your decision making skills when it comes to multithreading your applications. You must always keep in mind the fact that threads require resources. Before you consume those resources, analyze what affect their use will have on the system and how you can minimize that overhead. You should consider creating a thread if you are accessing outside resources such as a network share or remote databases. You should also consider spawning a new thread when you plan to execute a lengthy process such as printing, I/O operations, or background data processing.

Whatever your situation, keep the number of your threads to a minimum. You will reduce the overhead on your processor, increase the amount of time that your time slice uses to process instructions within your thread, and reduce the amount of memory required by your application.

VB.NET

Threading

Handbook

3

3

Working with Threads

In the previous chapters, we discussed how threads play an important role in developing multiuser applications. We used threads to solve some significant problems, like giving multiple users or clients access to the same resource at the same time. However in the learning process, we ignored one issue that we now need to address: what would happen to the resource if one user changes the state of the resource and at the same time another user wants to change the state of the same resource?

Let's take the example of an ATM. Mr. X and his wife Mrs. X both decide to empty their checking account by withdrawing $1000 from an ATM. Unfortunately they forget to decide who will actually do the job. So, ironically, Mr. X and Mrs. X both access the checking account from different ATMs, at exactly the same time. If two users access the same account at the same time, and if the application is not thread-safe, it may possible that both the ATMs detect that there is enough amount in the checking account and dispense $1000 to each of their users. The two users are causing two threads to access the account database at the same time.

> **The .NET Framework provides specific mechanisms to deal with such problems. The phenomenon of allowing only one thread to access a resource at any point of time is called Synchronization. Synchronization is a feature available to developers for creating thread-safe access to critical resources.**

Why Worry About Synchronization?

There are two main reasons why any .NET developer needs to keep synchronization in mind design when designing a multithreaded application:

❑   To avoid **race conditions**

❑   To ensure **thread-safety**

Since the .NET Framework has built-in support for threading, there is a possibility that any class we develop may eventually be used in a multithreaded application. We don't need to (and shouldn't) design every class to be threadsafe, because threadsafety doesn't come for free. But we should at least *think* about threadsafety every time we design a .NET class. The costs of threadsafety and guidelines concerning when to make classes threadsafe are discussed later in the chapter. We need not worry about multithreaded access to local variables, method parameters, and return values, because these variables reside on the stack and are inherently threadsafe. But instance and class variables will only be threadsafe if we design our class appropriately.

Before we examine the nuts and bolts of synchronization, let's consider in detail the ATM example that we discussed at the beginning of the chapter where Mr. X and Mrs.X are both trying to withdraw the last $1000 from the same account at the same time. Figure 1 depicts the ATM scenario with more clarity. Such a condition, where two or more threads try to access the same resource to change its state at the same time and produce an undesirable effect, is called a *race condition.* To avoid the race condition, we need to make the `Withdraw()` method *thread-safe* so that only one thread can access the method at any point of time.

Figure 1

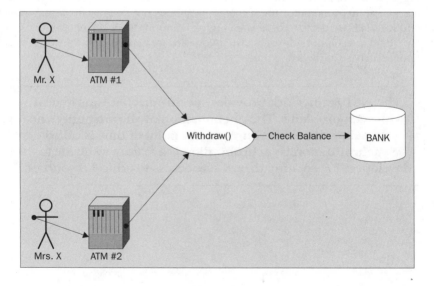

There are at least three ways to make an object thread-safe:

- ❏ Synchronize critical sections within the code
- ❏ Make the object immutable
- ❏ Use a thread-safe wrapper

Synchronize Critical Sections

To avoid undesirable effects caused by multiple threads updating a resource at the same time, we need to restrict the resource such that only one thread can update the resource at any point of time, or in other words, make the resource thread-safe. The most straightforward way to make an object or an instance variable thread-safe is to identify and synchronize its critical sections. For example, in the above scenario where Mr. X and Mrs. X both are both trying to access the same Withdraw() method at the same time, the Withdraw() method becomes the critical section and needs to be thread-safe. The easiest way to do this is to synchronize the method Withdraw() so that only one thread (either Mr. X or Mrs. X) can enter it at any one time. A transaction that cannot be interrupted during its execution is **Atomic**. By making the Withdraw() method atomic, we ensure that it is not possible for another thread to check the balance of the same account until the first thread has finished changing the state of the account (emptying in our case). The following code listing is a pseudo-code representation of a non-thread-safe Account class:

```
Class Account

    Sub ApprovedOrNot Withdraw (Amount)

        1.  Make sure that the user has enough cash (Check the Balance)
        2.  Update the Account with the new balance
        3.  Send approval to the ATM

    End Sub

End Class
```

This next listing represents a threadsafe pseudo-code version of the Account class:

```
Class Account

    Sub ApprovedOrNot Withdraw (Amount)

        lock this section (access for only one thread)

            1.  Check the Account Balance
            2.  Update the Account with the new balance
            3.  Send approval to the ATM

        End lock

    End Sub

End Class
```

In the first listing, two or more threads can enter the critical section at the same time so there is a possibility that both the threads check the balance at the same time, with both the threads receiving the balance ($1000) of the account. Due to this, there is a possibility that the ATM might dispense the $1000 amount to both the users, thus causing the account to go overdrawn unexpectedly.

On the contrary, in the second listing, only one thread is allowed access to the critical section at any one time. So, when Mr. X's thread begins to execute the Withdraw() method, Mrs. X's thread is not allowed access to the critical section and has to wait until Mr. X's thread returns. As a result, Mr. X's thread checks the balance of the account, updates the account with the new balance, which is $0 in this case, and then returns the approval Boolean value (True in this case) to the ATM for dispensing the cash. Until the cash is dispensed, no other thread has access to the critical section of Mr. and Mrs. X's Account object. After Mr. X receives the cash, Mrs. X's thread enters the critical section of the withdraw() method. Now, when the method checks for the account balance, the returned amount is $0 and, as a result, the method returns a Boolean value of False indicating insufficient balance and the ATM denies the withdrawal.

Making the Account Object Immutable

An alternative way to make an object threadsafe is to make the object immutable. An *immutable object* is one whose state can't be changed once the object has been created. This can be achieved by not allowing any thread to modify the state of the Account object once it is created. In this approach, we separate out the critical sections that read the instance variables from those that write to instance variables. The critical sections that only read the instance variables are left as they are and the critical sections that change the instance variables of the object are changed, such that, instead of changing the state of the current object, a new object that embodies the new state is created, and a reference to that new object is returned. In this approach, we don't need to lock the critical section because no methods (only the constructor) of an immutable object actually writes to the object's instance variables, thus, an immutable object is by definition thread-safe.

Using a Thread-Safe Wrapper

Another approach to making an object thread-safe is to write a wrapper class over the object that will be thread-safe rather than making the object itself thread-safe. The object will remain unchanged and the new wrapper class will contain synchronized sections of thread-safe code. The following listing is a wrapper class over the Account object:

```
Class AccountWrapper

   Private _a As Account

   public Sub New (Account a)
     Me._a = a
   End Sub
   Public Sub Withdraw(Double amount) As Boolean
     SyncLock Me
```

```
        return this._a.Withdraw(amount)
      End SyncLock
    End Sub

  End Class
```

The `AccountWrapper` class acts as a thread-safe wrapper of the `Account` class. The `Account` class is declared as a `Private` instance variable of the `AccountWrapper` class so that no other object or thread can access the `Account` variable. In this approach, the `Account` object does not have any thread-safe features, since all the thread-safety is provided by the `AccountWrapper` class. This approach is typically useful when we are dealing with a third-party library and the classes in that library are not designed for threadsafety. For example, let's assume that the bank already has an `Account` class that it used for developing software for its mainframe system and, for the sake of consistency, wants to use the same `Account` class for writing the ATM software. From the documentation of the `Account` class that the bank has provided us, it is clear that the `Account` class is not thread-safe. Also, we are not given access to the `Account` sourcecode for security reasons. In such a case, we would have to adopt the thread-safe wrapper approach where we develop the thread-safe `AccountWrapper` class as an extension to the `Account` class.

.NET Synchronization Support

The .NET Framework provides a few classes in the `System.Threading` and `System.EnterpriseServices` namespaces that allow the programmer to develop thread-safe code. The table below briefly describes some of the synchronization classes in the .NET Framework.

Class	Description
Monitor	Monitor objects are used to lock the critical sections of the code so that one and only one thread has access to the critical section at any point of time. Monitor objects help ensure the *atomicity* of critical sections of code.
Mutex	Mutex objects are similar to Monitor objects with the exception that they grant exclusive access to a resource shared across processes to only one thread. The Mutex overloaded constructor can be used to specify Mutex ownership and name.
AutoResetEvent, ManualResetEvent	AutoResetEvent and ManualResetEvent are used to notify one or more waiting threads that an event has occurred. Both these classes are NotInheritable.

Table continued on following page

Class	Description
Interlocked	The Interlocked class has the methods: CompareExchange(), Decrement(), Exchange(), and Increment() that provide a simple mechanism for synchronizing access to a variable that is shared by multiple threads.
SynchronizationAttribute	SynchronizationAttribute ensures that only one thread at a time can access an object. This synchronization process is automatic and does not need any kind of explicit locking of critical sections.

.NET Synchronization Strategies

The Common Language Infrastructure provides three strategies to synchronize access to instance and Shared methods and instance fields, namely:

- ❑ Synchronized contexts

- ❑ Synchronized code regions

- ❑ Manual synchronization

Synchronized Contexts

A context is a set of properties or usage rules that are common to a collection of objects with related run-time execution. The context properties that can be added include policies regarding synchronization, thread affinity, and transactions. In this strategy, we use the SynchronizationAttribute class to enable simple, automatic synchronization for ContextBoundObject objects. Objects that reside in a context and are bound to the context rules are called context-bound objects. .NET automatically associates a synchronization lock with the object, locking it before every method call and unlocking it (to be used by other threads) when the method returns. This is a huge productivity gain, because thread synchronization and concurrency management are among the most common development pitfalls. There is a lot more to this attribute than mere synchronization, including strategies for sharing the lock with other objects. The SynchronizationAttribute class is good for programmers who do not have experience of dealing with synchronization manually because it covers the instance variables, instance methods, and instance fields of the class to which this attribute is applied. It does not, however, handle synchronization of Shared fields and methods. It also does not help if we have to synchronize specific code blocks; synchronizing the entire object is the price we have to pay of for ease of use.

Coming back to our `Account` example, we can make our `Account` class thread-safe using the `SynchronizationAttribute`. The listing below shows an example of synchronizing the `Account` class using the `SynchronizationAttribute`:

```
[SynchronizationAttribute] Public Class Account
   Inherits ContextBoundObject

Sub ApprovedOrNot Withdraw (Amount)

   1.  Check the Account Balance
   2.  Update the Account with the new balance
   3.  Send approval to the ATM

   End Sub
End Class
```

Synchronized Code Regions

The second synchronization strategy concerns the synchronization of specific code regions. This section will look at the `Monitor` and `ReaderWriterLock` classes.

Monitors

Monitors are used to synchronize sections of code by acquiring a lock with the `Monitor.Enter()` method and then releasing the lock using the `Monitor.Exit()` method. The concept of a lock is normally used to explain the `Monitor` class. One thread gets a lock, while others wait until the lock is released. Once the lock is acquired on a code region, we can use the following methods within the `Monitor.Enter()` and `Monitor.Exit()` block:

❑   `Monitor.Wait()` – The method releases the lock on an object and blocks the current thread until it reacquires the lock

❑   `Monitor.Pulse()` – This method notifies a thread that is waiting in a queue that there has been a change in the object's state

❑   `Monitor.PulseAll()` – This method notifies all threads that are waiting in a queue that there has been a change in the object's state

The Enter() and Exit() Methods

Note that the `Monitor` methods are `Shared` and can be called on the `Monitor` class itself rather than an instance of that class. In the .NET Framework, each object has a lock associated with it that can be obtained and released so that only one thread at any time can access the object's instance variables and methods. Similarly, each object in the .NET Framework also provides a mechanism that allows it to be in a waiting state. Just like the lock mechanism, the main reason for this mechanism is to aid communication between threads. The need for such mechanism arises when one thread enters the critical section of an object and needs a certain condition to exist and assumes that another thread will create that condition from the same critical section.

The trick is now that only one thread is allowed in any critical section at any point of time, and when the first thread enters the critical section, any other thread cannot. So, how will the second thread create a condition in the critical section when the first thread is already in it? This is achieved by the "Wait and Pulse" mechanism. The first thread enters the critical section and executes the Wait() method. The Wait() method releases the lock prior to waiting and the second thread is now allowed to enter the critical section, changes the required condition, and calls the Pulse() method to notify the waiting thread that the condition has been reached and it can now continue its execution. The first thread then reacquires the lock prior to returning from the Monitor.Wait() method and continues execution from the point where it called Monitor.Wait().

No two threads can ever enter the Enter() function simultaneously. It is analogous to an ATM machine where only one person is allowed to operate at any point of time and another person can get their chance only after the first person leaves. You can see that the names Enter and Exit have been chosen very aptly. Figure 2 illustrates the Monitor functionality:

Figure 2

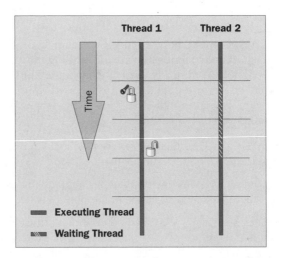

Let's see an example of using the Enter() and Exit() methods, MonitorEnterExit.vb:

```
Imports System
Imports System.Threading

Namespace MonitorEnterExit

    Public Class EnterExit
        Private result As Integer = 0
```

```
Public Sub NonCriticalSection()

  Console.WriteLine(("Entered Thread " & _
        Thread.CurrentThread.GetHashCode().ToString))
  Dim i As Integer
  For i = 1 To 5
    Console.WriteLine(("Result = " & result & " ThreadID " + _
          Thread.CurrentThread.GetHashCode().ToString))
    result += 1
    Thread.Sleep(1000)
  Next i

  Console.WriteLine(("Exiting Thread " & _
        Thread.CurrentThread.GetHashCode()))
End Sub

Public Sub CriticalSection()
  Monitor.Enter(Me)

  Console.WriteLine(("Entered Thread " & _
        Thread.CurrentThread.GetHashCode()))
  Dim i As Integer
  For i = 1 To 5
    Console.WriteLine(("Result = " & result & " ThreadID " + _
          Thread.CurrentThread.GetHashCode()))
    result += 1
    Thread.Sleep(1000)
  Next i

  Console.WriteLine(("Exiting Thread " & _
        Thread.CurrentThread.GetHashCode()))

  'Exit the Critical Section
  Monitor.Exit(Me)
End Sub

Public Overloads Shared Sub Main(ByVal args() As [String])
  Dim e As New EnterExit()

  If args.Length > 0 Then
    Dim nt1 As New Thread(New ThreadStart(AddressOf _
                                      e.NonCriticalSection))
    nt1.Start()

    Dim nt2 As New Thread(New ThreadStart(AddressOf _
                                      e.NonCriticalSection))
    nt2.Start()
  Else
    Dim ct1 As New Thread(New ThreadStart(AddressOf _
                                      e.CriticalSection))
    ct1.Start()
```

```
            Dim ct2 As New Thread(New ThreadStart(AddressOf _
                                        e.CriticalSection))
            ct2.Start()
        End If
    End Sub
  End Class
End Namespace
```

When we run the application without providing an input parameter we will get the output from the `CriticalSection()` method as follows:

```
Entered Thread 2
Result = 0   ThreadID 2
Result = 1   ThreadID 2
Result = 2   ThreadID 2
Result = 3   ThreadID 2
Result = 4   ThreadID 2
Exiting Thread 2
Entered Thread 3
Result = 5   ThreadID 3
Result = 6   ThreadID 3
Result = 7   ThreadID 3
Result = 8   ThreadID 3
Result = 9   ThreadID 3
Exiting Thread 3
```

When we do provide an input parameter, the corresponding output from the `NonCriticalSection()` method will be:

```
Entered Thread 2
Result = 0   ThreadID 2
Entered Thread 3
Result = 1   ThreadID 3
Result = 2   ThreadID 2
Result = 3   ThreadID 3
Result = 4   ThreadID 2
Result = 5   ThreadID 3
Result = 6   ThreadID 2
Result = 7   ThreadID 3
Result = 8   ThreadID 2
Result = 9   ThreadID 3
Exiting Thread 2
Exiting Thread 3
```

In the above example, we declare a `EnterExit` class with a global `result` variable and two methods: `NonCriticalSection()` and `CriticalSection()`. In the `NonCriticalMethod()` section, we don't specify any monitors to lock the section, while in the `CriticalSection()` method we lock the critical section using a monitor. Both the methods modify the value of `result`.

The critical section is defined between the code block `Monitor.Enter(Me)` and `Monitor.Exit(Me)`. The `Me` parameter indicates that the lock should be held on the current object in consideration. In the `Main()` method, we run the appropriate methods based on the arguments provided. If no argument is supplied, we use the `CriticalSection()` method and, if any argument is supplied, we use the `NonCriticalSection()` method. In both the cases, we have two threads accessing the methods, started from the `Main()` section, at the same time and changing the `result` variable. Though they are declared sequentially, the `For` loop and the sleep time will ensure that the threads will try to compete for resources.

Comparing the outputs of the critical and non-critical sections makes the concept of critical sections clear. If you observe the output from the `NonCriticalSection()` method, both the threads `nt1` and `nt2` are changing the `result` variable at the same time, thus resulting in a mixed output. This is because there are no locks in the `NonCriticalSection()`method and thus the method is not threadsafe. Multiple threads can access the method and so the global variable at the same time. On the contrary, if you observe the output from the `CriticalSection()` method, it is clear that until the thread `ct` exits the critical section (`Monitor.Enter()` and `Monitor.Exit()`) block, no other thread (`ct2` in this case) is allowed access to the critical section.

The Wait() and Pulse() Mechanism

The `Wait()` and `Pulse()` mechanism is used for interaction between threads. When a `Monitor.Wait()` is issued on an object, the thread that is accessing that object waits until it gets a signal to wakeup. The `Monitor.Pulse()` and `Monitor.PulseAll()` are used for signaling the waiting thread(s). The following listing is an example of how the `Wait()` and `Pulse()` methods work, `WaitAndPulse.vb`:

> **`Wait()` and `Pulse()` methods can be called only in the `Enter()` and `Exit()` code block.**

```
Imports System
Imports System.Threading

Namespace WaitAndPulse

    Public Class LockMe
    End Class

    Public Class WaitPulse1
        Private result As Integer = 0
        Private _lM As LockMe

        Public Sub New(ByVal l As LockMe)
            Me._lM = l
        End Sub
```

```
    Public Sub CriticalSection()
      Monitor.Enter(Me._lM)
      'Enter the Critical Section
      Console.WriteLine(("WaitPulse1: Entered Thread " + _
            Thread.CurrentThread.GetHashCode().ToString))
      Dim i As Integer
      For i = 1 To 5
        Monitor.Wait(Me._lM)
        Console.WriteLine("WaitPulse1: WokeUp")
        Console.WriteLine(("WaitPulse1: Result = " + _
            result.ToString + "  ThreadID " + _
            Thread.CurrentThread.GetHashCode().ToString))
        result += 1
        Monitor.Pulse(Me._lM)
      Next i

      Console.WriteLine(("WaitPulse1: Exiting Thread " + _
            Thread.CurrentThread.GetHashCode().ToString))

      'Exit the Critical Section
      Monitor.Exit(Me._lM)
    End Sub
End Class

Public Class WaitPulse2
  Private result As Integer = 0
  Friend _lM As LockMe

  Public Sub New(ByVal l As LockMe)
    Me._lM = l
  End Sub 'New

  Public Sub CriticalSection()
    Monitor.Enter(Me._lM)
    'Enter the Critical Section
    Console.WriteLine(("WaitPulse2: Entered Thread " + _
          Thread.CurrentThread.GetHashCode().ToString))
    Dim i As Integer
    For i = 1 To 5
      Monitor.Pulse(Me._lM)
      Console.WriteLine(("WaitPulse2: Result = " + _
          result.ToString + "  ThreadID " + _
          Thread.CurrentThread.GetHashCode().ToString))
      result += 1
      Monitor.Wait(Me._lM)
      Console.WriteLine("WaitPulse2: WokeUp")
    Next i

    'Wait for 10 seconds
    Console.WriteLine(("WaitPulse2: Exiting Thread " + _
          Thread.CurrentThread.GetHashCode().ToString))
```

```
        'Exit the Critical Section
        Monitor.Exit(Me._lM)
      End Sub
   End Class


Public Class ClassForMain

   Public Shared Sub Main()
      Dim l As New LockMe()

      Dim e1 As New WaitPulse1(l)
      Dim e2 As New WaitPulse2(l)

      Dim t1 As New Thread(New ThreadStart(AddressOf _
                                       e1.CriticalSection))
      t1.Start()

      Dim t2 As New Thread(New ThreadStart(AddressOf _
                                       e2.CriticalSection))
      t2.Start()
   End Sub
   End Class

End Namespace
```

The output from `WaitAndPulse` is:

```
WaitPulse1: Entered Thread 2
WaitPulse2: Entered Thread 3
WaitPulse2: Result = 0   ThreadID 3
WaitPulse1: WokeUp
WaitPulse1: Result = 0   ThreadID 2
WaitPulse2: WokeUp
WaitPulse2: Result = 1   ThreadID 3
WaitPulse1: WokeUp
WaitPulse1: Result = 1   ThreadID 2
WaitPulse2: WokeUp
WaitPulse2: Result = 2   ThreadID 3
WaitPulse1: WokeUp
WaitPulse1: Result = 2   ThreadID 2
WaitPulse2: WokeUp
WaitPulse2: Result = 3   ThreadID 3
WaitPulse1: WokeUp
WaitPulse1: Result = 3   ThreadID 2
WaitPulse2: WokeUp
WaitPulse2: Result = 4   ThreadID 3
WaitPulse1: WokeUp
WaitPulse1: Result = 4   ThreadID 2
WaitPulse1: Exiting Thread 2
WaitPulse2: WokeUp
WaitPulse2: Exiting Thread 3
```

In the `Main()` function, we create a LockMe object called 1. Then we create two objects of type `WaitPulse1` and `WaitPulse2`, and pass them as delegates, so that the threads can call the `CriticalSection()` method of both the objects. Note that the LockMe object in `WaitPulse1` is the same as the LockMe object in `WaitPulse2`, as the object has been passed by reference to their respective constructors. After initializing the objects, we create two threads, t1 and t2, and pass them the two created objects respectively. Assuming that `WaitPulse1.CriticalSection()` gets called first, the thread t1 enters the critical section of the method with a lock on the LockMe object and then executes `Monitor.Wait()` in the For loop. By executing `Monitor.Wait()`, it is waiting for a run-time notification (`Monitor.Pulse()`) from another thread to be woken up. Please note that when the thread executes the `Monitor.Wait()` method, it releases the lock on the LockMe object temporarily, so that other threads can access it. After thread t1 goes into the waiting state, thread t2 is free to access the LockMe object. Even though the LockMe object is a separate object (`WaitPulse1` and `WaitPulse2`), they both refer to the same object reference. Thread t2 acquires the lock on the LockMe object and enters the `WaitPulse2.CriticalSection()` method. As soon as it enters the For loop, it sends a run-time notification (`Monitor.Pulse()`) to the thread that is waiting on the LockMe object (t1 in this case) and goes off to the waiting state. As a result, t wakes up and acquires the lock on the LockMe object. Thread t1 then accesses the `result` variable and sends a runtime notification to the thread waiting on the LockMe object (thread t2 in this case). This cycle continues until the For loop ends. If you compare the description above with the output of the program, the concept will be crystal clear. It is important to note that every `Monitor.Enter()` function should be accompanied by a `Monitor.Exit()` function or else the program will never quit.

`Monitor.Enter()` takes an object as a parameter. If the object parameter is null, a variable, or an object of a value type like an integer an exception will be thrown.

The TryEnter() Method

The `Monitor.TryEnter()` method is similar to the `Enter()` method in that it tries to acquire an exclusive lock on an object; however, it does not block like the `Enter()` function. If the thread enters successfully then the `TryEnter()` method will return True. Let's see an example of this, `MonitorTryEnter.vb`:

```
Imports System
Imports System.Threading

Namespace MonitorTryEnter

  Public Class TryEnter

    Public Sub New()
    End Sub

    Public Sub CriticalSection()
      Dim b As Boolean = Monitor.TryEnter(Me, 1000)
      Console.WriteLine("Thread " & _
        Thread.CurrentThread.GetHashCode() & " TryEnter Value " & b)
      Dim i As Integer
```

```
        For i = 1 To 3
          Thread.Sleep(1000)
          Console.WriteLine(i & " " & _
                  Thread.CurrentThread.GetHashCode())
        Next i
        Monitor.Exit(Me)
      End Sub 'CriticalSection

      Public Shared Sub Main()
        Dim a As New TryEnter()
        Dim t1 As New Thread(New ThreadStart(AddressOf _
                                          a.CriticalSection))
        Dim t2 As New Thread(New ThreadStart(AddressOf _
                                          a.CriticalSection))
        t1.Start()
        t2.Start()
      End Sub
    End Class
End Namespace
```

The output from `MonitorTryEnter` is:

```
Thread 2 TryEnter Value True
Thread 3 TryEnter Value False
1 2
1 3
2 2
2 3
3 2
3 3
```

The SyncLock Statement

The `SyncLock` keyword can be used as an alternative to the `Monitor` methods. The following two blocks of code are equivalent:

```
Monitor.Enter(x)
  ...
Monitor.Exit(x)
```

```
SyncLock Me
  ...
End SyncLock
```

The following example, `Locking.vb`, uses the `SyncLock` keyword instead of the explicit `Monitor` methods:

```
Imports System
Imports System.Threading
```

```
Namespace Locking

  Public Class Locking

    Private result As Integer = 0

    Public Sub CriticalSection()

      SyncLock Me
        Console.WriteLine("Entered Thread " & _
                          Thread.CurrentThread.GetHashCode())
        Dim i As Integer
        For i = 1 To 5
          Console.WriteLine("Result = " & result & "  ThreadID " & _
                            Thread.CurrentThread.GetHashCode())
          result += 1
          Thread.Sleep(1000)
        Next i

        Console.WriteLine("Exiting Thread " & _
                          Thread.CurrentThread.GetHashCode())
      End SyncLock
    End Sub

    Public Overloads Shared Sub Main(ByVal args() As [String])
      Dim e As New Locking()

      Dim t1 As New Thread(New ThreadStart(AddressOf _
                                           e.CriticalSection))
      t1.Start()

      Dim t2 As New Thread(New ThreadStart(AddressOf _
                                           e.CriticalSection))
      t2.Start()
    End Sub
  End Class
End Namespace
```

The output from Locking.vb will be the same as for MonitorEnterExit (when a parameter has been supplied):

```
Entered Thread 2
Result = 0   ThreadID 2
Result = 1   ThreadID 2
Result = 2   ThreadID 2
Result = 3   ThreadID 2
Result = 4   ThreadID 2
Exiting Thread 2
Entered Thread 3
Result = 5   ThreadID 3
Result = 6   ThreadID 3
Result = 7   ThreadID 3
Result = 8   ThreadID 3
Result = 9   ThreadID 3
Exiting Thread 3
```

The ReaderWriterLock Class

ReaderWriterLock defines the lock that implements single-writer and multiple-reader semantics. The four main methods in the ReaderWriterLock class are:

❑ AcquireReaderLock(): This overloaded method acquires a reader lock, using either an integer or a TimeSpan for the timeout value

❑ AcquireWriterLock(): This overloaded method acquires a writer lock, using either an integer or a TimeSpan for the timeout value

❑ ReleaseReaderLock(): Releases the reader lock

❑ ReleaseWriterLock(): Releases the writer lock

> **Using the ReaderWriterLock class, any number of threads can safely read data concurrently. Only when threads are updating is data locked. Reader threads can acquire a lock only if there are no writers holding the lock. Writer threads can acquire lock only if there are no readers or writers holding the lock.**

The following listing, ReadWriteLock.vb, shows the use of the ReaderWriterLock() lock:

```vb
Imports System
Imports System.Threading

Namespace ReadWriteLock

  Public Class ReadWrite

    Private rwl As ReaderWriterLock
    Private x As Integer
    Private y As Integer

    Public Sub New()
      rwl = New ReaderWriterLock()
    End Sub 'New

    Public Sub ReadInts(ByRef a As Integer, ByRef b As Integer)
      rwl.AcquireReaderLock(Timeout.Infinite)
      Try
        a = Me.x
        b = Me.y
      Finally
        rwl.ReleaseReaderLock()
```

```
            End Try
        End Sub

        Public Sub WriteInts(ByVal a As Integer, ByVal b As Integer)
            rwl.AcquireWriterLock(Timeout.Infinite)
            Try
                Me.x = a
                Me.y = b
                Console.WriteLine("x = " & Me.x & " y = " & Me.y & _
                        " ThreadID = " & Thread.CurrentThread.GetHashCode())
            Finally
                rwl.ReleaseWriterLock()
            End Try
        End Sub
    End Class

    Public Class RWApp
        Private rw As New ReadWrite()

        Public Overloads Shared Sub Main(ByVal args() As [String])
            Dim e As New RWApp()

            'Writer Threads
            Dim wt1 As New Thread(New ThreadStart(AddressOf e.Write))
            wt1.Start()
Dim wt2 As New Thread(New ThreadStart(AddressOf e.Write))
            wt2.Start()

            'Reader Threads
            Dim rt1 As New Thread(New ThreadStart(AddressOf e.Read))
            rt1.Start()
Dim rt2 As New Thread(New ThreadStart(AddressOf e.Read))
            rt2.Start()
        End Sub

        Private Sub Write()
            Dim a As Integer = 10
            Dim b As Integer = 11
            Console.WriteLine("******** Write *********")

            Dim i As Integer
            For i = 0 To 4
                Me.rw.WriteInts(a, b)
                a += 1
                b += 1
                Thread.Sleep(1000)
            Next i
        End Sub

        Private Sub Read()
            Dim a As Integer = 10
            Dim b As Integer = 11
```

```
        Console.WriteLine("******** Read  *********")
        Dim i As Integer
        For i = 0 To 4
          Me.rw.ReadInts(a, b)
          Console.WriteLine("For i = " & i & " a = " & a & " b = " & _
            b & " ThreadID = " & Thread.CurrentThread.GetHashCode())
          Thread.Sleep(1000)
        Next i
      End Sub
    End Class
End Namespace
```

An example output from ReadWriteLock could be as follows:

```
******** Write *********
******** Write *********
******** Read  *********
For i = 0 a = 0 b = 0 ThreadID = 4
******** Read  *********
For i = 0 a = 0 b = 0 ThreadID = 5
x = 10 y = 11 ThreadID = 2
x = 10 y = 11 ThreadID = 3
For i = 1 a = 10 b = 11 ThreadID = 4
For i = 1 a = 10 b = 11 ThreadID = 5
x = 11 y = 12 ThreadID = 2
x = 11 y = 12 ThreadID = 3
For i = 2 a = 11 b = 12 ThreadID = 4
For i = 2 a = 11 b = 12 ThreadID = 5
x = 12 y = 13 ThreadID = 2
x = 12 y = 13 ThreadID = 3
For i = 3 a = 12 b = 13 ThreadID = 4
For i = 3 a = 12 b = 13 ThreadID = 5
x = 13 y = 14 ThreadID = 2
x = 13 y = 14 ThreadID = 3
For i = 4 a = 13 b = 14 ThreadID = 4
For i = 4 a = 13 b = 14 ThreadID = 5
x = 14 y = 15 ThreadID = 2
x = 14 y = 15 ThreadID = 3
```

In the above listing, threads wt1 and wt2 are writer threads that acquire writer locks in the WriteInts() method and threads rt1 and rt2 are reader threads that acquire reader locks in the ReadInts() method. In the WriteInts() method, the instance variables x and y are changed to the new values a and b respectively. When thread wt1 or wt2 acquires a writer lock by calling AcquireWriterLock(), no other thread (including the reader threads rt1 and rt2) is allowed access to the object until the thread releases the lock by calling the ReleaseWriterLock() method. This behavior is similar to that of Monitors. In the ReadInts() method, threads rt1 and rt2 acquire reader locks by calling the AcquireReaderLock() method. In the ReadInts() method, both the threads rt1 and rt2 can be given concurrent access to the instance variables x and y. Until the reader threads release the reader lock, neither of the writer threads (wt1 and wt2) is given access to the object. Only reader threads can have concurrent access to the object after acquiring the reader lock.

Monitors might be "toosafe" for threads that plan only to read the data rather than modify it. Monitors also have a performance hit associated with them and, for read-only type access, this performance hit is not necessary. The `ReaderWriterLock` class offers an elegant solution to dealing with read and write access to data by allowing any number of concurrent threads to read the data. It locks the data only when threads are updating the data. Reader threads can acquire a lock if and only if there are no writer threads holding the lock. Writer threads can acquire the lock if and only if there are no reader or writer threads holding the lock.

Manual Synchronization

The third synchronization strategy concerns manual techniques and the .NET Framework provides a classic suite of techniques. They give the programmer the ability to create and manage multithreaded applications using a low-level threading API analogous to the WIN32 Threading API.

The table below shows some of the classes in the `System.Threading` namespace that can be used for Manual Synchronization.

Class	Description
AutoResetEvent	The `AutoResetEvent` class is used to make a thread wait until some event puts it in the signaled state by calling the `Set()` method. The `AutoResetEvent` is automatically reset to nonsignaled by the system after a single waiting thread has been released. If no threads are waiting, the event object's state remains signaled. The `AutoResetEvent` corresponds to a Win32 `CreateEvent` call, specifying `False` for the `bManualReset` argument.
ManualResetEvent	The `ManualResetEvent` class is also used to make a thread wait until some event puts it in the signaled state by calling `Set()` method. The state of a `ManualResetEvent` object remains signaled until it is set explicitly to the non-signaled state by the `Reset()` method. The `ManualResetEvent` corresponds to a Win32 `CreateEvent` call, specifying `True` for the `bManualReset` argument.

Class	Description
Mutex	Mutex lock provides cross-process as well as cross-thread synchronization. The state of the Mutex is signaled if no thread owns it. Mutex doesn't have all of the wait and pulse functionality of the Monitor class, but it does offer the creation of named mutexes (using the overloaded constructor) that can be used between processes. The benefit of using Mutex over Monitors is that Mutex can be used across processes whereas Monitors cannot.
Interlocked	The Interlocked class provides methods for atomic, non-blocking integer updates that are shared between multiple threads. The threads of different processes can use this mechanism if the variable is in shared memory.

The ManualResetEvent Class

A ManualResetEvent object can possess only one of the two states, signaled (True) or non-signaled (False). The ManualResetEvent class inherits from the WaitHandle class and occurs when notifying one or more waiting threads that an event has occurred. The following listing, NETThreadEvents.vb, shows the use of the ManualResetEvent class with a non-signaled state. First we create an object called mansig and give it a value of False. As such, the function WaitOne() will wait until the mansig turns into True or the time value expires. Since the time duration elapsed while waiting, and the value of mansig was not set to True, it stopped blocking and returned with a value of False:

```
Imports System
Imports System.Threading

Namespace NETThreadEvents

  Public Class NonSignaledManual

    Public Shared Sub Main()
      Dim mansig As ManualResetEvent
      mansig = New ManualResetEvent(False)
      Console.WriteLine("Before WaitOne ")
      Dim b As Boolean = mansig.WaitOne(1000, False)
      Console.WriteLine("After WaitOne " & b)
    End Sub

  End Class

End Namespace
```

The output from NETThreadEvents with a value of False is:

```
Before WaitOne
After WaitOne False
```

In NETThreadEvents, we construct a ManualResetEvent object with a value of False.
The Boolean value False set the initial state of the ManualResetEvent object to non-
signaled. Then we call the WaitOne() method of the base-class WaitHandle. The
WaitOne() method takes two parameters. The first one is the number of milliseconds for
which we want the thread to wait at the WaitOne() method; the thread therefore waits for
one second before quitting. The second parameter is the exitContext, which is set to
True if we want to exit the synchronization domain for the context before the wait (if in a
synchronized context), and reacquire it; otherwise it's False.

The program blocks for one second at the WaitOne() method and then quits because
of the timeout. The state of the ManualResetEvent is still False, thus the Boolean b
returned by WaitOne() is False. Now let's figure out what will happen if we set the
state of ManualResetEvent to signaled (True) when we create it:

```
Imports System
Imports System.Threading

Namespace NETThreadEvents

   Public Class NonSignaledManual

      Public Shared Sub Main()
         Dim mansig As ManualResetEvent
         mansig = New ManualResetEvent(True)
         Console.WriteLine("Before WaitOne ")
         Dim b As Boolean = mansig.WaitOne(1000, False)
         Console.WriteLine(("After WaitOne " & b))
      End Sub

   End Class

End Namespace
```

The output from NETThreadEvents with a value of True is:

```
Before WaitOne
After WaitOne True
```

By changing initial state of the ManualResetEvent to signaled, the thread does not
wait at the WaitOne() method even though we specified the timeout value of 1000
milliseconds. When the ManualResetEvent was non-signaled, the thread waited for
the state to change to signaled, but it timed out after 1000 milliseconds. The state is
already signaled, so the thread has no reason to wait on the WaitOne() method. To
change the state of the ManualResetEvent to non-signaled, we have to call the
Reset() method of ManualResetEvent, and to change the state to signaled, we
have to call the Set() method.

The following listing, `ManualReset.vb`, shows the usage of the `Reset()` method, and the next, `ManualSet.vb`, shows the usage of the `Set()` method:

```vb
Imports System
Imports System.Threading

Namespace ManualReset

  Class Reset

    <STAThread> Shared Sub Main()
      Dim manRE As ManualResetEvent
      manRE = New ManualResetEvent(True)
      Console.WriteLine("Before WaitOne ")
      Dim state As Boolean = manRE.WaitOne(1000, True)
      Console.WriteLine("After first WaitOne " & state)

      'Change the state to signaled
      manRE.Reset()
      state = manRE.WaitOne(5000, True)
      Console.WriteLine("After second WaitOne " & state)

    End Sub

  End Class

End Namespace
```

The output from `ManualReset` is:

```
Before WaitOne
After first WaitOne True
After second WaitOne False
```

In `ManualReset`, we set the state of the `ManualResetEvent` object to signaled (`True`) in its constructor. As a result, the thread does not does not wait at the first `WaitOne()` method and returns `True`. Then we reset the state of the `ManualResetEvent` object to non-signaled (`False`), so we see that the thread has to wait for five seconds until it times out.

In `ManualSet.vb` we use the `Set()` method:

```vb
Imports System
Imports System.Threading

Namespace ManualSet

  Class ManualSet

    <STAThread> Shared Sub Main()
      Dim manRE As ManualResetEvent
      manRE = New ManualResetEvent(False)
      Console.WriteLine("Before WaitOne ")
      Dim state As Boolean = manRE.WaitOne(1000, True)
      Console.WriteLine("After first WaitOne " & state)
```

```
        'Change the state to signaled
        manRE.Set()
        state = manRE.WaitOne(5000, True)
        Console.WriteLine("After second WaitOne " & state)

    End Sub

End Class

End Namespace
```

The output from ManualSet is:

```
Before WaitOne
After first WaitOne False
After second WaitOne True
```

In ManualSet, we set the initial state of the ManualResetEvent object to non-signaled (False). As a result, the thread has to wait on the first WaitOne() method. Then we set the state to signaled using the Set() method, and the thread refuses to wait on the second WaitOne() method, and quits.

Just as the WaitOne() method waits for a single event object to become signaled, the WaitAll() function waits for all the event objects to become True or signaled, or it will stay there until the timeout occurs and the WaitAny() method waits for any of the event objects to become True or signaled.

The AutoResetEvent Class

The AutoResetEvent class works in a similar way to the ManualResetEvent class. It waits for the timeout to take place or the event to be signaled and then notifies the waiting threads about the event. One important difference between ManualResetEvent and AutoResetEvent is that AutoResetEvent changes state at the WaitOne() method. The following listing shows the usage of the AutoResetEvent class:

```
Imports System
Imports System.Threading

Namespace AutoReset

  Class AutoReset

    <STAThread> Shared Sub Main()
      Dim aRE As AutoResetEvent
      aRE = New AutoResetEvent(True)
      Console.WriteLine("Before first WaitOne ")
      Dim state As Boolean = aRE.WaitOne(1000, True)
      Console.WriteLine(("After first WaitOne " & state))
      state = aRE.WaitOne(5000, True)
      Console.WriteLine(("After second WaitOne " & state))
    End Sub
```

```
    End Class

End Namespace
```

The output from `AutoReset` is the same as that from the `ManualReset` example shown earlier:

```
Before first WaitOne
After first WaitOne True
After second WaitOne False
```

In `AutoReset`, the differences between the `AutoResetEvent` and `ManualResetEvent` are clear. The state of the event object changes from signaled to non-signaled at the first `WaitOne()`, and then it again changes state from non-signaled to signaled at the second `WaitOne()` method. As a result, the thread does not wait at the first `WaitOne()` method and has to wait at the second `WaitOne()` method until the time expires.

The Mutex Class

Like the `ManualResetEvent` and the `AutoResetEvent` classes, the `Mutex` class is also derived from the `WaitHandle` class. It is very similar to the `Monitor` class with the exception that it can be used for *interprocess* synchronization. Let's look at an example, `WroxMutex.vb`:

```
Imports System
Imports System.Threading

Namespace WroxMutex

  Class NETMutex
    Private Shared myMutex As System.Threading.Mutex

    Public Shared Sub Main()
      myMutex = New System.Threading.Mutex(True, "WROX")
      Dim nm As New NETMutex()
      Dim t As New Thread(New ThreadStart(AddressOf nm.Run))
      t.Start()
      Console.WriteLine("Thread will sleep for 5 seconds")
      Thread.Sleep(5000)
      Console.WriteLine("Thread Woke Up")
      myMutex.ReleaseMutex()
      Console.WriteLine("Before WaitOne")
      myMutex.WaitOne()
      Console.WriteLine("Lock owned by Main Thread")
    End Sub
```

```
Public Sub Run()
  Console.WriteLine("In Run method")
  myMutex.WaitOne()
  Console.WriteLine("Thread will sleep for 10 seconds")
  Thread.Sleep(10000)
  Console.WriteLine("End of Run method")
End Sub

End Class

End Namespace
```

The output from WroxMutex is:

```
Thread will sleep for 5 seconds
In Run method
Thread Woke Up
Thread will sleep for 10 seconds
Before WaitOne
End of Run method
Lock owned by Main Thread
```

In WroxMutex, we construct a Mutex with a Boolean value indicating that the calling thread should have initial ownership of the Mutex, and a string that is the name of the Mutex. We then create a thread, which calls the Run() method. The Mutex is still owned by the main thread. In the Run() function, the thread t has to wait until the main thread releases the ownership of the Mutex. Thus, the thread t waits at the WaitOne() method call in the Run() method. After sleeping for five seconds, the main thread releases the Mutex lock. Thread t then gets the ownership of the Mutex lock and then goes off for a sleep. Now, the Main() function will not be able to acquire the ownership of the Mutex until the thread t releases the ownership or aborts. In this case, the thread t times out and dies, so the ownership of the Mutex is transferred back to the main thread.

The Interlocked Class

Interlocked synchronizes access to a variable that is being shared by a number of threads. The operation is carried out in an *atomic* manner. Let's see an example, WroxInterlocked.vb:

```
Imports System
Imports System.Threading

Namespace WroxInterlocked

  Class WinterLocked
    Public a As New ManualResetEvent(False)
    Private i As Integer = 5
```

```
      Public Sub Run(ByVal s As Object)
        Interlocked.Increment(i)
          Console.WriteLine(Thread.CurrentThread.GetHashCode() & " " & i)
      End Sub
    End Class

    Public Class MainApp

      Public Shared Sub Main()
        Dim mR As New ManualResetEvent(False)
        Dim wL As New WinterLocked()

        Dim i As Integer
        For i = 1 To 10
          ThreadPool.QueueUserWorkItem(New WaitCallback(AddressOf _
                                        wL.Run), 1)

        Next i
        mR.WaitOne(5000, True)
      End Sub
    End Class
End Namespace
```

The output for WroxInterLocked is:

```
2  6
2  7
2  8
2  9
2  10
2  11
2  12
2  13
2  14
2  15
```

WroxInterLocked shows the use of the Interlocked class. We increment the value of the global variable (i) in an atomic manner. Like the Increment() method, there is also a Decrement() method that reduces the value of a variable by one. In the same manner, the Exchange() method changes the value of two variables passed to it as ByRef parameters.

Shared Variables and Methods and Synchronization

Shared variables and methods are affected differently from instance variables and methods in a synchronization lock. Shared variables are class variables, whereas variables that belong to an object are object or instance variables. In other words, there will be only one instance of a Shared variable and a Shared method will be shared by multiple objects of the same class and every object of the same class has its own set of instance variables and methods. So, if we synchronize a Shared variable or a Shared method, the lock is applied on the *entire class* all of the objects created from that class. As a result, no other object will be allowed to use the Shared variables of the class.

The ThreadStaticAttribute Class

ThreadStaticAttribute is used on a Shared variable to create a separate variable for each thread executing it, rather than sharing (default behavior) the Shared variable across threads. This means that a Shared variable with the ThreadStaticAttribute is not shared across different threads accessing it. Each thread accessing it will have a separate copy of the same variable. If one thread modifies the variable, another thread accessing it will not be able to see the changes. This behavior is contrary to the default behavior of Shared variables. In short, ThreadStaticAttribute gives us the best of both worlds (Shared and instance).

> *The reason that the class is named* ThreadStaticAttribute *and not* ThreadSharedAttribute *is because most OO languages, such as C# and Java, use the keyword* Static *when VB.NET uses the keyword* Shared.

The following listing shows the use of ThreadStaticAttribute (WroxShared.vb):

```
Imports System
Imports System.Threading

Namespace WroxShared

  Class ThreadStatic

      <ThreadStaticAttribute()> Public Shared x As Integer = 1
      Public Shared y As Integer = 1

      Public Sub Run()
        Dim i As Integer
        For i = 1 To 10
          Dim t2 As Thread = Thread.CurrentThread
          x += 1
          y += 1
          Console.WriteLine("i = " & i & " ThreadID = " & _
                          t2.GetHashCode() & " x=" & x & " y=" & y)
          Thread.Sleep(1000)
        Next i
      End Sub

  End Class

  Public Class MainApp

      Public Shared Sub Main()
        Dim tS As New ThreadStatic()
        Dim t1 As New Thread(New ThreadStart(AddressOf tS.Run))
        Dim t2 As New Thread(New ThreadStart(AddressOf tS.Run))
        t1.Start()
        t2.Start()
      End Sub

  End Class

End Namespace
```

The output from WroxShared is:

```
i=1  ThreadID=2  x=1  y=2
i=1  ThreadID=3  x=1  y=3
i=2  ThreadID=2  x=2  y=4
i=2  ThreadID=3  x=2  y=5
i=3  ThreadID=3  x=3  y=6
i=3  ThreadID=2  x=3  y=7
i=4  ThreadID=3  x=4  y=8
i=4  ThreadID=2  x=4  y=9
i=5  ThreadID=3  x=5  y=10
i=5  ThreadID=2  x=5  y=11
i=6  ThreadID=3  x=6  y=12
i=6  ThreadID=2  x=6  y=13
i=7  ThreadID=3  x=7  y=14
i=7  ThreadID=2  x=7  y=15
i=8  ThreadID=3  x=8  y=16
i=8  ThreadID=2  x=8  y=17
i=9  ThreadID=3  x=9  y=18
i=9  ThreadID=2  x=9  y=19
i=10 ThreadID=3  x=10 y=20
i=10 ThreadID=2  x=10 y=21
```

We all know a Shared variable is a class variable and its value remains the same across multiple objects of the class. ThreadStaticAttribute allows each thread accessing a Shared variable to have its own copy. In WroxStatic, variable x has ThreadStaticAttribute applied to it. As a result, each of the threads t1 and t2 will have a separate copy of the Shared variable x and changes made to x by thread t1 will not be visible to thread t2. On the other hand, changes made to the variable y by thread t1 will be visible to thread t2. If you observe the output of the program, variable x is incremented separately for threads t1 and t2.

> **The difference between a shared variable with a ThreadStaticAttribute and an instance variable is that the Shared variable does not require an object to access it, whereas an exception will be thrown if we try to access an instance variable without creating the instance of an object.**

Synchronization and Performance

Synchronization carries the overhead of the time required to acquire the synchronization lock. As a result, the performance is always poorer than the non-thread-safe version. As multiple threads might be trying to access the objects at the same time to acquire the synchronization lock, the performance of the entire application might be affected inadvertently. This is a tradeoff a developer must be aware of when designing larger applications. The important part is that these thread contentions are not visible until a thorough stress test is performed. Stress testing is extremely important in designing large-scale multithreaded applications. The developer has to balance these factors:

- ❏ To be safe, synchronize as much as possible. This makes the program slower, at worst no better than its single threaded version.

- ❏ For performance, synchronize as little as possible.

Multithreaded design is a continual tradeoff between these two factors.

Beware of Deadlocks

Though essential for threadsafety, synchronization, if not used properly, can cause deadlocks. As such, it is very important to understand what deadlocks are and how to avoid them. Deadlock occurs when two or more threads are waiting for two or more locks to be freed and the circumstances in the program logic are such that the locks will never be freed. Figure 3 illustrates a typical deadlock scenario.

Figure 3

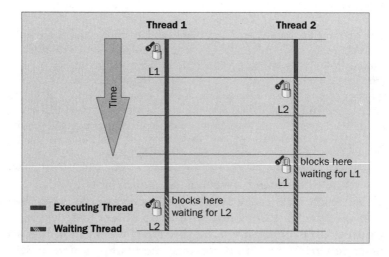

In the figure, Thread 1 acquires lock L1 on an object by entering its critical section. In this critical section, Thread 1 is supposed to acquire lock L2. Thread 2 acquires lock L2 and is supposed to acquire lock L1. So, now Thread 1 cannot acquire lock L2 because Thread 2 owns it and Thread 2 cannot acquire lock L1 because Thread 1 owns it. As a result, both the threads enter into an infinite wait or deadlock. One of the best ways to prevent the potential for deadlock is to avoid acquiring more than one lock at a time, which is often practicable. However, if that is not possible, you need a strategy that ensures you acquire multiple locks in a consistent, defined order. Depending on each program design, the synchronization strategies to avoid deadlocks may vary. There is no standard strategy that can be applied to avoid all deadlocks. Most of the time, deadlocks are not detected until the application is deployed on a full-scale basis. We can consider ourselves lucky if we are able to detect deadlocks in our program during the testing phase. A critical, but often overlooked element of any locking strategy is documentation. Unfortunately, even in cases where a good synchronization strategy is designed to avoid deadlocks, much less effort is made in documenting it. At the minimum, every method should have documentation associated with it that specifies the locks that it acquires and describes the critical sections within that method.

Let's take a look at an example, Deadlock.vb:

```vb
Imports System
Imports System.Threading

Namespace DeadLock

    Class DL
        Private field_1 As Integer = 0
        Private lock_1 As Object = New Integer(1) {}
        Private field_2 As Integer = 0
        Private lock_2 As Object = New Integer(1) {}

        Public Sub first(val As Integer)
            SyncLock lock_1
                Console.WriteLine("First:Acquired lock_1:" + _
                        Thread.CurrentThread.GetHashCode().ToString + _
                        " Now Sleeping")
                Thread.Sleep(1000)

                SyncLock lock_2
                    Console.WriteLine("First:Acquired lock_2:" + _
                            Thread.CurrentThread.GetHashCode().ToString)
                    field_1 = val
                    field_2 = val
                End SyncLock
            End SyncLock
        End Sub

        Public Sub second(val As Integer)
            SyncLock lock_2
                Console.WriteLine("Second:Acquired lock_2:" + _
                        Thread.CurrentThread.GetHashCode().ToString)
```

```
            SyncLock lock_1
                Console.WriteLine("Second:Acquired lock_1:" + _
                    Thread.CurrentThread.GetHashCode().ToString)
                field_1 = val
                field_2 = val
            End SyncLock
        End SyncLock
    End Sub
End Class

Public Class MainApp
    Private d As New DL()

    Public Shared Sub Main()
        Dim m As New MainApp()
        Dim t1 As New Thread(New ThreadStart(AddressOf m.Run1))
        t1.Start()
        Dim t2 As New Thread(New ThreadStart(AddressOf m.Run2))
        t2.Start()
    End Sub

    Public Sub Run1()
        Me.d.first(10)
    End Sub

    Public Sub Run2()
        Me.d.second(10)
    End Sub
End Class
End Namespace
```

The output from DeadLock is:

```
First:Acquired lock_1:2 Now Sleeping
Second:Acquired lock_2:3
```

In DeadLock, thread t1 calls the first() method, acquires lock_1, and goes to sleep
for one second. In the meantime, thread t2 calls the second() method and acquires
lock_2. Then it tries to acquire lock_1 in the same method. But lock_1 is owned by
thread t1, so thread t2 has to wait until thread t1 releases lock_1. When thread t1
wakes up, it tries to acquire lock_2. Now lock_2 is owned by thread t2 and thread t1
cannot acquire it until thread t2 releases lock_2. This results in a deadlock and a hang
program. Commenting out the Thread.Sleep() line from the method first() does
not result into deadlock, at least temporarily, because, thread t1 acquires lock_2 before
thread t2. But, in real-world scenarios, instead of Thread.Sleep(), we might connect
to a database resulting in thread t2 acquiring lock_2 before thread t1, and it will result
in a deadlock. The example shows how important it is to carve out a good locking
scheme in any multithreaded application. A good locking scheme may incorporate the
acquisition of lock by all the threads in a well defined manner. In case of the example
above, thread t2 should not acquire lock_2 until it is release by thread t2 or thread t2
should not acquire lock_1 until thread t1 releases it. These decisions depend on
specific application scenarios and cannot be generalized in any way. Testing of the
locking scheme is equally important, because deadlocks usually occur in deployed
systems due to lack of stress and functional testing.

End-to-End Examples

In this section of the chapter we will take a look at two larger examples. First, we'll take a look at creating thread-safe wrappers and then move on to a database connection pool.

Writing Your Own Thread-Safe Wrappers

The general idea of writing our own wrapper comes from the fact that we may not want to make every class in our library threadsafe, as synchronization has performance penalties associated with it. We would like to give the application developer a choice of whether to use a synchronized class or not. As the application developer would neither like to take the risk of a deadlock nor would want to pay the performance penalty of using a thread-safe class in a single-threaded environment, they might prefer to have a choice of having a built-in schronized wrapper for the same class in the library rather than writing a specific one. Collection classes like `ArrayList` and `Hashtable` in the `System.Collections` namespace already have this feature. We can decide whether we want to use a thread-safe `Hashtable` or not during initialization of the `Hashtable`. We can initialize a thread-safe `Hashtable` by calling the shared `Synchronized()` method of the `Hashtable` class as shown below:

```
Dim h as Hashtable
h = Hashtable.Synchronized(New Hashtable())
```

It would be good to give the application developer such a choice. In this example, we will attempt to develop a class and a synchronized wrapper for the class. We will develop a Book Collection library and Figure 4 shows the UML representation of the Book Collection library.

Figure 4

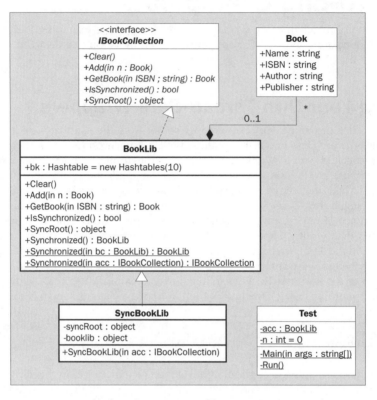

The program is very simple, but the concept of having intrinsic synchronization support is very important. By adding intrinsic synchronization support to our library, the developer will be able to choose between a synchronized and non-synchronized environment for the same class. For example, programmers who do not need synchronization can instantiate an object as follows:

```
Dim b As BookLib = New BookLib()
```

While programmers who use our type in a thread-hot environment can use the thread-safe wrappers as follows:

```
Dim b As BookLib = New BookLib()
b = b.Synchronized()
```

The following is the complete BookLib.vb source along with its synchronized wrapper:

```
Imports System
Imports System.Threading
Imports System.Collections
```

```vbnet
' Interface for dealing with collections of books.
Interface IBookCollection
  Sub Clear()
  Sub Add(ByVal n As Book)
  Function GetBook(ByVal ISBN As String) As Book
  ReadOnly Property IsSynchronized() As Boolean
  ReadOnly Property SyncRoot() As Object
End Interface

Public Class Book
  ' Properties and private variables avoided for code simplicity
  ' Real-World application should have private variables and
  ' properties accessing them.
  Public Name As String
  Public ISBN As String
  Public Author As String
  Public Publisher As String
End Class

' BookLib class. Non-Synchronized.
Class BookLib
  Implements IBookCollection

  Friend bk As New Hashtable(10)

  Public Overridable Sub Clear() _
        Implements WroxBookCollection.IBookCollection.Clear
    Me.bk.Clear()
  End Sub

  Public Overridable Sub Add(ByVal b As Book) _
        Implements WroxBookCollection.IBookCollection.Add

    Console.WriteLine("Adding Book for ThreadID:" + _
                  Thread.CurrentThread.GetHashCode().ToString)

    ' Sleep for 2 seconds so that in case of a synchronized wrapper,
    ' other threads will have to wait till this thread wakes up.
    Thread.Sleep(2000)
    'Add ISBN as the Key
    bk.Add(b.ISBN, b)

  End Sub

  Public Overridable Function GetBook(ByVal ISBN As String) As Book _
        Implements WroxBookCollection.IBookCollection.GetBook

    Console.WriteLine("Getting Book for ThreadID:" + _
                  Thread.CurrentThread.GetHashCode().ToString)
    Return CType(bk(ISBN), Book)

  End Function
```

113

```
   Public Overridable ReadOnly Property IsSynchronized() As Boolean _
         Implements WroxBookCollection.IBookCollection.IsSynchronized
      Get
         Return False
      End Get
   End Property

   Public Overridable ReadOnly Property SyncRoot() As Object _
         Implements WroxBookCollection.IBookCollection.SyncRoot
      Get
         Return Me
      End Get
   End Property

   Public Overloads Function Synchronized() As BookLib
      ' Return a thread-safe wrapper around this instance.
      Return Synchronized(Me)
   End Function

   Public Overloads Shared Function Synchronized( _
                                    ByVal bc As BookLib) As BookLib

      ' Return a thread-safe wrapper around the specified
      ' instance (which cannot be null).
      If bc Is Nothing Then
         Throw New ArgumentNullException("bc")
      End If

      If bc.GetType() Is GetType(SyncBookLib) Then
         Throw New InvalidOperationException( _
                  "BookLib reference is already synchronized.")
      End If

      Return New SyncBookLib(bc)
   End Function

   Public Overloads Shared Function Synchronized( _
                  ByVal acc As IBookCollection) As IBookCollection
      ' Return a thread-safe wrapper around the specified
      ' instance (which cannot be null).
      If acc Is Nothing Then
         Throw New ArgumentNullException("acc")
      End If

      If acc Is GetType(SyncBookLib) Then
         Throw New InvalidOperationException( _
                  "BookLib reference is already synchronized.")
      End If

      Return New SyncBookLib(acc)
   End Function

End Class
```

```
' SyncBookLib is the Synchronized wrapper around the BookLib class.
' This class will allow us to instantiate a synchronized wrapper.
NotInheritable Class SyncBookLib
   Inherits booklib
   Shadows MsyncRoot As Object
   Private booklib As Object

   Friend Sub New(ByVal acc As IBookCollection)
     booklib = acc
     MsyncRoot = acc.SyncRoot
   End Sub

   Public Overrides Sub Clear()
     SyncLock SyncRoot
       MyBase.Clear()
     End SyncLock
   End Sub

   Public Overrides Sub Add(ByVal b As Book)
     SyncLock SyncRoot
       MyBase.Add(b)
     End SyncLock
   End Sub

   Public Overrides Function GetBook(ByVal ISBN As String) As Book
     SyncLock SyncRoot
       Return CType(bk(ISBN), Book)
     End SyncLock
   End Function

   Public Overrides ReadOnly Property IsSynchronized() As Boolean
     Get
       Return True
     End Get
   End Property

   Public Overrides ReadOnly Property SyncRoot() As Object
     Get
       Return MsyncRoot
     End Get
   End Property

End Class

' This is the Main Application.
Class Test
   Private Shared acc As BookLib
   Private Shared n As Integer = 0

   Overloads Shared Sub Main(ByVal args() As String)

     acc = New BookLib()
```

115

```vb
' If the any argument is passed from the command-line
' Use a Synchronized Wrapper
If args.Length > 0 Then
  acc = acc.Synchronized()
End If

Dim threads As Thread() = _
              {New Thread(New ThreadStart(AddressOf Run)), _
               New Thread(New ThreadStart(AddressOf Run)), _
               New Thread(New ThreadStart(AddressOf Run))}

Dim t As Thread
For Each t In threads
  t.Start()
Next t

For Each t In threads
  t.Join()
Next t

Dim i As Integer
For i = 0 To n - 1
  Dim bk As Book = acc.GetBook(i.ToString())
  If Not (bk Is Nothing) Then
    Console.WriteLine("Book : " + bk.Name)
    Console.WriteLine("ISBN : " + bk.ISBN)
    Console.WriteLine("ISBN : " + bk.Publisher)
    Console.WriteLine("Author : " + bk.Author)
  End If
Next i
Console.WriteLine("Total Number of books added " + n.ToString)
Console.ReadLine()
End Sub

Shared Sub Run()
  Dim i As Integer
  For i = 0 To 1
    Dim bk As New Book()
    bk.Author = "Tejaswi Redkar"
    bk.Name = "A" & i.ToString
    bk.Publisher = "Wrox"
    bk.ISBN = n.ToString()
    n += 1
    acc.Add(bk)
  Next i
End Sub

End Class
```

In the above example, we first declare an interface IbookCollection, which has the following methods and properties for handling collection of books:

❑   Clear() – Method to clear the book collection

❑   Add() – Method to add a book to the book collection

❑   GetBook() – Method to get a book from the book collection

❑   IsSynchronized() – Read-only property used to check whether the collection is synchronized or not

❑   SyncRoot() – Read only property to get the synchronized root of the collection

Next we declare a class called Book representing a book in the collection. For example, the collection might be a library or a book store, but the representation of the Book class is the same in both.

The BookLib class implements the IBookCollection interface. As a result, the BookLib class must implement all the methods and properties of the IBookCollection interface. We declare a Hashtable called bk as the collection that will contain our books. The Key of the Book object will be its ISBN number. In the Add() method, we add a Book object to the Hashtable. In the GetBook() method, we retrieve the Book object if its ISBN number is supplied.

Now we must address any synchronization issues. In the Synchronized() method, we create an object of type SyncBookLib and return a reference to it. SyncBookLib is the synchronized version of the BookLib class. SyncBookLib inherits from the BookLib class, thus inheriting all the properties and methods that the BookLib class has already implemented. The difference between SyncBookLib and BookLib class is that in the SyncBookLib class, we lock all the critical sections using monitors. For example, the Clear(), GetBook(), and Add() methods have locks in their implementations thus making them thread-safe, whereas, in the BookLib class, there are no locks in any of the method.

In the Test class, we create a synchronized BookLib if we pass any command-line argument. If there are no command-line arguments passed, we create a non thread-safe BookLib object. Then we create three threads that add some books to our book library. When you run the application, the difference between the execution of synchronized BookLib and non-synchronized BookLib will be clear. In the synchronized version, only one thread can access the library at any point of time. So, the other two threads have to wait until the first thread has finished adding books to the BookLib. This is not the case if we use the non-synchronized version; all the threads are given concurrent access to the BookLib object instance.

The output from BookLib with a command-line argument (thread-safe) will be as follows:

```
Adding Book for ThreadID:2
Adding Book for ThreadID:3
Adding Book for ThreadID:4
Adding Book for ThreadID:2
Adding Book for ThreadID:3
Adding Book for ThreadID:4
Book : A0
ISBN : 0
ISBN : Wrox
Author : Tejaswi Redkar
Book : A0
ISBN : 1
ISBN : Wrox
Author : Tejaswi Redkar
Book : A0
ISBN : 2
ISBN : Wrox
Author : Tejaswi Redkar
Book : A1
ISBN : 3
ISBN : Wrox
Author : Tejaswi Redkar
Book : A1
ISBN : 4
ISBN : Wrox
Author : Tejaswi Redkar
Book : A1
ISBN : 5
ISBN : Wrox
Author : Tejaswi Redkar
Total Number of books added 6
```

The output from BookLib with no command-line argument (non-thread-safe) will be as follows:

```
Adding Book for ThreadID:3
Adding Book for ThreadID:4
Adding Book for ThreadID:2
Adding Book for ThreadID:3
Adding Book for ThreadID:4
Adding Book for ThreadID:2
Getting Book for ThreadID:7
Book : A0
ISBN : 0
ISBN : Wrox
Author : Tejaswi Redkar
Getting Book for ThreadID:7
Book : A0
ISBN : 1
ISBN : Wrox
Author : Tejaswi Redkar
Getting Book for ThreadID:7
Book : A0
ISBN : 2
ISBN : Wrox
Author : Tejaswi Redkar
Getting Book for ThreadID:7
Book : A1
```

```
ISBN : 3
ISBN : Wrox
Author : Tejaswi Redkar
Getting Book for ThreadID:7
Book : A1
ISBN : 4
ISBN : Wrox
Author : Tejaswi Redkar
Getting Book for ThreadID:7
Book : A1
ISBN : 5
ISBN : Wrox
Author : Tejaswi Redkar
Total Number of books added 6
```

A Database Connection Pool

Object pools are very common in enterprise software development where instantiation of objects has to be controlled in order to improve the performance of the application. For example, database connections are expensive objects to be created every time we need to connect to a database. So, instead of wasting resources in instantiating the database connection for every database call, we can pool and reuse some connection objects that we have already created and thus gain a performance advantage by saving the time and resources required to create a new connection object for every database call.

Object pooling can be thought of as similar to buying books. First we check whether the book is available within the company or the school library, then we check whether a "like-new" used book is posted somewhere on the internet for sale, and if we don't find it anywhere then we go and buy the new book (of course, if the company reimburses, nobody cares, just buy a new one). Object Pooling is similar; first we check the pool to see whether the object has already been created and pooled, if it is pooled, we get the pooled object; else we create a new one and pool it for future use. Object pooling is extensively used in large-scale application servers like Enterprise Java Beans (EJB) Servers, MTS/COM+, and even .NET Framework.

In this section, we will develop a database connection pool for pooling database connections. Database connections are expensive to create. In a typical web application there might be thousands of users trying to access the web site at the same time. If most of these hits need database access to serve dynamic data and we go on creating new database connection for each user, we are going to run out of the number of simultaneous connections supported by the database and, as a result, the web site will either slow down considerably in delivering the dynamic content, or crash after a critical point is reached. Connection pooling will help us balance the number of simultaneous users trying to access the database with the number of simultaneous connections supported by the database. The pool will also increase the performance of the web site considerably since we will not have to create a new connection for every user. Once data is served to one user, the connection will be returned back to the pool for future use.

Implementing the Pool

Let's start by taking a look at a UML diagram that depicts our database connection pool application. Figure 5 show the `ObjectPool` class and the `DBConnectionSingleton` class that inherits the `ObjectPool` class.

Figure 5

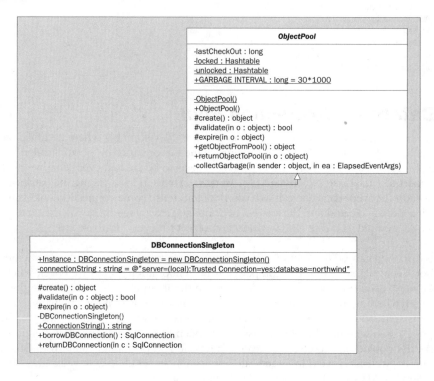

The ObjectPool Class

Let's start our discussion of the `ObjectPool` class by listing it in its entirety:

```
Imports System
Imports System.Collections
Imports System.Timers

Namespace WroxVB

   Public MustInherit Class ObjectPool
      'Last Checkout time of any object from the pool.
      Private lastCheckOut As Long

      'Hashtable of the checked-out objects
      Private Shared locked As Hashtable
```

```
'Hashtable of available objects
Private Shared unlocked As Hashtable

'Clean-Up interval
Friend Shared GARBAGE_INTERVAL As Long = 30 * 1000

Shared Sub New()
  locked = Hashtable.Synchronized(New Hashtable())
  unlocked = Hashtable.Synchronized(New Hashtable())
End Sub

Friend Sub New()
  lastCheckOut = DateTime.Now.Ticks
  'Create a Time to track the expired objects for cleanup.
  Dim aTimer As New System.Timers.Timer()
  aTimer.Enabled = True
  aTimer.Interval = GARBAGE_INTERVAL
  AddHandler aTimer.Elapsed, AddressOf collectGarbage
End Sub

' The derived class should implement this method
Protected MustOverride Function create() As Object

' The derived class should implement this method
Protected MustOverride Function validate(ByVal o As Object) _
                                         As Boolean

' The derived class should implement this method
Protected MustOverride Sub expire(ByVal o As Object)

' Get the object from the pool
Friend Function getObjectFromPool() As Object
  Dim now As Long = DateTime.Now.Ticks
  lastCheckOut = now
  Dim o As Object = Nothing

  SyncLock Me
    Try
      Dim myEntry As DictionaryEntry
      For Each myEntry In unlocked
        o = myEntry.Key

        If validate(o) Then
          unlocked.Remove(o)
          locked.Add(o, now)
          Return o
        Else
          unlocked.Remove(o)
          expire(o)
          o = Nothing
        End If
      Next myEntry
    Catch
```

```vb
                  ' Implement error handling
            End Try
            o = create()
            locked.Add(o, now)
        End SyncLock
        Return o
    End Function

    ' Return the object to the pool
    Friend Sub returnObjectToPool(ByVal o As Object)
        If Not (o Is Nothing) Then
            SyncLock Me
                locked.Remove(o)
                unlocked.Add(o, DateTime.Now.Ticks)
            End SyncLock
        End If
    End Sub

    ' Clean up the pool by deleting the expired objects.
    Private Sub collectGarbage(ByVal sender As Object, _
                ByVal ea As System.Timers.ElapsedEventArgs)
        SyncLock Me
            Dim o As Object
            Dim now As Long = DateTime.Now.Ticks
            Dim e As IDictionaryEnumerator = unlocked.GetEnumerator()

            Try
                While e.MoveNext()
                    o = e.Key
                    If now - CLng(unlocked(o)) > GARBAGE_INTERVAL Then
                        unlocked.Remove(o)
                        expire(o)
                        o = Nothing
                    End If
                End While
            Catch
                ' Implement error handling
            End Try
        End SyncLock
    End Sub
End Class

End Namespace
```

The ObjectPool base class contains two important methods;
getObjectFromPool(), which gets on object from the pool and
returnObjectToPool(), which returns object to the Pool. The object pool is
implemented as two Hashtables, one called locked and the other called unlocked.
The locked Hashtable contains all the objects that are currently in use and unlocked
contains all the objects that are free and available for use. The ObjectPool also
contains three MustOverride methods create(), validate(), and expire(), that
must be implemented by the derived classes.

In total, there are three critical sections in the `ObjectPool` class:

❑ While getting an object to the pool, `getObjectFromPool()` is used − A lock is needed while adding an object to the pool because the content of the `locked` and `unlocked` hashtables change and we do not want any race condition here.

❑ While returning an object to the pool, `returnObjectToPool()` is used − Again, a lock is needed while returning an object to the pool because the content of the `locked` and `unlocked` hashtables will change and a new object will be available for use. Here also we cannot afford to have a race condition, because, we do not want multiple threads accessing the same hashtable at the same time.

❑ While cleaning up the expired objects from the pool, `collectGarbage()` - In this method, we go over the `unlocked` hashtable to find and remove expired objects from the pool. The content of the `unlocked` hashtable may change and we need the removal of expired objects to be atomic.

In the `getObjectFromPool()` method, we iterate over the `unlocked` hashtable to get the first available object. The `validate()` method is used to validate the specific object. The `validate()` method may vary in specific implementations based on the type of the pooled object. For example, if the object is a database connection, the derived class of the object pool needs to implement the `validate()` method to check whether the connection to the database is open or closed. If the validation of the pooled object succeeds, we remove the object from the `unlocked` hash table and put it in the `locked` hashtable. The `locked` hash table contains the objects that are currently in use. If the validation fails, we kill the object with the `expire()` method. The `expire()` method also needs to be implemented by the derived class and is specific to the specific type of pooled object. For example, in the case of a database connection, the expired object will close the database connection. If a pooled object is not found, that is if the `unlocked` hash table is empty, we create a new object using the `create()` method and put the object in the `locked` hash table.

The `returnObjectToPool()` method implementation is much simpler. We just have to remove the object from the `locked` hashtable and put it back in the `unlocked` hash table for recycling. In this whole recycling process, we have to take into consideration the memory usage of the application. Object pooling is directly proportional to memory usage. So, the more objects we pool, the more memory we will be using. To control memory usage, we should periodically garbage-collect the objects that are pooled. This can be achieved by assigning a timeout period to every pooled object. If the pooled object is not used within the timeout period, it will be garbage -collected. As a result, the memory usage of the object pool will vary depending on the load on the system. The `collectGarbage()` method is used for handling the garbage collection of the pooled object. This method is called by the `aTimer` delegate that is initialized in the `ObjectPool` constructor. In our example, we the garbage-collection interval to 30 seconds in the `GARBAGE_COLLECT` constant.

> **We haven't implemented any database connection-specific code so we can assume that the `ObjectPool` class can be used for the pooling any type of .NET Framework objects.**

The DBConnectionSingleton Class

The `DBConnectionSingleton` class is the implementation of a database connection-specific object pool. The main purpose of this class is to provide database connection-specific implementations of the `create()`, `validate()`, and `expire()` methods inherited from the `ObjectPool` class. The class also provides methods called `borrowDBConnection()` and `returnDBConnection()` for borrowing and returning database connection objects from the object pool.

The complete listing of the `DBConnectionSingleton` class is as follows:

```vb
Imports System
Imports System.Data.SqlClient

Namespace WroxVB

   Public NotInheritable Class DBConnectionSingleton
      Inherits ObjectPool

      ' Private Constructor of the Singleton
      Private Sub New()
      End Sub

      ' This is how you get the instance of a Singleton
      Public Shared Instance As New DBConnectionSingleton()

      Private Shared _connectionString As String = _
         "server=(local);User ID=sa;Password=;database=northwind"

      Public Shared Property ConnectionString() As String
         Get
            Return _connectionString
         End Get

         Set(ByVal Value As String)
            _connectionString = Value
         End Set
      End Property

      ' Implemented create function of the ObjectPool class
      Protected Overrides Function create() As Object
         Dim temp As New SqlConnection(_connectionString)
         temp.Open()
         Return temp
      End Function
```

```vbnet
' Check whether the Connection is Open or Closed
Protected Overrides Function validate(ByVal o As Object) _
                                As Boolean
  Try
    Dim temp As SqlConnection = CType(o, SqlConnection)
    Return Not temp.State.Equals(ConnectionState.Closed)
  Catch
    ' Implement error handling
  End Try
End Function

' Close the Database Connection
Protected Overrides Sub expire(ByVal o As Object)
  Try
    CType(o, SqlConnection).Close()
  Catch
    ' Implement error handling
  End Try
End Sub

' Borrow a Database Connection from the Pool
Public Function borrowDBConnection() As SqlConnection
  Try
    Return CType(MyBase.getObjectFromPool(), SqlConnection)
  Catch e As Exception
    Throw e
  End Try
End Function

' Return a Database Connection to the Pool
Public Sub returnDBConnection(ByVal c As SqlConnection)
  MyBase.returnObjectToPool(c)
End Sub
End Class

End Namespace
```

As we are dealing with the `SqlConnection` object, the `expire()` method closes the `SqlConnection`, the `create()` method creates the `SqlConnection` and the `validate()` method checks whether the `SqlConnection` is open or not. The whole synchronization issue is hidden from the client application using the `DBConnectionSingleton` object instance.

Why Use a Singleton?

The Singleton is a popular creational design pattern, which is used when we need to have only one instance of an object. The intent of the Singleton pattern as defined in *Design Patterns (ISBN:020170265-7)* is to ensure a class has only one instance, and provide a global point of access to it. To implement a Singleton, we need a `Private` constructor so that the client application not be able to create a new object whenever it wants to, and the `Shared ReadOnly` property instance is used to create the only instance of the Singleton class. The .NET Framework, during the JIT process, will initialize the `Shared` property when (and only when) any method uses this `Shared` property. If the property is not used, then the instance is not created. More precisely, the class gets constructed and loaded when *any* `Shared` member of the class is used by *any* caller. This feature is called lazy initialization and gives the effect of the creation of the object only on the first call to the instance property. The .NET framework guarantees the threadsafety of shared type initializations inherently. So we do not have to worry about the threadsafety of the `DBConnectionSingleton` object because only one instance of it will ever be created during the lifetime of the application. The `Shared` variable instance holds the only instance of the `DBConnectionSingleton` class object.

Using the Database Connection Pool

The database connection pool is now ready for use and the `ObjectPoolTester` application in the code download for this chapter can be used to test it.

Below we show some code snippets of how to instantiate and use the database connection pool:

```
' Initialize the Pool
Dim pool As DBConnectionSingleton
pool = DBConnectionSingleton.Instance

' Set the ConnectionString of the DatabaseConnectionPool
DBConnectionSingleton.ConnectionString =
    " server=(local);User ID=sa;Password=;database=northwind"

' Borrow the SqlConnection object from the pool
Dim myConnection As SqlConnection = pool.borrowDBConnection()

' Return the Connection to the pool after using it
pool.returnDBConnection(myConnection)
```

In the above examples, we initialize the `DBConnectionSingleton` object from the instance property of the `DBConnectionSingleton` class. As discussed above, we are assured that with the use of the Singleton design pattern we have one and only one instance of the `DBConnectionSingleton` object. We set the `ConnectionString` property of the database connection to the Northwind database on the local SQL Server machine. Now, we can borrow database connections from the object pool using the `borrowDBConnection()` method of the pool object, and return the database connection by calling the `returnDBConnection()` method of the pool object. The following screenshot shows the `ObjectPoolTester` application in action. If you really want to explore how the pooling application works, the best way is to open the project in Visual Studio .NET and step through the `ObjectPoolTester` application in Debug mode.

126

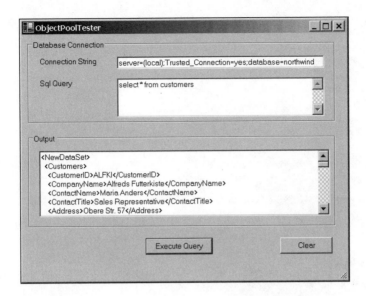

Summary

Synchronization is an extremely important concept in this multithreaded world of enterprise computing. It is extensively used in popular applications like the databases, message queues, and even web servers. Any developer developing multithreaded applications needs to have their synchronization concepts crystal clear. Rather than getting overwhelmed with the locking features and trying to make every object threadsafe, the developer should focus on deadlock scenarios and try to resolve as many deadlock conditions as possible right from the design stage of the application. It is also important to understand the performance hit associated with synchronization and how it will affect the overall performance of your application. In this chapter, along with the synchronization support in the .NET Framework, we also developed a couple of useful applications:

❑ A custom thread-safe wrapper. In this example, we learned how we can add intrinsic synchronization support to our library and give the application developer the choice of using synchronization or not. This will help the developer focus on their own application rather than worrying about the threadsafety of the library.

❑ A database connection pool. In this example, we developed a generic object pool that can be used for pooling any type of similar objects. Following that, we developed a database connection pool inheriting from the object pool. The object pool can be reused to pool any kind of object.

These applications offer a good start in developing your own thread-safe APIs.

VB.NET

Threading

Handbook

4

Design Patterns

Most highly scalable systems are highly concurrent in nature (concurrency is the existence of more than one request for the same object at the same time). However, writing code that is highly concurrent and thread safe (meaning when one or more threads are accessing shared data, there is no possibility that the data could be corrupted or made inconsistent) is a huge challenge.

If we use multithreading techniques with a formal threading model, we can write highly scalable code that can work in a concurrent fashion. In the previous chapters, we learned when to use threading and all the details about threading, including the threading traps. In this chapter, we'll learn all about the threading models supported by .NET and how to take advantage of these threading models, as well as some models we can impose on top of .NET to help us design our code.

By default all the .NET applications are multithreaded, which was not the case in VB6. In WinForms, there is a special thread called the UI thread that controls all the user interface-related functions such as keyboard activities and mouse activities. When you start running long-running, time-consuming processes on the UI thread, the application becomes unresponsive. If we can run tasks on a thread different from the UI thread, the application will behave better and the user interface will respond well. In addition, if you thought that creating numerous thread objects is the only way to achieve this, you would be wrong. We can use several techniques in addition to multithreading, including implementing asynchronous programming and using Timer-based functions, as we saw in Chapter 2.

Multiple Threads in Applications

If you programmed in the earlier version of VB, you might know that VB supported multiple threads within a COM container, such as MTS or COM+. Well although multiple threads were supported by VB5/6, the threading model they supported was **STA** (Single Threaded Apartments). However, the .NET Framework does not have the concept of Apartments and it manages all of the threads within AppDomains. By default, all .NET applications are multithreaded and any code can access any object at any time. So we have to be very careful with shared resources in the managed code.

The .NET Framework supports both managed and unmanaged threads and all the Win32 threading models. When you are trying to access COM components from managed code, unmanaged threads are created by the legacy COM components. Threads in the .NET Framework are created using the `Thread` object, whether managed or unmanaged.

If you have ever programmed multithreaded programs using in Win32 APIs, you may remember that Win32 supported *user-interface* threads and *worker* threads. As you learned in Chapter 1, the threading names have now changed into **Apartment Model Threading** and **Free Threading** respectively. The .NET Framework supports two basic threading models, which are *Apartment Model Threaded* or **Single Threaded Apartment** (**STA**) components, and *Free Threaded* or **Multiple Threaded Apartment** (**MTA**) components. When we create a thread in .NET, by default it is an MTA thread.

> **You should only use the STA threading model when you're going to access STA-based COM components such as VB6 COM components. Otherwise, you shouldn't mark the current thread as STA, since it involves a significant performance hit to the application.**

To reiterate what has been learned earlier, an apartment is the logical container within the `AppDomain` for sharing threads in the same context. A context is an order of sequence. Objects reside inside an `AppDomain` and the context is created when an object is created during the activation process.

STA Threading Model

An STA thread apartment works on a concept called **Object-per-Client** model, meaning the code that creates the STA thread apartment owns its threads. There will only be one thread in any apartment as shown in Figure 1.

In STA threading, all the calls to a thread will be placed in a queue and the calls will be processed one by one. Therefore, the STA thread will never execute multiple methods simultaneously. STA threads have their own private data and they don't share data between threads. This makes the threading model safe and avoids any data corruption and synchronization problems. However, this does restrict the capabilities available to the developer, and performance suffers, as data has to be copied with every thread created.

Figure 1

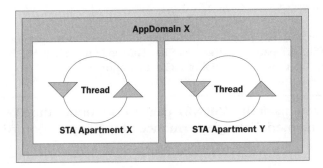

As you can see from the diagram, AppDomain X had two STA Threads, X and Y, running inside, and each of the STA Apartments has only one thread. The term **Thread Affinity** is used when defining the relationship between the thread and the code that creates the thread. When a call is made to an STA apartment thread, then calls between the caller and the thread are handled by the contexts in the AppDomain, and the contexts maintain the thread affinity.

If your managed application is going to use unmanaged legacy COM components, then it is very important to know the threading model of the COM components before accessing them. The threading model information can be found in the registry under the HKEY_CLASSES_ROOT\CLSID\{Class ID of the COM component} \InProcServer32 key.

If you want to specify that you are using the Apartment Threading model, then apply the STAThreadAttribute attribute on the Main() method.

```
<STAThreadAttribute> _
Sub Main()
   ...
End Sub
```

This attribute should only used if we're trying to access legacy STA components from the managed code. Otherwise, mark Main() as MTAThreadAttribute:

```
<MTAThreadAttribute> _
Sub Main()
    ...
End Sub
```

The same principal applies for ASP.NET applications. If your ASP.NET page is accessing an STA COM component, then you have to use the ASPCompact directive at the top of the ASP.NET page.

```
<%@ Page  AspCompact="true" %>
```

By default all the ASP.NET pages are multithreaded and when we use the AspCompact directive, the ASP.NET page is marked as STA. This will ensure the ASP.NET page is compatible with the threading model of a COM component.

> **When you mark the ASP.NET page to run under the STA threading model, the performance of the application will suffer.**

MTA Threading Model

The biggest difference between an STA and an MTA threaded apartment is that an MTA apartment can have more than one thread running simultaneously in the same apartment using all the shared data available in the apartment. This is illustrated in Figure 2.

Figure 2

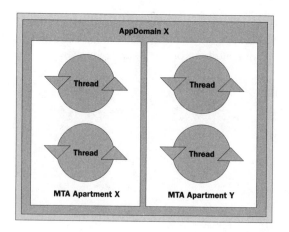

Since the MTA model supports simultaneous multiple thread execution, it becomes the caller's responsibility to synchronize the global data between multiple threads. Many of these issues were covered in the previous chapter.

Specifying the Threading Model

The threading model for a thread can be set using the `ApartmentState` property of the `Thread` class. The `ApartmentState` enumeration defines the types of threading models supported by .NET.

Enumeration Value	Meaning
MTA	Creates a multi-threaded apartment
STA	Creates a single-threaded apartment
Unknown	The apartment property of the `Thread` class is not set

As we've already learned, you should only mark the thread as STA thread if you are going to access an STA threaded legacy COM component. Otherwise, your threading model is in the default MTA threading model.

Designing Threaded Applications

A multithreaded program has two or more threads (flows of control). It can achieve significant performance gains with concurrency, with or without parallel thread execution. Concurrent thread execution means that two or more threads are executing at the same time. Parallelism occurs when two or more threads execute simultaneously across two or more processors.

In this section we'll talk about real threading considerations and issues. Before you start developing applications, you should ask yourself these questions:

1. Is it possible to subdivide the application to run on different threads?

2. If it is possible to subdivide, how do I subdivide and what are the criteria for subdividing?

3. What would be the relationship between the main thread and the worker threads? This defines how the one or more tasks in the application will relate to each other.

We can find out the answer to the first question by inspecting the application. For example, if your application does heavy I/O operation (such as reading an XML file or querying a database) that blocks the main thread, or it performs a lot of CPU intensive processing (such as encrypting and decrypting data, hashing, etc.) that can also block the main thread.

If you've identified the parts of your application that are potential candidates for separate threads, then you should ask yourself the following questions:

1. Does each of the tasks identified use separate global resources?

    For example, if you've identified two potential threads for your application and if both are going to use the same global resource, such as a global variable or a DataSet object, then if both threads try to access the global resource at the same time, we could get inconsistent or corrupt data, as shown in the previous chapter. The only way to prevent this kind of problem is by using locks on the global resources, which could leave the other thread waiting. If both of the tasks are going to use the same global resource then it is not a good idea to break the task into two. For some resources, you could use the Monitor class to prevent the threads from locking up. Again, this was shown in Chapter 3.

2. Over how long a period could the thread be blocked?

    It is not always possible to build applications that use independent global resources. For example, let's say both tasks in your application rely on a single global DataSet object. If the first task takes a lot of time to fill the DataSet object (let's say it fills about 50,000 rows from the database), then you would ordinarily lock the DataSet object to prevent concurrency problems. Here a pseudo-code version of the first task.

```
1. Open the Database connection
2. Lock the DataSet object
3. Perform the query
4. Fill the DataSet with 50,000 rows from the database
5. Unlock the DataSet object
```

In this case, the second task needs to wait for a long time to get access to the DataSet object, which happens only when the first task finishes its execution and releases the lock. This is a potential problem and it will likely remove the concurrency of your application. There is a better way to address this problem:

```
1. Open the Database connection
2. Perform the query
3. Fill the local DataSet with 50,000 rows from the database
4. Lock the global DataSet object
5. Set the local database to global dataset (DSGlobal = DSLocal)
6. Unlock the global DataSet object
```

In this way, we're not locking the global DataSet object until we need to update it. This way we're reducing the time waited for the lock on the global object to release.

3. Does the execution of one task depend on the other task?

For example, the tasks that you've identified could be querying the database and displaying the data in a DataGrid control. You can split the task into two by querying the database as the first task, and displaying the result in the DataGrid as the second task. The second task does not want to start until the first task is complete. Therefore, separating the querying and displaying the data in a DataGrid into two separate concurrently running tasks is not a viable option. One way around this is to have the first task raise an event when completed, and fire a new thread when this happens. Alternatively, you could use a timer that checks to see if is completed through a public field, and continues the execution of the thread when it has.

Threads and Relationship

The threads spun from a multithreaded application may or may not be related to each other. For example in every application there will be a main thread that spins other threads. So the main thread becomes the controller of all other threads in the application. There are few common methods that can be used to define the relationship between the threads in a multithreaded application.

- ❏ Main and Worker thread model
- ❏ Peer thread model
- ❏ Pipeline thread model

We will detail each of these models, including some code so that you can see how they might be implemented in your applications

Main and Worker Thread Model

This is the common model, used throughout this book so far. It is illustrated in Figure 3:

Figure 3

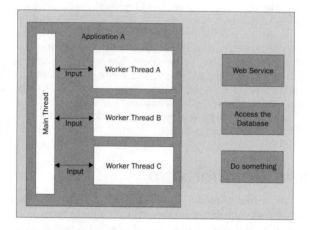

In the main and worker thread model, the main thread receives all the input and it passes the input to other threads to perform some task. The main thread may or may not wait for the worker threads to finish. In this model, the worker threads don't interact with the input sources and they read the input from the main thread to perform the task. For example, we could have three buttons on a `WinForm` application that triggers three events.

❑   Get data from a web service

❑   Get data from a database

❑   Do something else when the last button is clicked such as parsing an XML file

This is the simplest threading model. The main thread is that which is contained within the `Main()` method, and is very common in client GUI applications.

Below is some code to test this. The form used looks as follows:

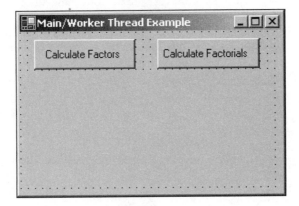

If you click on a button, it will fire off a worker thread that will perform some calculations and return the results in the space below the buttons. We shan't detail the UI code here; the full code can be downloaded from the Wrox web site, but shown below are the relevant sections:

```
Public Class MainWorker
    Public Function CalculateFactors(ByVal number As Integer) _
                    As ArrayList
        If number < 3 Then Return Nothing
        Dim current As Integer
        Dim factors As New ArrayList()
        factors.Add("1")
        For current = 2 To number - 1
            If Math.Floor(number / current) * current = number Then
                factors.Add(current.ToString())
            End If
        Next
        factors.Add(number.ToString())
        Return factors
    End Function

    Public Function CalculateFactorial(ByVal number As Integer) _
                    As Long
        If number < 0 Then Return -1
        If number = 0 Then Return 1
        Dim returnValue As Long = 1
        Dim current As Integer
        For current = 1 To number
            returnValue *= current
        Next
        Return returnValue
    End Function
End Class
```

The above methods are quite straightforward. They are wrapped in a class for modularity reasons. The first returns an `ArrayList` containing all of the factors of the number passed in, whereas the second just returns a `Long`. Remember that factorials very quickly get very large. The factorial of 13 is 6,227,020,800. The factorial method doesn't tie up the processor for very long, but it can be used to illustrate this model.

```vb
Public Sub New()
  MyBase.New()

  'This call is required by the Windows Form Designer.
  InitializeComponent()

  'Add any initialization after the InitializeComponent() call
  threadMethods = New MainWorker()
End Sub
```

The constructor just contains an instantiation of a new `MainWorker` object that will be used in the methods. Below are the methods used for the button click events:

```vb
Private Sub cmdFactors_Click(ByVal sender As System.Object, _
                            ByVal e As System.EventArgs) _
                            Handles cmdFactors.Click
  Dim calculateFactors As New Threading.Thread(AddressOf _
                                               FactorsThread)
  calculateFactors.Start()
End Sub

Private Sub FactorsThread()
  Dim value As ArrayList = threadMethods.CalculateFactors(200)
  lblResult.Visible = False
  lblResult.Text = String.Empty
  Dim count As Integer
  For count = 0 To value.Count - 1
    lblResult.Text &= CType(value.Item(count), String)
    If count < value.Count - 1 Then lblResult.Text &= ", "
  Next
  lblResult.Visible = True
End Sub
```

The `cmdFactors_Click()` method instantiates a new thread with the next method, which formats and acts upon the result contained in `MainWorker.CalculateFactors()`. It needs to be wrapped because thread methods cannot have return values.

```vb
Private Sub cmdFactorial_Click(ByVal sender As System.Object, _
                              ByVal e As System.EventArgs) _
                              Handles cmdFactorial.Click
  Dim calculateFactorial As New Thread(AddressOf FactorialThread)
  calculateFactorial.Start()
End Sub
```

```
Private Sub FactorialThread()
    Dim value As Long = threadMethods.CalculateFactorial(20)
    lblResult.Text = value.ToString()
End Sub
```

The above method is much simpler – whenever the cmdFactorial button is clicked, the Main thread fires off a new thread and updates the lblResult text label when the results have been achieved. This is a straightforward example of Main/Worker threads in actions. Obviously, this example can easily be changed to deal with connection to a database, or other more time-consuming activities.

We have to take care of issues relating to threads when you use this mode. You can have threads spawning threads, threads accessing the same resource, and threads going into an infinite loop. This is the simplest model, but also the one that requires most work from the developer. In addition, the threads are completely independent of each other, all being controlled entirely by the parent, in this case, the Main thread.

Peer Thread Model

The next threading model we will describe is the Peer threading model.

Figure 4

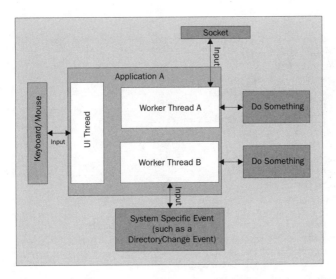

In this threading model, each thread will receive its own input from the appropriate sources and it will process the input accordingly. For example, the UI thread will receive the input from the keyboard and mouse and it can work accordingly. On the other hand, the Worker Thread A will listen to a particular socket and it will process the input as it comes in from the socket. In the same way, the Worker Thread B will wait for a system event and act accordingly. In this model, all the threads execute concurrently without blocking or waiting for other threads.

139

We can amend the previous example so that the `CalculateFactors()` method notices when the factorial thread finishes, and discovers the factorials of this number. We will use the factorial of 8 in this example. In this example, however, we shan't be using a socket but just the setting of a variable. The principles will be the same for sockets; you would either continuously listen, or to save processor cycles, sleep intermittently.

So, let's change the `WorkerThread` class first:

```
Public Class PeerThread
    Private factorial As Integer

Public Overloads Function CalculateFactors(_
                         ByVal number As Integer) As ArrayList
    If number < 3 Then Return Nothing
    Dim current As Integer
    Dim factors As New ArrayList()
    factors.Add("1")
    For current = 2 To number - 1
      If Math.Floor(number / current) * current = number Then
        factors.Add(current.ToString())
      End If
    Next
    factors.Add(number.ToString())
    Return factors
End Function

Public Overloads Function CalculateFactors() As ArrayList
    Dim count As Integer
    For count = 1 To 30
      Thread.CurrentThread.Sleep(TimeSpan.FromSeconds(1))
      If factorial > 0 Then
        Exit For
      ElseIf count = 30 And factorial = 0 Then
        Return Nothing
      End If
    Next
    Dim returnValue As ArrayList = CalculateFactors(factorial)
    Return returnValue
End Function

Public Function CalculateFactorial(ByVal number As Integer) As Long
    factorial = 0
    If number < 0 Then Return -1
    If number = 0 Then Return 1
    Dim returnValue As Long = 1
    Dim current As Integer
    For current = 1 To number
      returnValue *= current
    Next
    factorial = returnValue
    Return returnValue
End Function
```

First, we'll explain the small changes. A private field has been created that will store the result of the factorial when created. In addition, the class has been renamed to `PeerThread`. The `CalculateFactors()` method now has an overload, so that if it isn't passed an argument it performs the business end of this model.

All that happens is that the thread monitors the state of the `factorial` field, as if it were a socket. It checks to see if it is anything other than 0, and if so, then it calls the `CalculateFactors()` method with the value of `factorial` as its argument and returns the `ArrayList` that it produces. We have also made a change in that we reset the `factorial` field at the start of the `CalculateFactorial()` method so there will always be some work to do. At the end of this method, we set `factorial` to equal the factorial.

Now, the `frmCalculate` class needs altering also. Observe the following changes:

```
. . .
    Private threadMethods As PeerThread
    . . .
Public Sub New()
   MyBase.New()
   'This call is required by the Windows Form Designer.
   InitializeComponent()

   'Add any initialization after the InitializeComponent() call
   threadMethods = New PeerThread()
End Sub


    . . .
      Private Sub NewFactorsThread()
         Dim value As ArrayList = threadMethods.CalculateFactors()
         lblResult.Visible = False
         lblResult.Text = String.Empty
         Dim count As Integer
         For count = 0 To value.Count - 1
             lblResult.Text &= CType(value.Item(count), String)
             If count < value.Count - 1 Then lblResult.Text &= ", "
         Next
         lblResult.Visible = True
      End Sub


    . . .

   Private Sub cmdFactorial_Click(ByVal sender As System.Object, _
                             ByVal e As System.EventArgs) _
                             Handles cmdFactorial.Click
      Dim calculateFactors As New Thread(AddressOf NewFactorsThread)
      Dim calculateFactorial As New Thread(AddressOf FactorialThread)
      calculateFactors.Start()
      calculateFactorial.Start()
   End Sub
```

Apart from defining the new `threadMethods` field as a new `PeerThread` class, there are two main changes. We define a new method called `NewFactorsThread()`, which will call the `PeerThread`'s `CalculateFactors()` method with no arguments. The rest of this method is the same. In the `cmdFactorial_Click()` method, instead of just firing up the `FactorialThread` method in a thread, we fire up the `FactorsThread` too, and execute them out of sequence so that `FactorsThread` may have to wait for the factorial. You should be able to see how this can be tied into a network socket, and we see an example of monitoring such a socket in Chapter 7.

The common errors that could occur with this kind of model are those of deadlocks and blocking. If you have a thread continually listening at a socket and getting its parameters from that socket, then that socket may need to be locked from other threads. This means, therefore, that this is a very good model to use for manager classes. We could use a thread to monitor a socket and then fire off new threads to process the contents. Do not have more than one thread monitoring the same socket. In addition, if the thread is continually checking the socket or other resource, then it may consume more processor cycles than is necessary. As seen in the above example, you can use `Thread.Sleep()` to reduce the processor cycles expended.

As you will see, this example is also very similar to Pipeline Thread Model in concept, but we are simulating a Peer Thread Model. If you click on the Calculate Factorials button, unless you have a very fast machine, you should have time to click on Calculate Factors, which will enable you to calculate and display the factors of 200, before it overwrites the textbox with the factors of 8!, or 40320.

Pipeline Thread Model

Look at Figure 5:

Figure 5

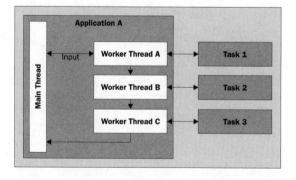

The pipeline thread model is based on a series of tasks and each of the tasks depend on the previous task. For example, the main thread creates a series of threads and each other thread will wait until the previous thread is finished executing. This kind of threading relationship is good if your task has certain stages and each of these stages is dependent on another. For example, your task could be processing input data and the process could have a few sub-tasks like:

❑ Filter all the non-valid characters such as <, >, !, etc.

❑ Check if the data is formatted corrected

❑ Format all the numbers with currency sign and decimal points

❑ Process the input

In this kind of situation, the next task can only be started if the previous task has finished. In the previous model, this is in effect what we were doing, as the `factorial` field was only set at the end of the thread. However, the proper way to implement the Pipeline Thread Model is to test to explicitly test that the thread has ended.

A few changes need to be made to the Peer Thread example to make it part of the Pipeline Model. First, we'll show the code for `frmCalculate`:

```
. . .
Private threadMethods As PipelineThread
Private calculateFactorial As Thread
. . .
Public Sub New()
. . .
    threadMethods = New PipelineThread()
. . .
Private Sub NewFactorsThread()
   calculateFactors.Join()
    . . .
```

As you can see, the changes are minimal here. The only interesting changes are the line that rescopes `calculateFactorial`, and the `calculateFactors.Join()` line. This instructs the `calculateFactors` thread to wait until `calculateFactorial` has completed before executing. The `Join()` call has to be within the thread that you want a pause in execution, and it is called on the thread it is waiting for. This inevitably means that the thread variable has to be rescoped to be at least class wide so that it can be accessed from other threads.

```
Class PipelineThread
   . . .

   Public Overloads Function CalculateFactors() As ArrayList
      Dim returnValue As ArrayList = CalculateFactors(factorial)
      Return returnValue
   End Function
```

Again, the changes here are small. The above method no longer has to check to see if factorial has been set, and so can execute as it can assume the factorial has been calculated. This example could be useful when, for instance, you are waiting on a DataSet to fill, before performing some further calculations. This would enable the thread to fire as soon as the thread that fills the DataSet is complete. Of course in a real application, error checking would have to be implemented as the thread could have completed but ended abruptly because of an error, or because of an Abort() instruction from another thread.

The traps you have to watch out for are the same traps that can occur with any thread. The first thread could be placed in an infinite loop, in which case, the second thread would never execute. By ensuring this can never happen in your first thread, you ensure that the second thread will execute and complete. In addition, you have to watch out for the thread ending unpredictably, due to an error or otherwise, as mentioned in the previous paragraph.

This concludes the discussion of the three models that can be applied to threading. By modeling your application to one of these, you should become familiar with the structure of the code you would need to use.

Summary

In this chapter, the various threading models that can be applied to your application, why you should use them, and how to implement them have been described. You should now be confident in your knowledge of:

❑ Different types of basic threading model, such as STA and MTA apartments

❑ How to specify the threading model

❑ The different models of threads that can be applied and their relationships to each other

This chapter should help you design your threaded application, as it will fit into one or more of the models described above and so the code examples given should help you to build the code you need. With the .NET Framework, threads are far more powerful, but also far more prone to errors than they used to be. By being aware of which model your application fits into, you can look out for these potential errors.

VB.NET

Threading

Handbook

5

5

Scaling Threaded Applications

For some situations where the threads are short-lived, it is efficient to use a pool of threads for performing tasks rather than creating and then subsequently deleting an entirely new thread for each task. A task, in this chapter, could be a single method or a number of methods. The process of pre-allocating a collection, or pool, of threads prior to their actual usage in an application is known as **thread pooling**.

This chapter aims to provide a detailed insight into thread pooling, and covers the following topics:

- ❑ What thread pooling is?
- ❑ The need for thread pooling
- ❑ The concept of thread pooling
- ❑ The role of the CLR in thread pooling
- ❑ Glitches involved in thread pooling and their solutions
- ❑ The size of a thread pool
- ❑ Exploring the .NET ThreadPool class
- ❑ Programming thread pools in VB.NET

As you'll discover, the Common Language Runtime (CLR) of the .NET Framework plays a major role in the thread pooling process.

What is Thread Pooling?

Thread pooling is the process of creating a collection of threads during the initialization of a multithreaded application, and then reusing those threads for new tasks as and when required, instead of creating new threads. The number of threads for the process is usually fixed. However, it is possible to increase the number of available threads. Each thread in the pool is given a task and, once that task has completed, the thread returns to the pool and waits for the next assignment.

The Need for Thread Pooling

Thread pooling is essential in multithreaded applications for the following reasons (it also makes their coding a lot easier:

- ❑ Thread pooling improves the response time of an application as threads are already available in the thread pool waiting for their next assignment and do not need to be created from scratch

- ❑ Thread pooling saves the CLR from the overhead of creating an entirely new thread for every short-lived task and reclaiming its resources once it dies

- ❑ Thread pooling optimizes the thread time slices according to the current process running in the system

- ❑ Thread pooling enables us to start several tasks without having to set the properties for each thread

- ❑ Thread pooling enables us to pass state information as an object to the procedure arguments of the task that is being executed

- ❑ Thread pooling can be employed to fix the maximum number of threads for processing the client's request

The Concept of Thread Pooling

One of the major problems affecting the responsiveness of a multithreaded application is the time involved in spawning threads for each task.

For example, a web server is a multithreaded application that can service several client requests simultaneously. Let's suppose that ten clients are accessing the web server at the same time:

- ❑ If the server operates a thread per client policy, it will spawn ten new threads to service these clients, which entails the overhead of first creating those threads and then of managing them throughout their lifetime. It's also possible that the machine will run out of resources at some point.

❏	Alternatively, if the server uses a pool of threads to satisfy those requests, then it will save the time involved in the spawning of those threads each time a request from a client comes in. This is the exact concept behind thread pooling.

The Windows operating system maintains a pool of threads for servicing requests. If our application requests a new thread, Windows will try to fetch it from the pool. If the pool is empty, it will spawn a new thread and give it to us. Windows will dynamically manipulate the thread pool size to increase the response time of our applications.

To recap then, the factors affecting the threading design of a multithreaded application are:

❏	The responsiveness of the application

❏	The allocation of thread management resources

❏	Resource sharing

❏	Thread synchronization

Responsiveness of the application and resource sharing are addressed by this chapter on thread pooling. The remaining factors have been covered in the previous chapters of this book.

The CLR and Threads

The CLR was designed with the aim of creating a managed code environment offering various services such as compilation, garbage collection, memory management, and, yes, thread pooling to applications targeted at the .NET platform.

Indeed, there is a remarkable difference between how Win32 and the .NET Framework defines a process which hosts the threads that our applications use. In a traditional multithreaded Win32 application, each process is made up of collections of threads. Each thread in turn consists of Thread Local Storage (TLS) and Call Stacks for providing time slices in the case of machines that have a single CPU. Single processor machines allot time slices for each thread to execute based on the thread priority. When the time slice for a particular thread is exhausted, it is suspended and some other thread is allowed to perform its task. In the case of the .NET Framework, each process can be sub-divided into what are known as Application Domains that host the threads along with the TLS and call stack. It's worthwhile to note that inter process communication is handled by a concept called Remoting in .NET Framework.

Having gained a basic understanding on concepts of thread pooling and the .NET process, let's dig into how the CLR provides us with thread pooling functionality for .NET applications.

149

The Role of the CLR in Thread Pooling

The CLR forms the heart and soul of the .NET Framework offering several services to managed applications, thread pooling being one of them. For each task queued in the thread pool (**work items**), the CLR assigns a thread from the pool (a **worker thread**) and then releases the thread back to the pool once the task is done.

Thread pools are always implemented by the CLR using a multithreaded apartment (MTA) model by employing high performance queues and dispatchers through **preemptive multitasking.** This is a process in which CPU time is split into several time slices. In each time slice, a particular thread executes while other threads wait. Once the time slice is exhausted, other threads are allowed to use the CPU based on *the highest priority of the remaining threads.* The client requests are queued in the task queue and each item in this queue is dispatched to the first available thread in the thread pool.

Once the thread completes its assigned task, it returns to the pool and waits for the next assignment from the CLR. The thread pool can be fixed or of dynamic size. In the former case, the number of threads doesn't change during the lifetime of the pool. Normally, this type of pool is used when we are sure of the amount of resources available to our application, so that a fixed number of threads can be created at the time of pool initialization. This would be the case when we are developing solutions for an intranet or even in applications where we can tightly define the system requirements of the target platform. Dynamic pool sizes are employed when we don't know the amount of resources available, as in the case of a web server that will not know the number of client requests it will be asked to handle simultaneously.

Glitches Involved in Thread Pooling

There is no doubt that thread pooling offers us a lot of advantages when building multithreaded applications, but there are some situations where we should avoid its use. The following list indicates the drawbacks and situations where we should avoid using thread pooling:

❑ The CLR assigns the threads from the thread pool to the tasks and releases them to the pool once the task is completed. There is no direct way to cancel a task once it has been added to the queue.

❑ Thread pooling is an effective solution for situations where tasks are short lived, like in the case of web server satisfying the client requests for a particular file. A thread pool should not be used for extensive or long tasks.

❑ Thread pooling is a technique to employ threads in a cost-efficient manner, where cost efficiency is defined in terms of quantity and startup overhead. Care should be exercised to determine the utilization of threads in the pool. The size of the thread pool should be fixed accordingly.

❑ All the threads in the thread pool are in multithreaded apartments. If we want to place our threads in single-thread apartments then a thread pool is not the way to go.

❑ If we need to identify the thread and perform various operations, such as starting it, suspending it, and aborting it, then thread pool is not the way of doing it.

❑ Also, it is not possible to set priorities for tasks employing thread pooling.

❑ There can be only one thread pool associated with any given process.

❑ If the task assigned to a thread in the thread pool becomes locked, then the thread is never released back to the pool for reuse. These kinds of situations can be avoided by employing effective programmatic skills.

The Size of the Thread Pool

The .NET Framework provides the `ThreadPool` class located in the `System.Threading` namespace for using thread pools in our applications. The number of tasks that can be queued into a thread pool is limited by the amount of memory in your machine. Likewise, the number of threads that can be active in a process is limited by the number of CPUs in your machine. That is because, as we already know, each processor can only actively execute one thread at a time. By default, each thread in the thread pool uses the default task and runs at default priority in a multithreaded apartment. The word default seems to be used rather vaguely here. That is no accident. Each system can have default priorities set differently. If, at any time, one of the threads is idle then the thread pool will induce worker threads to keep all processors busy. If all the threads in the pool are busy and work is pending in the queue then it will spawn new threads to complete the pending work. However, the number of threads created can't exceed the maximum number specified. By default, 25 thread pool threads can be created per processor. However, this number can be changed by editing the `CorSetMaxThreads` member defined in `mscoree.h` file. In case of additional thread requirement, the requests are queued until some thread finishes its assigned task and returns to the pool. The .NET Framework uses thread pools for asynchronous calls, establishing socket connections, and registered wait operations.

Exploring the ThreadPool Class

In this section, we will be exploring the various aspects of the `ThreadPool` class and will see how they can be employed to create thread pools in our .NET applications. The `ThreadPool` class provides a pool of threads that can be used to do the following things:

❑ Process work items

❑ Process asynchronous I/O calls

❑ Process timers

❑ Wait on behalf of other threads

The following table gives the list of methods of the `ThreadPool` class and their functionality.

Method Name	Functionality
BindHandle	This method binds the OS handle to the thread pool
GetAvailableThreads	This method indicates the number of work items that can be added to the work items queue
GetMaxThreads	This method indicates the number of requests that the thread pool can queue simultaneously
QueueUserWorkItem	This method queues a work item to the thread pool
RegisterWaitForSingleObject	This method registers a delegate, which waits for a `WaitHandle`
UnsafeQueueUserWorkItem	This is the unsafe version of the `QueueUserWorkItem()` method
UnsafeRegisterWaitForSingleObject	This is the unsafe version of the `RegisterWaitForSingleObject()` method

Of the above methods, `QueueUserWorkItem()` and `RegisterWaitForSingleObject()` play the most important roles in thread pooling. Let's dig into the details of each method. Here we'll see both their syntax and a sample call in VB.NET:

The `BindHandle()` method binds an operating system handle to the thread pool:

```
Public Shared Function BindHandle(ByVal osHandle As IntPtr) _
                      As Boolean
```

`osHandle` refers to the `IntPtr` type holding the OS handle. The return value is a Boolean where `True` indicates binding to the handle. This method throws a `SecurityException` if the caller does not have the required permission.

The `GetAvailableThreads()` method indicates the number of thread pool requests that can be added before reaching the maximum specified limit:

```
Public Shared Sub GetAvailableThreads( _
              ByRef workerThreads As Integer, _
              ByRef completionPortThreads As Integer)
```

workerThreads refers to the number of worker threads of the thread pool while completionPortThreads refers to the number of asynchronous I/O threads.

The GetMaxThreads() method returns the maximum number of concurrent requests that a thread pool can handle. Any requests above this limit are queued until some of the threads in the thread pool are freed up:

```
Public Shared Sub GetMaxThreads(ByRef workerThreads As Integer, _
                ByRef completionPortThreads As Integer)
```

workerThreads refers to the number of worker threads of the thread pool while the completionPortThreads refers to the number of asynchronous I/O threads.

QueueUserWorkItem() is an overloaded method that queues a work item to the thread pool. It may be called in the following two forms. In the first case, the method queues the specified work item to the thread pool and calls the specified delegate associated with it. This case has the following syntax:

```
Overloads Public Shared Function QueueUserWorkItem( _
                ByVal callBack As WaitCallback) As Boolean
```

Here callBack refers to the delegate to be invoked when the thread in the thread pool takes the work item. The return value true indicates the method succeeded and False indicates failure.

In the second case, the method queues the specified work item to the thread pool, invokes the specified delegate, and specifies the object to be passed to the delegate when the work item is executed in the pool. In this case the method call has the following syntax:

```
Overloads Public Shared Function QueueUserWorkItem( _
                ByVal callBack As WaitCallback, _
                ByVal state As Object) As Boolean
```

callBack refers to the delegate to be invoked when the thread in the thread pool services the work item, while state refers to the object containing the state that is being passed to the delegate when the servicing of the work item occurs. The return value True indicates the method succeeded and False indicates failure.

RegisterWaitForSingleObject() is also an overloaded method. It registers a delegate that waits for a WaitHandle. This class encapsulates all the objects of the operating system that wait for exclusive access to shared resources.

The method takes the following four forms. In the first case, the method registers a delegate and waits for the WaitHandle indicated by the timeout in milliseconds, which is given by a 32-bit signed integer. This overloaded form of the method has the following syntax in VB.NET:

153

```
Overloads Public Shared Function RegisterWaitForSingleObject( _
        ByVal waitObject As WaitHandle, _
        ByVal callBack As WaitOrTimerCallback, _
        ByVal state As Object, _
        ByVal millisecondsTimeOutInterval As Integer, _
        ByVal executeOnlyOnce As Boolean) As RegisteredWaitHandle
```

In the above syntax, the waitObject refers to the WaitHandle and the callBack refers to the WaitOrTimerCallback delegate to be invoked. The state parameter refers to the Object to be passed to the delegate.The millisecondsTimeOutInterval parameter refers to the timeout in milliseconds; if its value is 0 then the function tests the object state and returns immediately, on the other hand if its value is -1 the function waits forever. The executeOnlyOnce parameter indicates whether the thread has to wait on the waitObject parameter after the delegate has been invoked or not. The RegisteredWaitHandle parameter encapsulates the native handle.

This method throws an ArgumentOutOfRangeException if the millisecondsTimeOutInterval parameter is less than -1.

In the second case, the method does the same thing as specified in the first case but waits for the WaitHandle indicated by timeout in milliseconds that is given by 32-bit unsigned integer. This overloaded form of the method has the following syntax:

```
Overloads Public Shared Function RegisterWaitForSingleObject( _
        ByVal waitObject As WaitHandle, _
        ByVal callBack As WaitOrTimerCallback, _
        ByVal state As Object, _
        ByVal millisecondsTimeOutInterval As Long, _
        ByVal executeOnlyOnce As Boolean) As RegisteredWaitHandle
```

In the third case, the method waits for the WaitHandle indicated by the timeout given by the TimeSpan value. This overloaded form of the method has the following syntax:

```
Overloads Public Shared Function RegisterWaitForSingleObject( _
        ByVal waitObject As WaitHandle, _
        ByVal callBack As WaitOrTimerCallback, _
        ByVal state As Object, _
        ByVal timeout As TimeSpan, _
        ByVal executeOnlyOnce As Boolean) As RegisteredWaitHandle
```

In the fourth case, the timeout is given in milliseconds by an unsigned integer and this method, given by the following syntax, is non CLS compliant:

```
Overloads Public Shared Function RegisterWaitForSingleObject( _
        ByVal waitObject As WaitHandle, _
        ByVal callBack As WaitOrTimerCallback, _
        ByVal state As Object, _
        ByVal millisecondsTimeOutInterval As UInt32, _
        ByVal executeOnlyOnce As Boolean) As RegisteredWaitHandle
```

The UnsafeQueueUserWorkItem() method is the unsafe version of the QueueUserWorkItem() method and hence does not propagate the calling stack to the worker thread. This means that the code can lose the calling stack and, in doing so, elevate its security privileges. It has the following syntax:

```
Public Shared Function UnsafeQueueUserWorkItem( _
                ByVal callBack As WaitCallback, _
                ByVal state As Object) As Boolean
```

The UnsafeRegisterWaitForSingleObject() method is the unsafe version of the RegisterWaitForSingleObject() method and takes the following four forms:

```
Overloads Public Shared Function UnsafeRegisterWaitForSingleObject( _
                WaitHandle, WaitOrTimerCallback, Object, Long, _
                Boolean) As RegisteredWaitHandle
```

```
Overloads Public Shared Function UnsafeRegisterWaitForSingleObject( _
                WaitHandle, WaitOrTimerCallback, Object, Long, _
                Boolean) As RegisteredWaitHandle
```

```
Overloads Public Shared Function UnsafeRegisterWaitForSingleObject( _
                WaitHandle, WaitOrTimerCallback, Object, TimeSpan, _
                Boolean) As RegisteredWaitHandle
```

```
Overloads Public Shared Function UnsafeRegisterWaitForSingleObject( _
                WaitHandle, WaitOrTimerCallback, Object, UInt32, _
                Boolean) As RegisteredWaitHandle
```

Programming the Thread Pool in VB.NET

The previous sections of the chapter dealt with theoretical aspects of using thread pools in the .NET Framework. Now it's time for us to cover the programmatic aspects of creating and using thread pools in .NET applications from a VB.NET perspective. As described in the previous section, the System.Threading namespace contains the ThreadPool class that we can use to create a thread pool in .NET applications.

Before we start coding, there are three important rules that we must be clear about concerning the ThreadPool class. They are:

❑ There can be only one working thread per ThreadPool object

❑ There can be only one ThreadPool object per process

❑ A ThreadPool object is created for the first time when we call the ThreadPool.QueueUserWorkItem() method, or when a callback method is called through a timer or registered wait operation

One common use of the `ThreadPool` class is to start many separate tasks without setting the properties of each thread. The following console example (`ThreadModule.vb`) shows how to add the tasks to a queue and how a `ThreadPool` object assigns the threads for each task currently waiting:

```
Imports System
Imports System.Threading

Module ThreadModule
  Public Sub longtask1(ByVal obj As Object)
    Dim i As Integer
    For i = 0 To 999
      Console.WriteLine("Long Task 1 is being executed")
    Next
  End Sub

  Public Sub longtask2(ByVal obj As Object)
    Dim i As Integer
    For i = 0 To 999
      Console.WriteLine("Long Task 2 is being executed")
    Next
  End Sub

  Sub Main()
    Dim thrPool As ThreadPool
    thrPool.QueueUserWorkItem(New WaitCallback(AddressOf longtask1))
    thrPool.QueueUserWorkItem(New WaitCallback(AddressOf longtask2))
    Console.Read()
  End Sub
End Module
```

Let's dissect the above example. It comprises two separate tasks called `longtask1` and `longtask2` that do the simple job of outputting a message to the console in a loop. A `ThreadPool` class can be employed to start these two tasks without setting the properties of threads for each individual task by passing the delegate of the procedure to the `WaitCallback()` method, as given by the following block of code:

```
Dim thrPool As ThreadPool
thrPool.QueueUserWorkItem(New WaitCallback(AddressOf longtask1))
thrPool.QueueUserWorkItem(New WaitCallback(AddressOf longtask2))
```

The example also has a `Console.Read()` statement, which holds the input on the console until the user presses the *Enter* key (or any other key).

The next example (`ThreadAppModule.vb`) shows how to pass and return values from a thread in a thread pool. It should be noted that only `Sub` procedures can be queued to a `ThreadPool`, hence we cannot return values directly, as in the case of functions. However, we can wrap up all these parameters into a class and can pass an instance of that class as an argument to the `QueueUserWorkItem()` method:

```
Imports System
Imports System.Threading

Friend Class ObjState
  Friend inarg1 As String
  Friend inarg2 As String
  Friend outval As String
End Class

Module ThreadAppModule

  Sub Task1(ByVal StateObj As Object)
    Dim StObj As ObjState
    'cast the parameter object to the type ObjState
    StObj = CType(StateObj, ObjState)
    Console.WriteLine("Input Argument 1 in task 1: " & StObj.inarg1)
    Console.WriteLine("Input Argument 2 in task 1: " & StObj.inarg2)
    'The class variables can be employed for returning values
    StObj.outval = "From Task1 " & StObj.inarg1 & " " & StObj.inarg2
  End Sub

  Sub Task2(ByVal StateObj As Object)
    Dim StObj As ObjState
    'cast the parameter object to the type ObjState
    StObj = CType(StateObj, ObjState)
    Console.WriteLine("Input Argument 1 in task 2: " & StObj.inarg1)
    Console.WriteLine("Input Argument 2 in task 2: " & StObj.inarg2)
    'The class variables can be employed for returning values
    StObj.outval = "From Task2 " & StObj.inarg1 & " " & StObj.inarg2
  End Sub

  Sub Main()
    Dim TPool As System.Threading.ThreadPool
    Dim StObj1 As New ObjState()
    Dim StObj2 As New ObjState()
    ' Set some fields that act like parameters in the state object.
    StObj1.inarg1 = "String Param1 of task 1"
    StObj1.inarg2 = "String Param2 of task 1"
    StObj2.inarg1 = "String Param1 of task 2"
    StObj2.inarg2 = "String Param2 of task 2"

    ' Queue a task
    TPool.QueueUserWorkItem(New System.Threading.WaitCallback _
                        (AddressOf Task1), StObj1)
    ' Queue another task
    TPool.QueueUserWorkItem(New System.Threading.WaitCallback _
                        (AddressOf Task2), StObj2)
    Console.Read()
  End Sub

End Module
```

The output from `ThreadAppModule` will be:

```
Input Argument 1 in task 1: String Param1 of task 1
Input Argument 2 in task 1: String Param2 of task 1
Input Argument 1 in task 2: String Param1 of task 2
Input Argument 2 in task 2: String Param2 of task 2
```

Let's explore the above example step by step. This example is pretty similar to the previous example except for the passing of an object; we are passing the input and output parameters to tasks queued in the thread pool using the `ObjState` object.

The `ObjState` object contains two input parameters and one output parameter, all of type `String`, as given by the following code block:

```
Friend Class ObjState
   Friend inarg1 As String
   Friend inarg2 As String
   Friend outval As String
End Class
```

Next we define two procedures, `task1` and `task2`, and pass an instance of `ObjState` as a parameter to each of them. The procedures `task1` and `task2` concatenate the values of the input parameters `inarg1` and `inarg2` of the passed `ObjState` object and store the result in the `outval` class variable. This is given by the following code block:

```
Sub Task1(ByVal StateObj As Object)
   Dim StObj As ObjState
   'cast the parameter object to the type ObjState
   StObj = CType(StateObj, ObjState)
   Console.WriteLine("Input Argument 1 in task1 " & StObj.inarg1)
   Console.WriteLine("Input Argument 2 in task1 " & StObj.inarg2)
   'The class variables can be employed for returning values
   StObj.outval = "From Task1 " & StObj.inarg1 & " " & StObj.inarg2
End Sub

Sub Task2(ByVal StateObj As Object)
   Dim StObj As ObjState
   'cast the parameter object to the type ObjState
   StObj = CType(StateObj, ObjState)
   Console.WriteLine("Input Argument 1 in task 2 " & StObj.inarg1)
   Console.WriteLine("Input Argument 2 in task2 " & StObj.inarg2)
   'The class variables can be employed for returning values
   StObj.outval = "From Task2 " & StObj.inarg1 & " " & StObj.inarg2
End Sub
```

In the `Sub Main()` method we queue these two tasks in the thread pool employing the `QueueUserWorkItem()` method of the `ThreadPool` class, as given by the following code block:

```
Sub Main()
   Dim thrPool As ThreadPool
   thrPool.QueueUserWorkItem(New WaitCallback(AddressOf longtask1))
   thrPool.QueueUserWorkItem(New WaitCallback(AddressOf longtask2))
   Console.Read()
End Sub
```

We can also queue work items that have wait operations involved with them to the thread pool by employing `RegisterWaitForSingleObject()` to which `WaitHandle` is passed as an argument. This `WaitHandle` signals the method wrapped in a `WaitOrTimerCallback` delegate. In this case, the thread pool creates a background thread to invoke the callback method. The following example (vbThreadPool.vb) demonstrates this concept:

```
Imports System
Imports System.Threading

Public Class vbThreadPool
   Private Shared i As Integer = 0

   Public Shared Sub Main()
      Dim arev As New AutoResetEvent(False)
      ThreadPool.RegisterWaitForSingleObject(arev, _
              New WaitOrTimerCallback(AddressOf workitem), _
              Nothing, 2000, False)
      arev.Set()
      Console.Read()
   End Sub

   Public Shared Sub workitem(ByVal O As Object, _
                      ByVal signaled As Boolean)
      i += 1
      Console.WriteLine("Thread Pool Work Item Invoked: " & i.ToString)
   End Sub

End Class
```

The output from the above example will be something like:

```
Thread Pool Work Item Invoked: 1
Thread Pool Work Item Invoked: 2
Thread Pool Work Item Invoked: 3
Thread Pool Work Item Invoked: 4
.....
```

The output will continue with a new line printed every 2 seconds and the value of i incremented by one until the user presses the *Enter* key to invoke the `Console.Read()` statement.

To start, an `AutoResetEvent` object called `arev` is created to signal the execution of queued work items:

```
Dim arev As New AutoResetEvent(False)
```

We invoke the `RegisterWaitForSingleObject()` method, which registers a delegate and signals the work item at the specified time interval. In our example, it is set to 2 seconds as given by the following piece of code:

```
ThreadPool.RegisterWaitForSingleObject(arev, _
         New WaitOrTimerCallback(AddressOf workitem), _
         Nothing, 2000, False)
```

To raise the event we need to use the `set()` method of the `AutoResetEvent` object:

```
arev.Set()
```

This example concludes the practical session on using thread pools in VB.NET applications; in the next section we will examine scalability and build a thread pool manager application.

Scalability in .NET

If you have a multiprocessor system, then you'll see threads really show their worth. The Windows OS manages the allocation of threads to processors and, as you have seen throughout this book, firing any process automatically starts a thread. The .NET Framework does not provide fine-grained control of the processor allocation, preferring to allow the operating system to control the scheduling, as it will have more information on the loading of the processors than the CLR would. It does, however, provide some control over which processor an entire process runs on. However, this applies to *all* of its threads, so its use is not applicable to this book.

If you have only one thread, the main thread, then every task within that thread will operate on the same processor. However, if a new thread is fired, then the operating system schedules which processor it should be executed on. This decision as to which processor will run the thread does itself consume some processor resources and so, for small tasks, it isn't generally worth it as the time to execute may be only as long as the time it takes for the OS to allocate the task to a processor. However, this allocation has been taking less and less time in successive versions of Windows, and for anything other than the most trivial of tasks, when using threads, you should find a performance improvement by creating a new thread to execute your task. It is in symmetric multi-processor (SMP) systems that the benefits of threading are really shown, as the processors can be used to their full effect to distribute the load of the application.

In the next section, we describe how to create a thread pool manager with which you can create and manage threads, and which will ensure that a maximum and minimum number of threads exist in a pool and that idle threads get reused.

A Thread Pool Manager

Throughout this book, you have seen different ways of creating threads and in this chapter we have described the `ThreadPool` class to make use of the operating system's own thread pool for short-lived threads. We can implement a half-way house between the two, however. We can create a class that will keep a pool of a specified number of threads to be supplied to any requesting application. This will enable the threads to be managed more easily by your code, and also allow for faster thread execution as you may be able to use a previously instantiated thread object. This class will draw together much of the knowledge acquired so far, and you will be able to use it in your own multithreaded applications. We will explain this class as we go along, and at the end provide an application to test that this assembly is working as expected.

So, let's get started and explain the code of our thread pool manager contained in a file named `ThreadPool.vb`:

```
Imports System
Imports System.Collections
Imports System.Threading
Imports System.Text
Imports Microsoft.VisualBasic


Namespace GenThreadPool
```

The above declarations show that the only additional external assembly needed is `System.dll`. The `GenThreadPool` namespace is defined to contain all of the relevant classes for this project. Below we show the interface called `IThreadPool` that will be used for the `GenThreadPoolImpl` class:

```
Public Interface IThreadPool
   Sub AddJob(jobToRun As System.Threading.Thread)
   Function GetStats() As Stats
End Interface
```

This defines two methods for the thread pool, `AddJob()` and `GetStats()`, which will be detailed in the following definitions of the `GenThreadPoolImpl` class, which generates the thread pool that we will be using:

```
Public Class GenThreadPoolImpl
   Implements IThreadPool
   Private m_maxThreads As Integer
   Private m_minThreads As Integer
   Private m_maxIdleTime As Integer
   Private Shared m_debug As Boolean
   Private m_pendingJobs As ArrayList
   Private m_availableThreads As ArrayList
```

```vb
      Public Property PendingJobs As ArrayList
        Get
           Return m_pendingJobs
        End Get

        Set
           m_pendingJobs = value
        End Set
    End Property

    Public Property AvailableThreads As ArrayList
        Get
           Return m_availableThreads
        End Get

        Set
           m_availableThreads = value
        End Set
    End Property

    Public Property Debug() As Boolean
        Get
           Return m_debug
        End Get

        Set
           Me.m_debug = value
        End Set
    End Property

    Public Property MaxIdleTime() As Integer
        Get
           Return Me.m_maxIdleTime
        End Get

        Set
           Me.m_maxIdleTime = value
        End Set
    End Property

    Public Property MaxThreads() As Integer
        Get
           Return Me.m_maxThreads
        End Get

        Set
           Me.m_maxThreads = value
        End Set
    End Property

    Public Property MinThreads() As Integer
        Get
           Return Me.m_minThreads
        End Get

        Set
           Me.m_minThreads = value
        End Set
    End Property
```

This class implements the `IThreadPool` interface, which we defined earlier, and then goes on to define a few `Private` fields. The properties are just wrappers around the relevant `Private` members to prevent users from altering the values directly, in case further rules need to be added later. The fields `m_maxThreads`, `m_minThreads`, and `m_maxIdleTime` specify the maximum and minimum number of threads in the pool, and how long in milliseconds to allow a thread to remain idle before removing it from the pool. There are three constructors for this class:

```
Public Sub New()

    m_maxThreads = 1
    m_minThreads = 0
    m_maxIdleTime = 300
    Me.m_pendingJobs = ArrayList.Synchronized(New ArrayList())
    Me.m_availableThreads = ArrayList.Synchronized(New ArrayList())
    m_debug = False

End Sub
```

The default constructor only permits one thread to be present in the pool, and will destroy it after only 0.3 seconds. It also performs some lazy initialization, creating an array list to contain the jobs awaiting a thread, and the threads not yet allocated to a method call. The m_debug flag, when set to `True`, would allow further debugging information while testing.

```
Public Sub New(maxThreads As Integer, minThreads As Integer, _
            maxIdleTime As Integer)

    m_maxThreads = maxThreads
    m_minThreads = minThreads
    m_maxIdleTime = maxIdleTime
    Me.m_pendingJobs = ArrayList.Synchronized(New ArrayList())
    Me.m_availableThreads = ArrayList.Synchronized(New ArrayList())
    m_debug = False
    InitAvailableThreads()

End Sub
```

When a `GenThreadPoolImpl` class is instantiated with three integers, we specify how the minimum and maximum number of threads, and the idle time of the threads. It also fires off the `InitAvailableThreads()` method, detailed below:

```
Private Sub InitAvailableThreads()

    If Me.m_maxThreads > 0 Then
        Dim i As Integer
        For i = 1 To (Me.m_maxThreads)
            Dim t As New Thread(AddressOf (New GenPool(Me,
Me)).run)
                                        Dim e As New ThreadElement(t)
            e.Idle = True
            Me.m_availableThreads.Add(e)
        Next
    End If

End Sub
```

163

This creates the threads needed for the pool on instantiation. The default constructor only specified one thread, so it wasn't necessary before. This cycles through, creating the maximum number of threads allowed by the pool, specified in m_maxThreads. Below is the constructor for four arguments

```
Public Sub New(maxThreads As Integer, minThreads As Integer, _
               maxIdleTime As Integer, debug_ As Boolean)

    m_maxThreads = maxThreads
    m_minThreads = minThreads
    m_maxIdleTime = maxIdleTime
    Me.m_pendingJobs = ArrayList.Synchronized(New ArrayList())
    Me.m_availableThreads = ArrayList.Synchronized(New ArrayList())
    Me.m_debug = debug_
    InitAvailableThreads()

End Sub
```

This constructor does the same as the above, only allowing us to set the debugging flag. We now go on to describe the business end of this class, the AddJob() method:

```
Public Sub AddJob(job As Thread) Implements IThreadPool.AddJob
    If job Is Nothing Then
       Return
    End If

    SyncLock Me
```

The above subroutine actually adds a job to the pool. If the job passed as a parameter is non-existent, then it exits the method. Otherwise, it provides a lock on the GenThreadPoolImpl instance to ensure that no other thread or process can add or remove a job:

```
        m_pendingJobs.Add(job)
        Dim index As Integer = FindFirstIdleThread()

        If Me.m_debug Then
           Console.WriteLine(("First Idle Thread is " & _
                             index.ToString()))
        End If
        If index = - 1 Then
           If m_maxThreads = _
               - 1 Or m_availableThreads.Count < m_maxThreads Then
             If Me.m_debug Then
               Console.WriteLine("Creating a new thread")
             End If

             Dim t As New Thread(AddressOf (New GenPool(Me, Me)).Run)
```

The job is added to an `ArrayList`, which will store all the jobs awaiting execution and completion. The `FindFirstIdleThread()` function returns the index of a thread contained within m_availableThreads that is currently idle and so available for use. If the function returns -1, then there are no idle threads and the pool needs to attempt to create a new one. The `Run()` method of the `GenPool` class is fired inside this thread.

```
Dim e As New ThreadElement(t)

e.Idle = False
e.GetMyThread().Start()

Try
   m_availableThreads.Add(e)
Catch
   ex As OutOfMemoryException
   Console.WriteLine("Out of memory: " & ex.ToString())
   Thread.Sleep(3000)
   m_availableThreads.Add(e)
   Console.WriteLine("Added Job again")
End Try

   Return
End If

If Me.m_debug Then
   Console.WriteLine("No Threads Available..." & _
                    Me.GetStats().ToString())
End If
```

The `ThreadElement` class is another helper class that will be defined later. It adds some additional properties to a standard thread so that the pool can manage it effectively. The thread's `Start()` method is fired before it is added to the m_availableThreads collection.

```
Else
   Try
      If Me.m_debug Then
         Console.WriteLine("Using an existing thread...")
      End If
      CType(m_availableThreads(index), _
         ThreadElement).Idle = False
```

Above, we start to detail the condition whereby a thread is deemed idle and so free for allocation to a new job. Firstly, we convert the thread explicitly into a `ThreadElement` and change its idle flag:

```
SyncLock CType(m_availableThreads(index), _
         ThreadElement).GetMyThread()
   Monitor.Pulse(CType(m_availableThreads(index), _
            ThreadElement).GetMyThread())
End SyncLock
```

Here we lock the thread so that it cannot be affected by any other process. We then alert all waiting threads that it is now available for use, so we issue a `Monitor.Pulse()` instruction, and then release the lock:

```
        Catch ex As Exception
          Console.WriteLine(("Error while reusing thread " & _
                            ex.Message))

          If Me.m_debug Then
            Console.WriteLine(("Value of index is " & _
                              index.ToString()))
            Console.WriteLine(("Size of available threads is " & _
                Me.m_availableThreads.Count.ToString()))
            Console.WriteLine(("Available Threads is " & _
                Me.m_availableThreads.IsSynchronized.ToString()))
          End If
        End Try
      End If
    End SyncLock
  End Sub
```

Finally, we catch any exceptions and output the results to the commandline, providing more useful debugging information if the `Me.Debug` flag has been set. That completes the `AddJob()` method so now let's look at the implementation of the `GetStats()` function:

```
Public Function GetStats() As Stats _
                  Implements IThreadPool.GetStats
  Dim statsInstance As New Stats()

  statsInstance.MaxThreads = m_maxThreads
  statsInstance.MinThreads = m_minThreads
  statsInstance.MaxIdleTime = m_maxIdleTime
  statsInstance.PendingJobs = m_pendingJobs.Count
  statsInstance.NumThreads = m_availableThreads.Count
  statsInstance.JobsInProgress = _
    m_availableThreads.Count - FindIdleThreadCount()

  Return statsInstance
End Function
```

The `GetStats()` function returns a `Stats()` structure, which we will define later. As we will see, it contains the minimum and maximum number of threads, as well as other values set in the constructor. Now let's look at the `FindIdleThreadCount()` function:

```
Public Function FindIdleThreadCount() As Integer
  Dim idleThreads As Integer = 0
  Dim i As Integer

  For i = 0 To m_availableThreads.Count - 1
    ' Check for ThreadElements that have their Idle Property true
    If CType(m_availableThreads(i), ThreadElement).Idle Then
```

```
            idleThreads += 1
         End If
      Next
      Return idleThreads
   End Function
```

This function is one called earlier in the class and it simply goes through the array list of threads and returns the how many of them are idle. We also used the `FindFirstIdleThread()` function so let's see it:

```
Public Function FindFirstIdleThread() As Integer
   Dim i As Integer

   For i = 0 To m_availableThreads.Count - 1
      If CType(m_availableThreads(i), ThreadElement).Idle Then
         Return i
      End If
   Next

   Return - 1
End Function
```

As we can see, the function returns the index of the first idle thread in the array list. We will also need the following function:

```
Public Function FindThread() As Integer
   Dim i As Integer

   For i = 0 To m_availableThreads.Count - 1
      If CType(m_availableThreads(i), _
            ThreadElement).GetMyThread().Equals( _
            Thread.CurrentThread) Then
         Return i
      End If
   Next

   Return - 1
End Function
```

This method is used to determine in which index position in the array list the current thread is located. We'll also need the following method:

```
Public Sub RemoveThread()
   Dim i As Integer

   For i = 0 To m_availableThreads.Count - 1
      If CType(m_availableThreads(i), _
            ThreadElement).GetMyThread().Equals( _
            Thread.CurrentThread) Then
         m_availableThreads.RemoveAt(i)
         Exit Sub
      End If
   Next
End Sub
End Class
```

This removes the current thread from the array list of threads. This is, of course, used to remove a thread from the pool when it is finished with and has been idle for longer than the time specified in `Me.MaxIdleTime`. Now we start to define the rest of the classes for this assembly:

```
Public Class GenPool
    Private m_lock As [Object]
    Private m_gn As GenThreadPoolImpl

    Public Sub New(lock_ As [Object], gn As GenThreadPoolImpl)
        Me.m_lock = lock_
        Me.m_gn = gn
    End Sub
```

The `GenPool` class executes all of the pending threads, and once complete, after the period specified in `MaxIdleTime`, will remove them from the pool. It checks to see if there are any threads available on the `GenThreadPoolImpl` passed as a reference to the constructor, and it locks the values of the object passed as the first parameter. In general, this will be the same `GenThreadPoolImpl` object passed as the second argument.

```
Public Sub Run()
    Dim job As Thread

    While True
        While True
            SyncLock Me.m_lock
                If m_gn.PendingJobs.Count = 0 Then

                    Dim index As Integer = m_gn.FindThread()
                    If index = - 1 Then
                        Exit Sub
                    End If

                    CType(m_gn.AvailableThreads(index), _
                            ThreadElement).Idle = True
                    Exit While
                End If

                job = CType(m_gn.PendingJobs(0), Thread)

                m_gn.PendingJobs.RemoveAt(0)
            End SyncLock
```

This `Run()` method starts a loop to attempt to find a thread in the pool that matches the current thread, and begin its execution. You can see above that it locks the object passed in as a parameter to the constructor, and if there are no pending jobs, then it just finds the thread in the pool that matches the current one, returning –1 if there isn't one. If there is a pending job, then it retrieves the first one, and then removes it from the queue.

```
            'run the job
            job.Start()
        End While
```

It then begins execution of the method on the pending thread, and returns to the start of the loop.

```
        Try
            SyncLock Me
                If m_gn.MaxIdleTime = - 1 Then
                    Monitor.Wait(Me)
                Else
                    Monitor.Wait(Me, m_gn.MaxIdleTime)
                End If
            End SyncLock
        Catch

        End Try
```

In the next part of the loop (once it has no more pending jobs), it locks the current object and waits for the thread to be free for execution for the period specified in MaxIdleTime.

```
        SyncLock m_lock
            If m_gn.PendingJobs.Count = 0 Then
                If m_gn.MinThreads <> - 1 And _
                    m_gn.AvailableThreads.Count > m_gn.MinThreads Then
                    m_gn.RemoveThread()
                    Return
                End If
            End If
        End SyncLock
    End While
End Sub
End Class
```

Finally, it locks the object again, and if there are no pending jobs and there are more than the minimum required number of threads, then it removes the thread from the pool. We now move on to the ThreadElement class:

```
Public Class ThreadElement
    Private m_idle As Boolean
    Private m_thread As Thread

    Public Sub New(th As Thread)
        Me.m_thread = th
        Me.m_idle = True
    End Sub
```

A `ThreadElement` is what is stored in the thread pool, and takes a thread as the parameter for its constructor. It sets the thread as idle on construction of this object.

```
Public Property Idle() As Boolean
  Get
    Return Me.m_idle
  End Get

  Set
    Me.m_idle = value
  End Set
End Property

Public Function GetMyThread() As Thread
  Return Me.m_thread
End Function
End Class
```

The above code is straightforward. The `Idle` property essentially defines when the thread's execution is complete, and the `GetMyThread()` method just returns the `Thread` object. Now look at the following structure:

```
Public Structure Stats
  Public MaxThreads As Integer
  Public MinThreads As Integer
  Public MaxIdleTime As Integer
  Public NumThreads As Integer
  Public PendingJobs As Integer
  Public JobsInProgress As Integer
```

Here we define the `Stats` structure that we mentioned earlier, which stores all of the statistics of the thread pool. The fields are self-describing. `ToString()` is the only method:

```
Public Overrides Function ToString() As String
  Dim sb As New StringBuilder("MaxThreads = ", 107)

  sb.Append(MaxThreads)
  sb.Append(ControlChars.Lf & "MinThreads = ")
  sb.Append(MinThreads)
  sb.Append(ControlChars.Lf & "MaxIdleTime = ")
  sb.Append(MaxIdleTime)
  sb.Append(ControlChars.Lf & "Pending Jobs = ")
  sb.Append(PendingJobs)
  sb.Append(ControlChars.Lf & "Jobs In Progress = ")
  sb.Append(JobsInProgress)

  Return sb.ToString()
  End Function
  End Structure
End Namespace
```

This `ToString()` method returns the structure in a string format, using
`StringBuilder` to build up the string. The `107` argument initilizes the
`StringBuilder`'s size to 107 characters, as it is fair to assume that there are not likely
to be more than 99,999 threads. If so, then `StringBuilder` will resize itself anyway.
This capacity specification allows a small performance boost.

If you have an application that is firing methods repeatedly on different threads, this
class can manage the process and help ensure that too many threads aren't spawned.
Apart from containing a maximum and minimum number of threads, it will reuse an
existing thread if possible. You can now compile this project into a DLL, and use this
class from within other projects. Below is code that will allow you to test this thread
pool class, `TestGenThreadPool.vb`:

```vb
Imports System
Imports System.Threading
Imports GenThreadPool

Namespace TestGenThreadPool
  Public Class TestPerformance
    Public count As Integer
    Private m_lock As New [Object]()

    Public Sub New(pool As IThreadPool, times As Integer)
      Console.WriteLine("Performance using Pool[in ms]: ")

      count = 0
      Dim start As Long = System.DateTime.Now.Millisecond

      Console.WriteLine(("Start Time for Job is " + _
                  System.DateTime.Now))

      Dim i As Integer
      For i = 0 To times - 1
        Dim tl As New Thread(AddressOf (New Job(Me)).Run)
        pool.AddJob(tl)
      Next

      While True
        SyncLock m_lock
          If count = times Then
            Exit While
          End If
        End SyncLock
        Try
          Thread.Sleep(5000)
        Catch
        End Try
      End While

      Console.WriteLine("" & _
            (System.DateTime.Now.Millisecond - start).ToString())
```

```
        Console.WriteLine("End Time for Job is " & _
                     System.DateTime.Now.ToString())

        Console.WriteLine("Performance using no Pool[in ms]: ")

        count = 0
        start = System.DateTime.Now.Millisecond

        Console.WriteLine("Start Time for JobThread is " & _
                     System.DateTime.Now.ToString())

        For i = 0 To times - 1
          Dim jt As New Thread(AddressOf (New JobThread(Me)).Run)
          jt.Start()
        Next

        While True
          SyncLock m_lock
            If count = times Then
              Exit While
            End If
          End SyncLock
          Try
            Thread.Sleep(5000)
          Catch
          End Try
        End While

        Console.WriteLine("" & _
             (System.DateTime.Now.Millisecond - start).ToString())

        Console.WriteLine("End Time for JobThread is " & _
                     System.DateTime.Now.ToString())
    End Sub

    NotInheritable Class JobThread
      Private m_lock As New [Object]()
      Private tpf As TestPerformance

      Public Sub New(tpf_ As TestPerformance)
        Me.tpf = tpf_
      End Sub

      Public Sub Run()
        SyncLock m_lock
          tpf.count += 1
        End SyncLock
      End Sub
    End Class

    NotInheritable Class Job
      Private m_lock As New Object()
      Private tpf As TestPerformance
```

```
      Public Sub New(tpf_ As TestPerformance)
        Me.tpf = tpf_
      End Sub 'New

      Public Sub Run()
        SyncLock m_lock
          tpf.count += 1
        End SyncLock
      End Sub
    End Class
End Class

Class TestPool
  Private Shared i As Integer = 0
  Private j As Integer = 0

  Public Sub Run()
    i += 1
    j = i

    Console.WriteLine("Value of i in run is {0} ", j)
  End Sub

  Public Shared Sub Main(args() As String)
    Dim tp = New GenThreadPoolImpl(1000, 1000, 300, True)

    Dim i As Integer
    For i = 0 To 99
      Dim td1 As New TestPool()
      Dim t1 As New Thread(AddressOf td1.Run)
      Dim td2 As New TestPool()
      Dim t2 As New Thread(AddressOf td2.Run)
      Dim td3 As New TestPool()
      Dim t3 As New Thread(AddressOf td3.Run)
      Dim td4 As New TestPool()
      Dim t4 As New Thread(AddressOf td4.Run)
      Dim td5 As New TestPool()
      Dim t5 As New Thread(AddressOf td5.Run)
      Dim td6 As New TestPool()
      Dim t6 As New Thread(AddressOf td6.Run)
      Dim td7 As New TestPool()
      Dim t7 As New Thread(AddressOf td7.Run)
      Dim td8 As New TestPool()
      Dim t8 As New Thread(AddressOf td8.Run)
      Dim td9 As New TestPool()
      Dim t9 As New Thread(AddressOf td9.Run)
      Dim td10 As New TestPool()
      Dim t10 As New Thread(AddressOf td10.Run)
      Dim td11 As New TestPool()
      Dim t11 As New Thread(AddressOf td11.Run)
```

173

```
                tp.AddJob(t1)
                tp.AddJob(t2)
                tp.AddJob(t3)
                tp.AddJob(t4)
                tp.AddJob(t5)

                tp.AddJob(t6)
                tp.AddJob(t7)
                tp.AddJob(t8)
                tp.AddJob(t9)
                tp.AddJob(t10)
                tp.AddJob(t11)
            Next

            Dim td12 As New TestPool()
            Dim t12 As New Thread(AddressOf td12.Run)
            tp.AddJob(t12)

            Dim p As New TestPerformance(tp, 1000)
        End Sub
    End Class
End Namespace
```

The above application just mechanically attempts to add new threads to an instance of the thread pool, with the debug flag set to true. It is quite straightforward, but the best way to see this thread pool in action is to try it out in your own applications. You can use this class, once compiled.

Summary

In this chapter, we have seen how thread pooling can be used when a thread is required for a relatively short duration. Thread pooling allows recycling of threads. A thread is assigned a task and, when that task has completed, it returns to the pool and waits for the next assignment. We also covered the various aspects of using thread pools in .NET applications. We started defining what a thread pool was and then why we might choose to use one in our applications. We also covered the role of CLR in creating the thread pool followed by the glitches involved in using a thread pool.

We later covered some more scalability issues, as the ThreadPool class isn't suitable for applications that may need to fire a number of long-lived threads. We discussed the creation of a ThreadPool manager class and mentioned how SMP systems can dramatically increase the performance of an application if it is threaded.

VB.NET

Threading

Handbook

6

6

Debugging and Tracing Threads

Debugging and tracing are two techniques frequently, and often necessarily, employed by developers. The former allows a developer to analyze an application's variables and code, and step through the program's code flow. The latter allows us to trace the behavior of our application, displaying information in a **listener** (a log file, the Windows event log, or similar). They are fundamental to creating robust applications because they provide an easy way to monitor and understand how our application is working. The big difference between the two techniques is that tracing can be done during an application's runtime, while the debugger is used at design time, before releasing the final version of our application. During recent years, developers have suffered from the lack of a debugger for ASP applications. In order to understand a variable's value, code's flow, and every common task usually done with a debugger, ASP developers often had to populate their code with Response.Write() statements, echoing messages like Entered the function, Exited from the loop, and so on. Then when we had finished testing the ASP application, we needed to remove all the undesired statements. That's not the best way to debug a program.

Fortunately, .NET brings debugging functionality to the next generation of ASP developers by providing four useful classes: Trace, Debug, BooleanSwitch, and TraceSwitch. In addition, any .NET language can use these classes; also, every developer who chooses to use Visual Studio .NET to create applications can perform debugging operations using its visual tools.

The various tracing and debugging techniques are especially useful for applications that use threads. If implemented well, these techniques allow developers to trace each thread's behavior, discovering any applications' anomalies such as unexpected resource consumption, bugs, and so on.

In this chapter, we will analyze both tracing and debugging aspects in the following order:

❏ Using Visual Studio .NET debug analysis, and using its powerful tools

❏ Using the .NET tracing classes in order to implement these features in our code

❏ Putting it all together by creating an application that uses tracing

For this chapter, Visual Studio .NET is necessary to make use of much of the tracing and debugging features shown. However, by using the /d:TRACE=TRUE switch, some tracing functionality can be achieved using the command line.

Creating the Application Code

Usually, when we create an application (or part of one), we write the code and then try to run the application. Sometimes it works as we expected it to; often it doesn't. When it doesn't, we try to discover what could be happening by examining more carefully the code that we wrote. In this case, we can use the debugger by choosing some breakpoints to stop the application's execution near or just before the guilty function, then step through lines of code, examining (perhaps modifying) variable values to understand precisely what went wrong. Finally, when all is working we can build the release version (a version without debugging components) of our application, and distribute it. In this type of program, during the development history, we need to insert the tracing functionalities. In fact, even if the program works very well, there will be always a case where something has not been foreseen (especially when some external, possibly third-party, components fail). In that case, if we have filled the code with tracing instructions, we could turn on tracing and examine the resulting log file to understand what might have happened. Moreover, tracing functionalities are useful in discovering where an application consumes resources or where it spends too much time to perform a task. In applications that use threads, we should use tracing functionalities because it can be difficult to observe each thread's behavior.

Tracing, debugging, and performance techniques are often known as **instrumentation**. This term refers to the capacity to monitor an application's performance, and diagnose errors and bugs. So, an application that supports instrumentation has to include:

❏ Debugging: Fixing errors and bugs during an application's development

❏ Code tracing: Receiving information in a listener program during an application's execution

❏ Performance counters: Using techniques to monitor an application's performance

Let's examine what the .NET Framework provides for us to add instrumentation to our applications.

Debugging Your Code

Usually, when you test your application and see that its behavior is not what you expect it to be, you start examining more carefully the code written. If you are using Visual Studio .NET to create your application, it provides many amazing tools to visually debug the application. In addition, whatever language you choose to develop your application in, it will use the same debugger with the same tools. Moreover, the basic debugger's functionalities have been inherited from the Visual Basic 6 and Visual C++ IDEs, resulting in something that should be intuitive for most developers. However, we shan't spend too much time on the debugger in general, and will focus this discussion mostly on those features directly relevant to threading.

The new debugger provides:

- ❏ The same tool to debug different applications created using different languages

- ❏ The possibility to debug SQL Server stored procedures

- ❏ The possibility to debug .NET Framework and Win32 native code, so that if you are debugging your Visual Basic .NET application and your thread uses a COM+ component, you can debug both the applications using the same debugger

- ❏ A more powerful and enhanced remote debugger

If you already have experience with the Visual Basic 6 debugger, you will know that some functionality has been removed. The most relevant is the ability to change the code and continue with its execution. Using the Visual Studio .NET debugger, this feature is no longer available, because each modification to the code requires a new compilation.

In this section of the book, we will analyze the debugging tools provided by the Visual Studio .NET IDE that can be especially useful during the testing and error discovery phase of multithreaded application development.

Visual Studio .NET Debugger

Using the Visual Studio .NET debugger, as you know, you can break the execution of your application at a specified point simply by inserting a breakpoint near the line of the code you wish to inspect. When the application is suspended, the debugger provides many tools to examine variables' content, edit their values, examine the memory and call stack, and more.

Configuring Debugger Parameters

In order to make use of the Visual Studio .NET debugger, we have to build the application using the Debug configuration. In that way, we will fill the application with symbolic debugging information rather than optimize the code. When everything appears to work fine, you would release your application after recompiling the code, choosing the Release configuration, which removes debugging information and optimizes the code.

When a new debugger session begins, a lot of resources are loaded into the memory. In fact, the debugger fills the memory with the various code to allow us to debug unmanaged code, SQL Server stored procedures, and more. It is therefore a good idea to remove these features when we don't need them. We can change the debugger's settings inside the Property Pages dialog box. The following dialog box will appear:

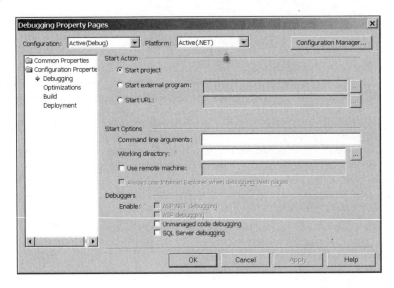

These configuration parameters are self explanatory, and not directly relevant to debugging threaded applications

After compiling a Debug configured project, the output directory will contain the EXE or DLL file and a PDB (program database) file. Because IL keeps the values of parameters and private members inside arrays, the original names of these variables are lost – as well as some other information relevant to debugging. When a project is compiled for debugging, or the /debug:full switch is used on the command-line compiler, a PDB file is generated at the same time. Within the EXE or DLL file is contained an absolute path pointing to the PDB file and if the debugger doesn't find the program database file, it starts to search in the same application path and in the directory specified in the Property Pages dialog box. Finally, if the debugger can't find the PDB file in any directory, it will regenerate a new one.

180

Debugger Tools

Once you have loaded your project into Visual Studio .NET you are ready to debug your application by simply hitting either the *F10* or *F11* key. If you are not working with the release version of your application, you will see the IDE showing many docked windows. During your debugging session these windows will be filled with the variables' values, objects' dumps, call stack, disassembly code, and more. Let's start examining more closely these debugging tools, and how they can be used to assist in the debugging of your threaded application.

The Locals Window

This window allows you to examine and modify each variable's content defined locally in the function you are debugging. For example, debugging the following `Main()` method of `TraceSwitchExample`, you will retrieve just the content of two variables: `fs` and `t`. Observe the following screenshot:

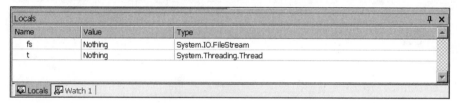

You can activate this window selecting the Locals menu within the Window menu contained in the Debug main menu. Alternatively, you can press *Ctrl+Alt+V*, release and press *L*.

The Watch Window

You can drag variables from the source code, dropping them over this window in order to inspect their values and structure. In the following screenshot, a `BooleanSwitch` object (which you will learn about in the next section) has been dropped into the window.

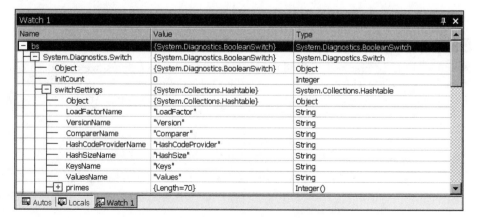

Expanding tree nodes by clicking over the plus sign you can examine and change object property values. You can activate up to four Watch windows by pressing *Ctrl+Alt+W*, then releasing and pressing a key between *1* and *4*.

> *You can also add a variable to the Watch window by selecting it in the source code and choosing* Add Watch *from the context menu.*

The Command Window – Immediate Window

This window provides a text field where you can query a variable's contents and change variables' values. When you need to retrieve the variable's content you have to use a question mark before the expression. In the following screenshot, the `Enabled` property of the `BooleanSwitch` object has been examined, changed to `False`, and displayed again.

In addition, this window allows us to make use of various IDE commands; such as creating a new file or a new project, finding a string, and whatever else you can usually do within the Visual Studio .NET menu. To switch from Immediate mode to Command mode you simply have to write the `>cmd` statement. Once in Command mode, you will be assisted by the IDE in finding the desired commands by the IntelliSense functionality. To switch back to the Immediate mode, the command is: `>immed`.

You can activate this window by selecting Debug | Window | Immediate, or you can press *Ctrl+Alt+I*.

Stepping Through the Code

Now that we have briefly described the more useful debug windows, we can focus our attention on code navigation. The Visual Studio .NET debugger allows developers to step between code lines, observing the program behavior at runtime. The debugger provides three different ways to step through the code:

❑ **Step Into**: Pressing the *F11* key you will go through the code one step at a time, entering function bodies that you find on your way.

❑ **Step Over**: Pressing the *F10* key you will go one step forward in the code executing every function you encounter but stepping over it (executing the function as one line).

❑ **Step Out**: Pressing *Shift+F11*, you will execute all the code within the body of the function that you are currently stepped into.

Each time you step to the next line of code by pressing these keys, you are executing the highlighted code.

> **You cannot use the stepping features to step through a thread's execution. These are only relevant to see what the code is doing around the thread.**

Another useful feature provided by the Visual Studio .NET debugger is the Run To Cursor functionality. Selecting it from the context menu over the source code, you can execute all the lines between the highlighted line and the line where the cursor is placed.

Finally, the Visual Studio .NET debugger provides a way to change the execution point of our application. You can decide to move your application's execution point by launching the debugger and choosing the Set Next Statement item in the context menu. Be careful when using this feature, because every line of code between the old and the new position will cease to be executed.

Setting Breakpoints

In large source code applications, you cannot step through all the code to arrive to the function you are interested in debugging. The debugger offers the possibility to set breakpoints in the code. As the name says, the breakpoint is a point where the execution of your program is to be suspended. You can specify breakpoints both before and after launching the debugger session, by simply placing the cursor on the line and pressing the *F9* key. A red highlight will be placed over the line to let you know that you have just added a breakpoint to the code, and a glyph will be added to the left margin of the source window. In order to remove a breakpoint you can either click over the glyph or press the *F9* key again.

You can manage all the disseminated breakpoints from a unique window by using the Breakpoints window.

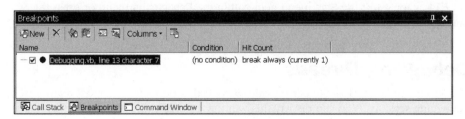

Using this window, you can add a new breakpoint, delete one or all breakpoints, disable all breakpoints, add and remove window's columns, and view breakpoint properties.

> **Breakpoints are the method you can use to suspend execution of a thread and examine its variables' contents.**

You can specify to activate a breakpoint only when a specific variable changes its content. You have to specify the variable's name choosing the has changed radio button in the breakpoint property pages. This again can be useful in threads, as you can detect when something unexpected occurs.

Finally, the Hit Count... allows developers to enable breakpoint when the breakpoint has reached the specified hit counter. Again this is useful in debugging threads as it allows you to see how often a thread is spawned.

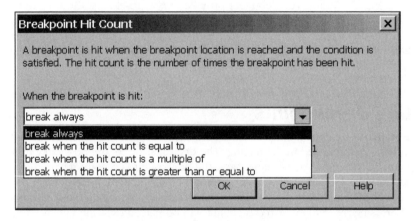

From the combo box, you can select the condition that you want to assign to the breakpoint. For example, you can activate the breakpoint in a loop only when you are near to exiting from it. You can select the break when the hit count is equal to an item by assigning a value to the text field that will appear next to the combo.

In order to execute all the code lines until the breakpoint is reached you have to press the *F5* key, or select the Start menu item within the Debug main menu or press the Start button on the standard toolbar.

Debugging Threads

The Visual Studio .NET debugger provides a special window to manage threads during debugging sessions. You can display this window by selecting Debug | Windows |Threads, or by simply pressing *Ctrl+Alt+H*.

The Threads window contains the following columns:

Column name	Description
ID	The thread's unique identifier assigned by the operating system.
Name	The thread's name. You can specify it in the code using the Name property of the Thread object.
Location	The function or memory address containing the thread.
Priority	The thread's priority.
Suspend	A counter for determining how often the thread has been suspended.

You can switch between threads by simply double clicking on the item within the Threads window. Moreover, by right clicking on a thread, you can choose the Freeze menu item that will pause the thread's execution. To roll back the frozen thread state, you select the Thaw menu item.

This covers the relevant sections of the debugger for our application.

Code Tracing

The next technique that we will analyze to instrument our code is tracing. In a multi-threaded application, this technique is especially important. You can trace a thread's behavior and interaction, when more than one task has been started. As we see later, this is not possible using the debugger. The .NET Framework provides some useful classes that allow developers to implement tracing functionality simply. Let's examine the tracing classes that the .NET Framework offers:

❑ Trace: This class has many shared methods that write messages to a listener. By default, the debug output windows will be used as the listener application, but thanks to the Listeners collection, we can add different listeners such as a text file listener, or the Windows event log listener.

❑   Debug: This class has the same methods as the Trace class, writing information to a listener application. The largest difference between these two classes is in their usage; Trace is useful at runtime, Debug is used at development time.

❑   BooleanSwitch: This class allows us to define a switch that turns on or off the tracing messages.

❑   TraceSwitch: This class provides four different tracing levels allowing developers to choose the severity of the messages to send to the listener.

The System.Diagnostics.Trace Class

In this section, we will analyze the most frequently used methods of the Trace class. It is provided by the .NET Framework and encapsulates all the necessary methods to implement the tracing functionality easily. The Trace class is contained in the System.Diagnostics namespace and provides many shared methods for sending messages to the listener application. As you know, the Shared declaration means that we do not have to instantiate a new object from the Trace class and can use the method directly. For example:

```
Sub Main()
   Trace.WriteLine(t.ThreadState)
End Sub
```

The code snippet above uses the WriteLine() method to output the thread state, followed by a carriage return, to the listener application. The following table lists all the shared methods provided by the Trace class:

Method	Description
Assert(*condition, message*)	Displays the specified string *message* when the *condition* provided to the method evaluates to False. When you do not specify the message text, the Call Stack is displayed instead.
Fail(*message*)	Similar to the Assert() method, this writes the specified text to the Call Stack when a failure occurs. The Assert() method differs because Fail() cannot specify a condition before displaying the error. In fact, the Fail() method is usually placed in the Catch statement of a Try-Catch-Finally instruction.
Write(*message | object*)	Writes the specified text *message*, or object name, to the listener application.

Method	Description
WriteIf(*condition, message*)	Writes the specified *message* text into the listener application if the specified *condition* is True.
WriteLine(*message* | *object*)	Writes the specified *message* text, or object name, followed by a carriage return.
WriteLineIf(*condition, message*)	Writes the specified *message* text followed by a carriage return if the specified *condition* is True.

The behavior of these methods depends on the listener application chosen. For example, the Assert() method displays a message box when the default listener is specified.

Default Listener Application

The Trace class provides a Listeners collection that allows us to add a new listener application. When no new listener object is added to the collection, the Trace class uses the default listener application: the Output debug window. This window is provided by the Visual Studio .NET IDE during debugging. Let's see a simple example, TraceExample1:

```
Sub Main()
    Trace.WriteLine("Entered Main()")
    Dim i As Integer
    For i = 0 To 5
        Trace.WriteLine(i)
    Next
    Trace.WriteLine("Exiting from Main()")
End Sub
```

The code is really simple; it writes tracing information when entering and exiting from the Main() method, plus the variable's values in the loop. In the next screenshot, you can see how the Visual Studio .NET Output listener shows the information:

The `Trace` class also provides two useful methods to assert error notification:
`Assert()` and `Fail()`. The former allows developer to check a condition provided as
parameter and write a message into the listener when this condition is `False`. The
latter writes a message into the listener each time a failure occurs. When no other
listener is added to the collection, the `Assert()` method displays a message box to
inform the user about an assertion. The following snippet of code, `TraceAssert.vb`,
can be tested when the SQL Server service has been stopped deliberately in order to
raise a connection exception:

```
Public Class TraceAssert
    Public Sub DBThread()
        ' Create a connection object
        Dim dbConn As New _
            SqlConnection("server=.;database=pubs;uid=sa;pwd=")

        ' Create a command object to execute a SQL statement
        Dim dbQuery As New SqlCommand("SELECT * FROM authors", dbConn)
        Dim dr As SqlDataReader

        Trace.WriteLine(DateTime.Now & " - Executing SQL statement")

        Try
            ' Open the connection to the database
            dbConn.Open()

            ' Execute the SQL statement
            dr = dbQuery.ExecuteReader(CommandBehavior.CloseConnection)

            While (dr.Read())
                ' Reading records
            End While
        Catch ex As Exception
            ' Trace an assertion if connection fails
            Trace.Assert(dbConn.State = ConnectionState.Open, "Error", _
                "Connection failed...")

            ' Trace an assertion if DataReader empty
            Trace.Assert(Not dr Is Nothing, "Error", _
                "The SqlDataReader is null!")
        Finally
            If (dr.IsClosed = False) And (Not dr Is Nothing) Then
                dr.Close()
            End If
        End Try
    End Sub

    Public Shared Sub Main()
        ' Create a thread
        Dim t As Thread
        t = New Thread(AddressOf DBThread)

        ' Start the thread
        t.Start()
    End Sub
End Class
```

In the `Main()` method, a new thread is created and started. The new thread runs the code within the `DBThread()` subroutine. This code simply tries to contact the pubs SQL Server database, and retrieve all the data contained within the `authors` table. If the SQL Server service were not available, the following assertion would be displayed upon execution of the code:

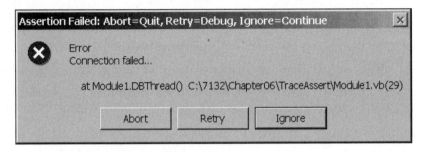

The row that raises that assertion is:

```
' Trace an assertion if something goes wrong
Trace.Assert(dbConn.State = ConnectionState.Open, "Error", _
    "Connection failed...")
```

As you can see, the first parameter checks whether the state of the connection is `Open`. It will be set to `False` when the connection has not been opened, so the assertion will be displayed. As you will see later in the chapter, you can deactivate tracing messaging using the application configuration file. In that way, you can decide whether to display assert messages at runtime.

Using Different Listener Applications

In this section we will see how to change the default listener application. The `Trace` class (and the `Debug` class as we will see later) exposes the `Listeners` collection, which contains a collection of listener applications. Without adding any new listener class, the `DefaultTraceListener` will point to the Output debug window provided by Visual Studio .NET. However, the .NET Framework provides another two classes that can be used as listener applications:

Class	Description
EventLogTraceListener	Using this class, you will redirect tracing messages to the Windows Event Log
TextWriterTraceListener	Using this class you will redirect tracing messages to a text file, or to a stream

In a multi-threaded application, we change the default listener with one of the listed listeners if we need to trace an application's behavior during its execution outside of Visual Studio. Naturally, the Output debug window is available only during the debug. Using these two classes, you could choose if trace messages are placed in the Windows Event log, or inside a text file. Usually, when you know that your application will run in an operating system equipped with the Event Log, the EventLogTraceListener class is the best solution to choose. The reasons include:

1. The Event Log is managed by the operating system

2. The Event Log allows administrators to specify security settings for the log

3. The Event Log has to be read with the Event Viewer. This displays in a better visual environment than occurs with text file in Notepad.

Changing the default listener is simple, so let's see an example, TraceEventLog.vb:

```
Module TraceEventLog
    Sub Main()
        ' Create a trace listener for the event log.
        Dim eltl As New EventLogTraceListener("TraceLog")

        ' Add the event log trace listener to the collection.
        Trace.Listeners.Add(eltl)

        ' Write output to the event log.
        Trace.WriteLine("Entered Main()")
    End Sub
End Module
```

Firstly, we have to create a new listener object. In the example above, a new EventLogTraceListener has been created in order to use the Windows event log as listener application. The class constructor accepts a string where we can specify the name of the source that has written an entry. The constructor will instantiate a new EventLog object assigning the specified source name to the Source property of the EventLog class, automatically.

The next step is adding the new listener object to the Listeners collection using the Add() method and providing the reference to the listener object. Finally, we can start to write tracing messages that will be redirected to the listener application.

Opening up the Windows event log using the Event Viewer application, we should see the new entry appearing in the Application Log section:

We can double-click the item inside the Application Log report to examine the message:

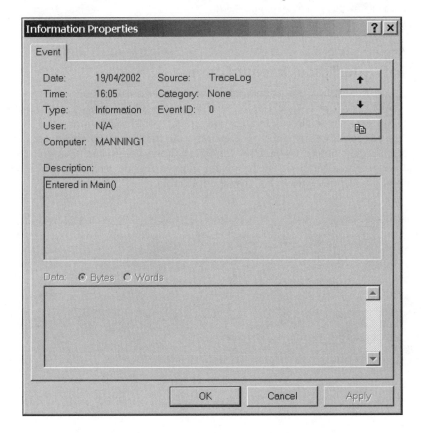

The code that we have examined above adds a new listener to the `Listeners` collection so that we will receive tracing messages both in the Output debug window, and in the event log. If we want to remove the default listener in order to use just the event log application, we have to call the `RemoveAt()` method, as illustrated in the code below:

```
Sub Main()
    ' Create a trace listener for the event log.
    Dim eltl As New EventLogTraceListener("TraceLog")

    ' Remove the default listener
    Trace.Listeners.RemoveAt(0)

    ' Add the event log trace listener to the collection.
    Trace.Listeners.Add(eltl)

    ' Write output to the event log.
    Trace.WriteLine("Entered in Main()")
End Sub
```

The TextWriterTraceListener Class

We are going to conclude our listener explanation by examining the `TextWriterTraceListener` class. It is useful when we have to write our tracing messages to a text file or directly in a console application. In fact, during the `TextWriterTraceListener` object's creation, you can specify either a `TextWriter` object, or a `Stream` object. Using a Stream object allows you to specify more details on how the file stream is handled. The following snippet of code, `TraceConsole.vb`, shows how to trace messages in a Console application:

```
Module TraceConsole
    Sub Main()
        ' Remove the default listener
        Trace.Listeners.RemoveAt(0)

        ' Add a console listener
        Trace.Listeners.Add(New TextWriterTraceListener(Console.Out))

        ' Write a trace message
        Trace.WriteLine("Entered Main()")
    End Sub
End Module
```

Specifying the `Console.Out` streaming in the class's constructor, our Console application will display tracing messages:

Finally, let's see how to add text log files as listener. We have to add a new `TextWriterTraceListener` object, specifying a `FileStream` object in its constructor. When the application ends, we have to use the static `Close()` method provided by the `Trace` class in order to close the log writing all the tracing messages. In the following code, `Debugging.vb`, a thread is started that traces both main and secondary thread messages:

```
Private Sub WritingThread()
    ' Trace an info message
    Trace.WriteLine(DateTime.Now & " - Entered WritingThread()")

    ' Sleeping for one sec....
    Thread.CurrentThread.Sleep(1000)

    ' Trace an info message
    Trace.WriteLine(DateTime.Now & " - Slept for 1 second...")
End Sub
```

The `WritingThread()` method is simply used by the thread to sleep for a second and write some tracing messages.

Here, we create a new `FileStream` object, either creating or opening the `Debugging.log` file, if it already exists. Then, we add the new listener into the `Listeners` collection by creating a new instance of the `TextWriterTraceListener` class within the `Add()` method:

```
Sub Main()
    ' Create a file listener
    Dim fs As New IO.FileStream("C:\Debugging.log", _
        IO.FileMode.OpenOrCreate)
    Trace.Listeners.Add(New TextWriterTraceListener(fs))
```

After starting the thread, the code waits for the carriage return key from the user and then closes the listener application and flushes all the tracing messages to the log file:

```
' Write the line only when the switch is on
Trace.WriteLine (DateTime.Now & " - Entered Main()")

' Create a thread
Dim newThread As Thread
t = New Thread(AddressOf WritingThread)

' Start the thread
t.Start()

' Wait for the user carriage return
Console.Read()

' Close the file listener flushing the trace messages
Trace.Close()
End Sub
```

The output of the code will be something similar to this:

```
30/04/2002 16:38:15 - Entered Main()
30/04/2002 16:38:15 - Entered into WritingThread()
30/04/2002 16:38:16 - Slept for one second...
```

The Trace class provides a useful property called IndentLevel for indenting tracing messages. For instance, we could use different indent levels for tracing messages written by the main and secondary threads. Adding the following lines to the code above, we can accomplish this task easily:

```
Private Sub WritingThread()
    ' Setting indent level
    Trace.IndentLevel = 2

    ' Trace an info message
    Trace.WriteLine(DateTime.Now & " - Entered in WritingThread()")

    ' Sleeping for one sec....
    Thread.CurrentThread.Sleep(1000)

    ' Trace an info message
    Trace.WriteLine(DateTime.Now & " - Slept for 1 second...")
End Sub
```

The output of the modified code is:

```
30/04/2002 16:40:07 - Entered Main()
     30/04/2002 16:40:07 - Entered into WritingThread()
     30/04/2002 16:40:08 - Slept for one second...
```

> You can increment or decrement the level of the indentation using the `Indent()` and `Unindent()` methods, respectively.

Tracing Switches

When we are near to the application deployment phase, we will probably want to remove all the tracing and debugging messages from the code. However, we do not have to look for every trace instruction and remove it. We can use compilation flags during the application building. From the Visual Studio .NET IDE, we can right-click on the project name within the Solution Explorer window, selecting the Properties item from the context menu. The following dialog box will appear:

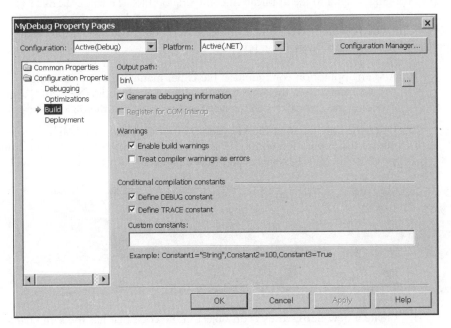

We simply need to uncheck the Define DEBUG constant and Define TRACE constant checkboxes, recompile the solution, and all the Trace and Debug statements will be stripped from the application.

> In order to remove tracing functionalities, you can even use the `vbc.exe` command-line compiler. Simply use the `/d:TRACE=FALSE /d:DEBUG=FALSE` switches when compiling.

Adding switches to the traced code allows us to activate/deactivate tracing messages at runtime. By simply declaring a value in the configuration file of our application, we can activate the trace functionality without rebuilding the entire solution. Naturally, we have to build the application to maintain tracing information, and this implicates a greater final application size and slower performance, even when the switches are turned off.

The `BooleanSwitch` and `TraceSwitch` classes are provided by the .NET Framework to implement these switches. Let's first examine the `BooleanSwitch` class.

The BooleanSwitch Class

Using this class in the traced code, we can decide to activate/deactivate messages by simply changing a value in the application configuration file. The `WriteLineIf()` and `WriteIf()` methods will be useful to write messages depending on the `Enabled` property provided by the `BooleanSwitch` class. In order to add switches to your application you have to follow these few steps:

1. Add an application configuration file either manually, or by selecting Add New Item... from the Project menu within Visual Studio .NET, and choosing the Application Configuration File template from the dialog box.

2. Open the configuration file in order to insert the necessary XML tags to inform the application about the switch name and value. Specifying a value equal to 0 will deactivate tracing functionality, and a value of 1 activate it:

```xml
<?xml version="1.0" encoding="utf-8" ?>
<configuration>
  <system.diagnostics>
    <switches>
      <add name="MySwitch" value="1" />
    </switches>
  </system.diagnostics>
</configuration>
```

3. Create a new `BooleanSwitch` object in the code that has the same name as that specified in the configuration file. We could also use the `Enabled` property in conjunction with the `Trace` static methods. Let's continue our Debugging example, by declaring a global `BooleanSwitch` object in order to use it everywhere in the code:

```vb
Dim bs As BooleanSwitch

Sub Main()
    ' Create a Boolean switch called MySwitch
    bs = New BooleanSwitch("MySwitch", _
        "Enable/Disable tracing functionalities")
```

```
' Create a file listener
Dim fs As New FileStream("C:\Debugging.log", FileMode.OpenOrCreate)
Trace.Listeners.Add(New TextWriterTraceListener(fs))
```

```
' Write the line only when the switch is on
Trace.WriteLineIf(bs.Enabled, DateTime.Now & _
    " - Entered in Main()")
```

```
...
End Sub
```

In the Main() method we create the object, specifying the same name used in the configuration file plus a brief description. The WriteLineIf() method will write the message only if the Enabled property has been set to 1 in the configuration file.

The TraceSwitch class

This class is an enhanced version of the BooleanSwitch class because it allows us to choose whether to deactivate tracing functionality or display messages using an importance-based hierarchy. The following table lists the levels:

Trace level	Description
0	None: Tracing is deactivated.
1	TraceError: Only the error messages will be written to the listener application.
2	TraceWarning: Error and warning messages will be written to the listener application.
3	TraceInformation: Error, warning, and information messages will be written to the listener application.
4	TraceVerbose: All kinds of messages will be written to the listener application.

So, when an error occurs, we can change the application configuration file specifying to write just the error messages that we have added to the code to focus our attention just on these messages. The configuration file is the same we have seen for the BooleanSwitch example. What changes is the code, as we have to instantiate an object from the TraceSwitch class. Moreover, we will use the enumeration values within the class to specify the level of the tracing messages. Let's see an example, TraceSwitchExample.vb:

```
Public Class TraceSwitchExample
    Private Shared TSwitch As TraceSwitch
```

```
Public Shared Sub Main()
  ' Create a Boolean switch called MySwitch
  TSwitch = New TraceSwitch("MySwitch", _
    "Four different trace levels")

  ' Create a file listener
  Dim fs As New FileStream("C:\Debugging.log", _
    FileMode.OpenOrCreate)
  Trace.Listeners.Add(New TextWriterTraceListener(fs))

  ' Write the line only when the switch is set
  Trace.WriteLineIf(TSwitch.TraceInfo, DateTime.Now & _
    " - Entered in Main()")

  ' Create a thread
  Dim threadInstance As Thread
  threadInstance = New Thread(AddressOf DBThread)

  ' Start the thread
  threadInstance.Start()
  ' Wait for the user carriage return
  Console.Read()

  ' Close the file listener flushing the trace messages
  Trace.Close()
End Sub
```

We start by declaring a global `TraceSwitch` object and then create a new object, giving it the name specified in the configuration file. We add a text file log listener to the application. We then start a new thread that contacts the pubs database within SQL Server in order to retrieve all the records from the authors table.

If the thread has been omitted, the `Open()` method raises an exception that generates a trace error message:

```
Public Shared Sub DBThread()
  ' Trace an info message
  Trace.WriteLineIf(TSwitch.TraceInfo, DateTime.Now & _
    " - Entered in DBThread()")

  ' Create a connection object
  Dim dbConn As New _
    SqlConnection("server=.;database=pubs;uid=sa;pwd=")

  ' Create a command object to execute a SQL statement
  Dim dbQuery As New SqlCommand("SELECT * FROM authors", dbConn)
  Dim dr As SqlDataReader

  Try
    Trace.WriteLineIf(TSwitch.TraceInfo, DateTime.Now & _
```

```
            " - Executing SQL statement")

        ' Execute the SQL statement
        dr = dbQuery.ExecuteReader(CommandBehavior.CloseConnection)

        While (dr.Read())
            ' Reading records
        End While
    Catch ex As Exception
        Trace.WriteLineIf(TSwitch.TraceError, DateTime.Now & _
            " - Error: " & ex.Message)
    Finally
        If (Not dr Is Nothing) AndAlso (dr.IsClosed = False)Then
            dr.Close()
        End If
    End Try
  End Sub
End Class
```

Here is the output from the code when the value 1 is specified in the configuration file, which specifies TraceError:

19/04/2002 17:52:23 - Error: ExecuteReader requires an open and available Connection. The connection's current state is Closed.
Slept for 1 second...

Here is the output when the value 3 is specified in the configuration file, which specifies TraceInformation:

19/04/2002 17:54:23 - Entered Main()
19/04/2002 17:54:23 - Entered DBThread()
19/04/2002 17:54:24 - Executing SQL statement
19/04/2002 17:54:24 - Error: ExecuteReader requires an open and available Connection. The connection's current state is Closed.

The Debug class

The Debug class provides the same functionality as the Trace class. You will find that it exposes the same methods and properties, with same tracing results.

> **When you change the listener application using the Listeners collection provided by the Trace class, you will change the listener application for Debug messages, as well.**

The big difference between these two classes is in the context in which we should use them. The Debug class is useful when we need to add information during debugging sessions. Before deploying our application, we will build the release version that will remove debug information from our code, automatically. Therefore, we would add Trace class functionalities when we need to check our application during the runtime phase.

The DataImport Example

At this point we are ready to concentrate our attention on a practical example that could be useful to demonstrate what we have seen thus far. The DataImport example, included here, is a typical application that waits for files to arrive in a specific directory before importing them into a SQL Server database. The code for this application, as with the rest of the code in this book, can be found at the Wrox web site. Below we outline the classes that will be used in this example:

❑ FileSystemWatcher: This allows developers to specify the directory to monitor, and to raise an event when something changes (for example a new file is created, or removed). This class is contained in the System.IO namespace of the .NET Framework class library.

❑ TextWriterTraceListener: This implements our own tracing functionality.

❑ Thread: That you've seen many times before, which allows us to start a new thread to import data into the database.

❑ Many classes from the SqlClient namespace necessary to manage the SQL Server database connection and update.

The first release of the DataImport application contains some logical errors that we will discover using tracing functionality. In that way we can have a good example about log (trace) files and their importance.

> **To learn more about the ADO.NET classes, please refer to one of the Wrox Press releases such as *Professional ADO.NET Programming* (ISBN 1-861005-27-X), or *ADO.NET Programmer's Reference (ISBN 1-861005-58-X)*.**

The Code

Let's start analyzing the code of the DataImport example:

```
Imports System.IO
Imports System.Threading
Imports System.Data.SqlClient
Imports Microsoft.VisualBasic


Class DataImport
```

First of all, we added all the necessary namespaces to use the FileSystemWatcher, Thread, and SQL Server classes:

```
' Global Boolean switch used to activate/deactivate tracing
' functionality
Private Shared BS As BooleanSwitch

Public Shared Sub Main()
  ' Remove the default listener
  Trace.Listeners.RemoveAt(0)

  ' Create and add the new listener
  BS = New BooleanSwitch("DISwitch", "DataImport switch")
  BS.Enabled = True
  Trace.Listeners.Add(New TextWriterTraceListener(New _
    FileStream("C:\DataImport.log", FileMode.OpenOrCreate)))
```

Then the code removes the default listener and creates a new TextWriterTraceListener object that points to C:\DataImport.log:

```
' Create a FileSystemWatcher object used to monitor the
' specified directory
Dim fsw As New FileSystemWatcher()

' Set the path to watch and specify the file
' extension to monitor for
fsw.Path = "C:\temp"
fsw.Filter = "*.xml"

' No need to go into subdirs
fsw.IncludeSubdirectories = False

' Add the handler to manage the raised event
' when a new file is created
AddHandler fsw.Created, _
  New FileSystemEventHandler(AddressOf OnFileCreated)

' Enable the object to raise the event
fsw.EnableRaisingEvents = True
```

Here the code creates a `FileSystemWatcher` object used to monitor the `C:\temp` directory specified in the `Path` property. The `Filter` property is useful to filter through each file within the directory looking for just the ones with the specified file extension. The `IncludeSubdirectories` property determines whether to extend the file monitoring to subdirectories. The `AddHandler` statement is used to specify the event that we want to manage in our code by providing the address of the function used as the event handler. In this case, we want to receive file creation events so we have to specify the `Created` event provided by the `FileSystemWatcher` class. Finally, the code enables the `FileSystemWatcher` object to raise events.

```
Try
    ' Call the WaitForChanged() method within an infinite loop.
    ' When the event is raised, OnFileCreated() will be called.
    Dim result As WaitForChangedResult
    Do
        result = fsw.WaitForChanged(WatcherChangeTypes.Created)
        Trace.WriteLineIf(bs.Enabled, DateTime.Now & _
            " - Found: " & result.Name & " file")
    Loop
```

The above code implements an infinite loop, which waits for the file creation event to be raised. The `WaitForChangedResult` object will contain information about the file created. For example, the code uses the `Name` property to trace the name of the discovered file.

```
    Catch e As Exception
        Trace.WriteLineIf(bs.Enabled, DateTime.Now & _
            " - An exception occurred while waiting for file: ")
        Trace.Indent()
        Trace.WriteLineIf(bs.Enabled, DateTime.Now & " - " & _
            e.ToString())
        Trace.Unindent()
    Finally
        fsw.EnableRaisingEvents = False
        Trace.WriteLineIf(bs.Enabled, DateTime.Now & _
            " - Directory monitoring stopped")
        Trace.Close()
    End Try
End Sub
```

The above `Main()` subroutine ends by tracing some useful messages and any exceptions. The `OnFileCreated()` shared method is detailed below:

```
Private Shared Sub OnFileCreated(ByVal source As Object, _
                                 ByVal eventArgs As _
                                      FileSystemEventArgs)
    Try
        ' Create a new object from the ImportData class to
        ' process the incoming file
```

```
        Dim id As New DataImport()
        id.FileName = eventArgs.FullPath

      ' Create and start the thread
      Dim threadInstance As New Thread(AddressOf id.Import)
      threadInstance.Name = "DataImportThread"
      threadInstance.Start()
```

Inside the OnFileCreated event handler a new thread will be started. This thread will use the Import method of the custom ImportData class to import the XML file into the database. Since at this point we know the full path of the discovered file (the FileSystemEventArgs parameter contains this information) and since we need it even in the ImportData class, we can use the m_strFileName variable provided by the class.

```
      Catch ex As Exception
        Trace.WriteLineIf(bs.Enabled, DateTime.Now & _
          " - An exception occurred while queuing file: ")
        Trace.Indent()
        Trace.WriteLineIf(bs.Enabled, DateTime.Now & " - " & _
          ex.ToString())
        Trace.Unindent()
      Finally
        Trace.Flush()
      End Try
    End Sub

    ' Path and filename of the retrieved file
    Public FileName As String = ControlChars.NullChar

    Public Sub Import()
      ' Declare Sql objects to contact the database
      Dim dbConn As New _
        SqlConnection("server=.;database=pubs;uid=sa;pwd=")
      Dim da As New SqlDataAdapter("SELECT * FROM authors", dbConn)
      Dim ds As New DataSet()
      Dim sa As New SqlCommandBuilder(da)
```

Inside the Import() method, the code starts by creating and setting all the necessary classes to contact the authors table within the SQL Server pubs database. The SqlConnection object allows us to specify database connection parameters. The SqlDataAdapter object connects to the database using the connection object executing the SQL statement specified as the first parameter. Finally, the SqlCommandBuilder examines the SQL statement specified in the SqlDataAdapter constructor, creating INSERT, MODIFY, and DELETE statements, automatically. They are needed when we use the Update() method exposed by the SqlDataAdapter class to physically change the database with new information.

```
Try
    Trace.WriteLineIf(BS.Enabled, DateTime.Now & _
        " - Filling the DataSet.")
    ' Fill a dataset with data within the authors table
    da.Fill(ds)
```

Here the `Fill()` method from the `SqlDataAdapter` class is used to fill the `DataSet` object specified in its parameter, with the results of the SQL query specified earlier. The `DataSet` is an in-memory representation of the database data and so it will be formatted as the `authors` table and filled with every record contained in the table:

```
' Read the XML file filling another dataset
Dim dsMerge As New DataSet()

Trace.WriteLineIf(BS.Enabled, DateTime.Now & _
    " - Reading XML file.")
dsMerge.ReadXml(FileName, XmlReadMode.InferSchema)
Trace.WriteLineIf(BS.Enabled, DateTime.Now & _
    " - DataSet filled with data.")
```

Here the code uses the discovered file to fill another `DataSet` object. This time the `ReadXml()` method has been used. The power of the `DataSet` object is just right in front of you. You can manage data provided by both database and XML document in the same exact way. The `DataSet` object maintains an XML data representation of the records within itself.

```
' Update the database, tracing the total time needed to
' conclude the operation
Dim time As Date = DateTime.Now
Trace.WriteLineIf(BS.Enabled, time & " - Updating database.")
da.Update(dsMerge)
Dim time2 As Date = DateTime.Now
Trace.WriteLineIf(BS.Enabled, time2 & _
    " - Database updated successfully.")
Trace.Indent()
Trace.WriteLineIf(BS.Enabled, DateTime.Now _
    & " - Total TIME: " & DateDiff(DateInterval.Second, _
    & time, time2) & " second/s")
Trace.Unindent()
```

Finally, the code uses the `Update()` method provided by the `SqlDataAdapter` class to write new records to the `authors` table. Note the tracing information used in this snippet of code; this provides detailed information by adding performance messages. The `DateTime` class has been used to retrieve the total time in seconds needed to update the database:

```
Catch sqlEx As SqlException
    Trace.WriteLineIf(BS.Enabled, DateTime.Now & _
```

```
          " - A SQL exception occurred during file processing: ")
        Trace.Indent()
        Trace.WriteLineIf(BS.Enabled, DateTime.Now & _
          " - " & sqlEx.ToString())
        Trace.Unindent()
      Catch ex As Exception
        Trace.WriteLineIf(BS.Enabled, DateTime.Now & _
          " - A general exception occurred during file processing: ")
        Trace.Indent()
        Trace.WriteLineIf(BS.Enabled, DateTime.Now & _
          " - " & ex.ToString())
        Trace.Unindent()
      Finally
        Trace.Flush()
      End Try
    End Sub
  End Class
```

Then, after writing the code for catching and dealing with any exceptions that may occur, the code is complete.

Testing the Application

To test the application you have to follow these steps:

- ❑ Create a C:\temp directory to contain the XML file

- ❑ Run the DataImport application

- ❑ Copy the authors.xml file into the C:\temp directory

As a final result you should find the DataImport.log file in the C:\ directory having content similar to this:

```
01/05/2002 12:23:01 - Found: authors.xml file
01/05/2002 12:23:01 - Filling the DataSet.
01/05/2002 12:23:02 - Reading XML file.
01/05/2002 12:23:02 - DataSet filled with data.
01/05/2002 12:23:02 - Updating database.
01/05/2002 12:23:02 - Database updated successfully.
01/05/2002 12:23:03 - Total TIME: 0 second/s
```

The authors.xml file is not that large so the total time is less than one second.

Logical Errors

All seems to be working well, but obviously, everything hasn't been accounted for. So far, we have tested our application with a very small file size, so when the application receives the file creation event and opens the file, the process that copies it into the directory finishes its task of closing the file. What happens when we receive a huge file? Well, when the thread tries to access the XML file and fill the `DataSet` object, it receives an access denied error caused by attempting to open a file already in use by the copier task. Try to test the application again by copying the `huge_authors.xml` file instead. Since we have used tracing messages, you may find the following error in the log file:

```
4/14/2002 1:29:00 PM - Found: huge_authors.xml file
4/14/2002 1:29:00 PM - Filling the DataSet.
4/14/2002 1:29:00 PM - Reading XML file.
4/14/2002 1:29:00 PM - A general exception occurred during file processing:
    4/14/2002 1:29:00 PM - System.IO.IOException: The process cannot access the file
"C:\temp\huge_authors.xml" because it is being used by another process.
    at System.IO.__Error.WinIOError(Int32 errorCode, String str)
    at System.IO.FileStream..ctor(String path, FileMode mode, FileAccess access, FileShare share,
Int32 bufferSize, Boolean useAsync, String msgPath, Boolean bFromProxy)
    at System.IO.FileStream..ctor(String path, FileMode mode, FileAccess access, FileShare share)
    at System.Xml.XmlDownloadManager.GetStream(Uri uri, ICredentials credentials)
    at System.Xml.XmlUrlResolver.GetEntity(Uri absoluteUri, String role, Type ofObjectToReturn)
    at System.Xml.XmlTextReader.CreateScanner()
    at System.Xml.XmlTextReader.Init()
    at System.Xml.XmlTextReader.Read()
    at System.Xml.XmlReader.MoveToContent()
    at System.Data.DataSet.ReadXml(XmlReader reader, XmlReadMode mode)
    at System.Data.DataSet.ReadXml(String fileName, XmlReadMode mode)
```

This is a kind of error that the debugger often fails to catch because the time used to launch it and the time to step through the code is often sufficient to copy the file. It may also not occur on your machine. It depends on the speed of your disk access and the amount of memory you have (so how much the application is slowed down).

The error message suggests a possible solution that we should add to the application to resolve the error. Before calling the `ReadXml()` method, we should try to open the file with exclusive access. If an error occurs, then we can suspend the thread for few seconds, trying again when the file can be processed. Let's see how the code changes in `DataImport2`, by adding the `GetFileAccess()` method:

```
    Private Function GetFileAccess() As Boolean
        Trace.WriteLineIf(BS.Enabled, DateTime.Now & _
            " - Trying to get exclusive access to the " & _
            FileName & " file.")
        Dim checkFile As File
```

```
Try
    Dim fs As FileStream = checkFile.Open(m_strFileName, _
        FileMode.Append, FileAccess.Write, FileShare.None)
    fs.Close()
    Trace.WriteLineIf(BS.Enabled, DateTime.Now & _
        " - Access to the " & FileName & " file allowed.")
    GetFileAccess = True
Catch
    Trace.WriteLineIf(bs.Enabled, DateTime.Now & _
        " - Access denied to the " & m_strFileName & " file.")
    GetFileAccess = False
End Try
End Function
```

The GetFileAccess() function has been added in order to return a Boolean value indicating whether you can have exclusive access to the file or not. The function simply tries to open the file with the share access property set to None:

```
Public Sub Import()
    ' Declare Sql objects to contact the database
    Dim dbConn As New _
        SqlConnection("server=.;database=pubs;uid=sa;pwd=")
    Dim da As New SqlDataAdapter("SELECT * FROM authors", dbConn)
    Dim ds As New DataSet()
    Dim sa As New SqlCommandBuilder(da)
```

```
Try
    Do While (GetFileAccess() = False)
        Thread.Sleep(3000)
        Trace.WriteLineIf(BS.Enabled, DateTime.Now & _
            " - Slept 5 seconds... Try to access to the " & _
            FileName & " file, again.")
    Loop
```

```
    Trace.WriteLineIf(bs.Enabled, DateTime.Now & _
        " - Filling the DataSet.")
    ' Fill a dataset with data within the authors table
    da.Fill(ds)
```

The Import() method provided by the ImportData class will try to get exclusive access to the file. If the file is still opened by the copier task, the thread will be suspended for five seconds. So, the GetFileAccess() function will be called until the source file can be opened:

We have seen practically how the tracing functionalities can be useful to understand the application behavior during run-time execution.

Summary

In this chapter we have seen how the Visual Studio .NET debugger can be used to observe an application's behavior during its execution. Also, we have seen which powerful tools the debugger provides, to allow us to examine and change a variable's value, and more.

In the second part of the chapter, we covered the tracing functionality provided by the .NET with three classes: Trace, Debug, and Switch. We started listing the most useful tracing functionalities focusing on the ability to activate tracing technique by modifying values within the application configuration file.

Finally, we have seen a practical example where the tracing technique helps developers to find and correct bugs and logical errors.

VB.NET

Threading

Handbook

7

7

Networking and Threading

In the previous chapters of this book, we've taken an in-depth look at threading in VB.NET and discussed the various concepts and techniques associated with programming multithreaded applications. Now that you are a threading expert, we're going to build a simple multithreaded client-server application in VB.NET and put to use some of the concepts that we have discussed thus far.

There are certain application needs for which the effective use of threads and asynchronous programming is indispensable, such as network communication, effective user interfaces, and disk input/output, to just name a few. In all these cases, a single-threaded application can freeze or appear to have crashed while it's waiting for an operation to complete. This is also true in the case of a network application where latency is often the most important criterion, especially with users that have low speed connections. In the sample application showcased in this chapter, we are going to utilize the System.Net namespace and briefly explore the networking capabilities of .NET, especially since the multi-user and asynchronous nature of network applications make them ideal candidates for threading.

In particular, we will discuss the following:

❑   Developing network applications in .NET using the System.Net namespace

❑   Developing a simple multithreaded client-server application based on TCP/IP

❑   Using intrinsic .NET functionality to implement asynchronous operations

❑   Using asynchronous message transfers between a client and a remote server

Networking in .NET

Prior to the advent of the .NET Framework, the ability to develop sophisticated Windows-based networking applications was limited to advanced C++ programmers using the convoluted WinSock library for the most part. There was, of course, the `WinInet` control that Visual Basic developers could utilize in order to accomplish relatively simple tasks. However, one did not have to attempt too much before facing functional impediments with the simple and limited services offered in that control.

Fortunately, the `System.Net` namespace within the .NET Framework brings a slew of effective functionality packaged in a simple and consistent object model. The ease of use of these classes does not compromise functionality, as almost all the core functions of WinSock 2.0 have been wrapped and abstracted in the `System.Net` namespace. Developers can easily develop at any level from sockets all the way up to HTTP. Also, unlike the raw use of the WinSock library, the `System.Net` namespace relieves developers from having the dubious pleasure of manually coding many imperative resource management tasks, such as dealing with overlapped IO and completion ports.

So, without further delay, let's briefly explore the `System.Net` namespace.

System.Net Namespace

The `System.Net` namespace actually comprises two namespaces, `System.Net` and `System.Net.Socket`.

We will primarily be using the `System.Net.Sockets` namespace in our application. The layered approach of the `System.Net` classes provides applications with the ability to access networks with various levels of control based on the demands of the application. In addition to the extensive support for sockets, `System.Net` classes also offer an impressive array of functionality to use with the HTTP protocol. For the most part, the `System.Net` offerings are categorized in three layers, Application protocols, Transport protocols, and Web protocols. The `System.Net.Sockets` namespace consists primarily of classes and utilities for dealing with the transport protocol. Let's look at some of the more important classes within the `System.Net` namespace, as listed in the table below.

Class	Description
`Authorization`	Provides authentication messaging for a web server.
`Cookie`	Provides a set of properties and methods used to manage cookies. This class cannot be inherited.

Class	Description
Dns	Simple domain name resolution functionality.
EndPoint	Identifies a network address. This is a MustInherit class.
GlobalProxySelection	Global default proxy instance for all HTTP requests.
HttpVersion	Defines the HTTP version numbers supported by the HttpWebRequest and HttpWebResponse classes.
HttpWebRequest	HTTP-specific implementation of the WebRequest class.
HttpWebResponse	HTTP-specific implementation of the WebResponse class.
IPAddress	Internet Protocol (IP) address.
IPEndPoint	A network endpoint consisting of an IP address and a port number.
IPHostEntry	Container class for Internet host address information.
NetworkCredential	Provides credentials for password-based authentication schemes such as basic, digest, NTLM, and Kerberos authentication.
SocketAddress	Stores serialized information from EndPoint-derived classes.
SocketPermission	Controls rights to make or accept socket connections.
WebClient	Provides common methods for sending data to and receiving data from a resource identified by a URI.
WebException	The exception that is thrown when an error occurs while accessing resources via the HTTP protocol.
WebPermission	Controls rights to access HTTP Internet resources.
WebPermissionAttribute	Specifies permission to access Internet resources.
WebProxy	Contains HTTP proxy settings for the WebRequest class.
WebRequest	Makes a request to a Uniform Resource Identifier (URI). This class must always be inherited (a MustInherit class).
WebResponse	Provides a response from a Uniform Resource Identifier (URI). This class must always be inherited (a MustInherit class).

As you can see, the System.Net namespace contains a cornucopia of classes and utilities that are quite useful for a wide range of web and network programming needs.

System.Net.Sockets Namespace

The System.Net.Sockets namespace primarily focuses on the transport layer: the socket layer for which it contains a comprehensive set of classes. These classes do an excellent job of abstracting much of the complexity associated with socket programming, while offering a powerful and productive socket stack that also adheres to the Berkeley socket. Lastly, built-in support for TCP and UDP is well integrated in the classes of the System.Net.Sockets. The table below lists the classes of the System.Net.Sockets namespace.

Class	Description
LingerOption	Contains information about the amount of time it will remain available after closing with the presence of pending data (the socket's linger time).
MulticastOption	Contains IP address values for IP multicast packets.
NetworkStream	Provides the underlying stream of data for network access.
Socket	Implements the Berkeley sockets interface.
SocketException	The exception that is thrown when a socket error occurs.
TcpClient	Provides client connections for TCP network services.
TcpListener	Listens for connections from TCP network clients. This is essentially the TCP server class.
UdpClient	Provides User Datagram Protocol (UDP) network services.

A varying level of control is offered to the developer, such as lower-level classes like the Socket class, and higher-level classes, such as the TcpClient class, which offers slightly less control with added productivity. An in-depth discussion of these classes would go beyond the scope of this book, but we will take a closer look at some of the above classes as we design and develop our sample application a little later in this chapter.

Creating the Sample Application

Now that you've had a brief introduction to networking in .NET, let's actually start discussing the application that we are going to build in this chapter. The purpose of this example is to create a simple application to familiarize you with the use of threading in building networking applications in .NET. The application will actually consist of two small Windows Form applications, with one acting as the server and the other as the client. We will be using Visual Studio .NET to design and implement these applications.

Design Goals

We want to create two autonomous and simple applications that interact with one another. The first application is a multithreaded/multi-user stock quote server program that looks up stock quotes from a database table and sends the data back to the requesting client asynchronously. The second application is the client and simply queries the server with a stock symbol for which it wishes to get the quote information. All this will happen asynchronously, such that the client's user interface is not paused while the server is responding to the request. The list below outlines and summarizes the basic requirements we are going to abide by when building the applications:

- ❏ There will be two autonomous applications (one serving as the client and the other as the server) that can communicate with each other over the Internet

- ❏ The user interface of the client should not pause or freeze because of slow network connections, or any other delays, when querying the server for stock quotes

- ❏ The server should be capable of handling numerous simultaneous client connections and queries and have the ability to communicate with the client in an asynchronous manner

- ❏ Network settings must be abstracted away from the application and be modifiable

To help us understand the typical user interaction within the application, let's look at a simple UML sequence diagram below.

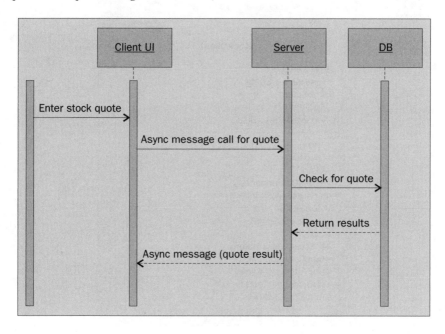

So far, we've discussed the basic design guidelines for the applications from a very high-level standpoint. If you are like most developers, you probably can't wait to see some code. So without further delay, let's actually start building the two applications and examining code segments and concepts as we go along (as always, the code is available at http://www.wrox.com).

Building the Application

As mentioned before, the sample application in this chapter really consists of two autonomous applications: a client and a server. The two applications will communicate with each other via a specific TCP/IP port, which can be changed by altering the configuration file of the application (as we'll see later, both the client and the server need the same configuration file). Enough said, let's start by building our client application, which performs the simple task of querying the server for the result of a stock quote.

Creating the Client

Before we start building the application, let's take a moment or two to see the UML view of the client form class, which is going to contain all the code for the client application:

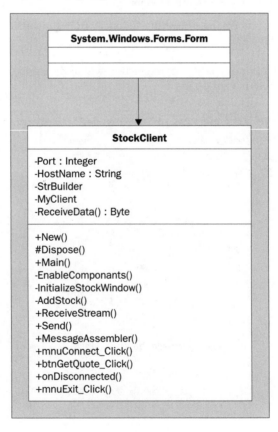

The `StockClient` application simply inherits from the `System.Windows.Forms.Form` namespace and contains all the code for the client application, such as the `Private` member variables and the methods. To create the `StockClient` application, we start by creating a new Windows Application project in Visual Studio .NET and naming it `StockClient`. On the default form, we create three controls on the page; a textbox called `txtStock`, a button called `btnGetQuote` with its `Text` property set to `Get Quote`, and a new `ListView` control from the Visual Studio .NET toolbox called `lstQuotes`. Change the `Name` and `Text` properties of the form to `StockClient`. Also, add a `MainMenu` control to your form, and create a menu item `&File` with two sub-items `&Connect` (called `mnuConnect`) and `E&xit` (called `mnuExit`). Lastly, ensure that all the controls on the form, except the menu, have their `Enabled` property set to `False`; these will remain invisible until the user connects to the server.

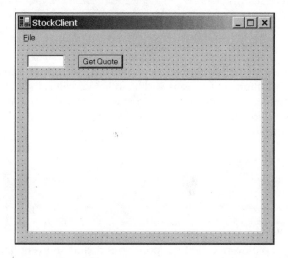

We'll start with the set of `Imports` statements to reference the namespaces we need:

```
Imports System.Threading
Imports System.Net
Imports System.Net.Sockets
Imports System.Text
Imports System.IO
Imports System.Configuration
```

We are going to need some `Private` member variables that will be used throughout the `StockClient` application:

```
Private Port As Integer
Private HostName As String
Private Const PacketSize As Integer = 1024
Private ReceiveData(packetSize) As Byte
Private MyClient As TcpClient
Private StrBuilder As New StringBuilder()
```

We will examine the variables and their use later on, but for now let's amend our `ListView` control so that it can keep track of all the stock quotes that we enter. We need it to contain six columns: one column for each of the returned fields for the stock quote. The desired fields are `Symbol`, `Price`, `Change`, `Bid`, `Ask`, and `Volume`. Let's create a method called `InitializeStockWindow()` to add these columns to the `ListView` control as shown below:

```
Private Sub InitializeStockWindow()
    lstQuotes.View = System.Windows.Forms.View.Details
    lstQuotes.Columns.Add("Symbol", 60, HorizontalAlignment.Left)
    lstQuotes.Columns.Add("Price", 50, HorizontalAlignment.Left)
    lstQuotes.Columns.Add("Change", 60, HorizontalAlignment.Left)
    lstQuotes.Columns.Add("Bid", 50, HorizontalAlignment.Left)
    lstQuotes.Columns.Add("Ask", 50, HorizontalAlignment.Left)
    lstQuotes.Columns.Add("Volume", 170, HorizontalAlignment.Left)
End Sub
```

The code segment above simply enables the grid lines of the `ListView` control, as well as assigning six columns of various widths to it. We will call this function upon connecting to the server when the application is ready to start retrieving stock quotes from the server. We also need a method to enable and disable the controls as required, for instance upon the successful connection, as listed below:

```
Private Sub EnableComponents(ByVal enable As Boolean)
    txtStock.Enabled = enable
    btnGetQuote.Enabled = enable
    lstQuotes.Enabled = enable
End Sub
```

Now we create a simple event called `Disconnected`, and an event handler for it called `OnDisconnected()` which would be called once the event is actually raised. The `OnDisconnected()` method simply disables the `Connect` option in the File menu as well as displaying an error message via a message box. It also disables the remaining input controls on the form:

```
Public Event Disconnected(ByVal sender As Object)

Private Sub OnDisconnected(ByVal sender As Object)
    mnuConnect.Enabled = True
    MessageBox.Show("The connection was lost!", "Disconnected", _
                    MessageBoxButtons.OK, MessageBoxIcon.Error)
    EnableComponents(False)
End Sub
```

To bind the `OnDisconnected()` method to the `Disconnected` event, we need to use an event handler as shown below:

```
AddHandler Disconnected, AddressOf OnDisconnected
```

As you may know, one of the greatest features of Visual Basic.NET is its ability to dynamically bind and unbind event handlers to events at runtime. You can use the `AddHandler` statement to assign a method to an event and, in much the same manner, use the `RemoveHandler` statement to detach an event handler method from an event. Indeed, the ability to dynamically assign functionality to an event is very useful when you need to start or stop the event handler for an event or need to overwrite the behavior of an event handler. In the case of the `Disconnected` event, we assign it to the `OnDisconnected` delegate. Technically, we have the opportunity to accomplish this anytime before the invocation of the event. However, it's usually best to declare all the event handlers early on in the application's execution, so we will declare it in our `mnuConnect_Click` event as soon as a connection to the server is established.

Speaking of the `mnuConnect_Click` event, double-click the **Connect** sub-item of the **File** menu to enter code for the actual connection to the server. This is where we start to get our feet wet in network programming. First we need to instantiate a `TcpClient` object, which is a member of the `System.Net.Sockets` namespace. In order to that, we are going to need a host address and a port with which the client contacts the server. We will abstract that information away from the core of the application by storing it in an external configuration file. .NET configuration files are well-formed XML files and are accompanied by a useful namespace in the .NET Framework, `System.Configuration`. With that in mind, let's look at the contents of the external configuration file that we can easily create in Notepad or Visual Studio.NET:

```
<configuration>
  <configSections>
    <section name="HostInfo"
             type="System.Configuration.SingleTagSectionHandler" />
  </configSections>
  <HostInfo hostname="localhost" port="6800" />
</configuration>
```

The XML above contains an entry with two attributes storing the host information. We used `localhost`, and the port could be just about any port (just as long as it's not a reserved port) and you can choose just about any port number between 1024 and 65000. Save the file as `StockClient.exe.config`, and place it in the `bin` subdirectory where the compiled version of the application is going to reside.

Now add the following code to the `mnuConnect_Click` event handler:

```
Private Sub mnuConnect_Click(ByVal sender As System.Object, _
                    ByVal e As System.EventArgs) _
                    Handles mnuConnect.Click
    Dim HostSettings As IDictionary

    Try
        HostSettings = ConfigurationSettings.GetConfig("HostInfo")
        HostName = CType(HostSettings("hostname"), String)
        Port = CType(HostSettings("port"), Integer)
```

219

```
      MyClient = New TcpClient(HostName, Port)
      MyClient.GetStream.BeginRead(ReceiveData, 0, PacketSize, _
                              AddressOf ReceiveStream, Nothing)
      EnableComponents(True)
      InitializeStockWindow()
      mnuConnect.Enabled = False
      AddHandler Disconnected, AddressOf onDisconnected

   Catch ex As Exception
     MessageBox.Show("Error: Unable to establish a connection!", _
          "Disconnected", MessageBoxButtons.OK, MessageBoxIcon.Error)
   End Try
End Sub
```

The first portion of the code above reads the host information from the configuration file. The HostName, Port, and MyClient fields have already been declared as Private at the start of the class. At this point we just declare a local dictionary object to read in all the attributes of the HostInfo node in the configuration file.

An instance of the TcpClient class is instantiated by passing the DNS host name and a port number into the constructor. As you probably know, the host name maps to a specific host (or, more accurately, interface) on the network; the port number identifies the specific service on that host to connect to. The combination of host name and a service port is typically called an endpoint, which is represented in the .NET Framework by the EndPoint class. The TcpClient class constructor may take in an instance of the IPEndPoint class, but is also overloaded to accept a host name and a service port number.

> **You can use the DNS class to resolve a host name into an IP address and then use a service port to construct an IPEndPoint class.**

If we've done everything right and there is a server running with the same host name and port, a new connection will be established. Upon the obtaining a connection, we must spawn a background thread to get data from the server asynchronously to enable the input controls for the user to receive stock symbols. Here's where things start to get a little interesting.

As mentioned previously, we need the receiving method of our application to be asynchronous. This is the only way the client can function without delays and serial user interaction. It is simply unacceptable to have the client application remain suspended while waiting for data to arrive from the server. Thanks to the .NET Framework, the solution is relatively simple and easy to implement. We first have to identify the `TcpClient`'s `NetworkStream` object. We can do that by calling the `GetStream()` method of the `TcpClient` object instance, which returns the underlying `NetworkStream` used to send and receive data. `GetStream()` creates an instance of the `NetworkStream` class using the underlying socket as its constructor parameter. In addition, the instance of the `NetworkStream` class inherits from the `Stream` class, which provides a number of methods and properties used to facilitate network communications. Once we have an underlying stream, we can use it to send and receive data over the network. Much like its cousin classes `FileStream` and `TextStream`, the `NetworkStream` class exposes read and write methods designed to send and receive data in a synchronous manner. `BeginRead()` and `BeginWrite()` are nothing more than the asynchronous versions of those methods. As a matter of fact, most of the methods in the .NET Framework classes beginning with `Begin`, such as `BeginRead()` and `BeginGetResponse()`, are intrinsically asynchronous without the programmer having to provide additional code when they are used with delegates. Therefore, there's no need to manually spawn new threads, and as the process reading the data is running on a background thread, the main thread of the application is free to remain attentive and responsive to UI interaction. Let's look at the signature of the `BeginRead()` method:

```
Overrides Public Function BeginRead(ByVal buffer() As Byte, _
          ByVal offset As Integer, ByVal size As Integer, _
          ByVal callback As AsyncCallback, ByVal state As Object) _
          As IAsyncResult
```

The table below explains each of the parameters of this method.

Parameter	Description
buffer	The data buffer in which the data will arrive
offset	The location in buffer to begin storing the data to
size	The size of buffer
callback	The delegate to call when the asynchronous call is complete
state	An object containing additional information supplied by the client

Before we proceed further, let's take a moment to have a word or two about asynchronous calls, since they are a very important concept. As mentioned earlier, the problem with synchronous operations is that the working thread can be blocked until a certain operation is complete and that's not always desirable. Asynchronous calls run in a background thread and allow the initial thread (the calling thread) to continue as normal. .NET allows asynchronous calls via the help of delegates to just about any class and/or method. However, certain classes, such as the `NetworkStream` class, contain methods like `BeginRead()` that have asynchronous capabilities built into them. Delegates are used to act as place holders for the functions against which asynchronous calls are made. In fact, delegates are nothing more than type-safe function pointers.

As you can see, the `BeginRead()` method requires byte arrays as opposed to strings or text streams and, as such, is going to require a little more processing. We have already defined a variable named `ReceiveData` and another integer constant for the size of the byte array named `PacketSize`. Now we need to pass in the name of the method that is going to actually receive the data – the method that is going to be invoked by the callback delegate when the data arrives. Bear in mind that this method is going to be running in a background thread, so we have to be careful if we wish to interact with the UI. Therefore, we simply spawn a background thread to receive the data as it arrives from the server over the network by just one line:

```
MyClient.GetStream.BeginRead(receiveData, 0, packetSize, _
                        AddressOf ReceiveStream, Nothing)
```

We create a method called `ReceiveStream()` that deals with the data in the byte packets as it arrives:

```
Private Sub ReceiveStream(ByVal ar As IAsyncResult)

    Dim ByteCount As Integer
    Try
        ByteCount = MyClient.GetStream.EndRead(ar)
        If ByteCount < 1 Then
            ' MessageBox.Show("Disconnected")
            RaiseEvent Disconnected(Me)
            Exit Sub
        End If

        MessageAssembler(ReceiveData, 0, ByteCount)

        MyClient.GetStream.BeginRead(ReceiveData, 0, PacketSize, _
                            AddressOf ReceiveStream, Nothing)

    Catch ex As Exception
        'Display error message
        Dim Params() As Object = {(("An error has occurred" + _
                            ex.ToString).ToString}
        Me.Invoke(New InvokeDisplay(AddressOf Me.DisplayData), Params)

    End Try
End Sub
```

First off, we have to check to see if there are any bytes in the byte array packet. There always has to be something in there. You can think of this as the pulse of the connection; as long as the client is connected to the server, there will be some data in that incoming packet, however small. We use the `EndRead()` method of the `Stream` object to check the current size of the byte array. We pass an instance of `IAsyncResult` into the `EndRead()` method. The `BeginRead()` method of the `GetStream()` method initiates an asynchronous call to the `ReceiveStream()` method, which is followed by a series of under-the-hood actions built in by the compiler in order to expedite the asynchronous operation. The `ReceiveStream()` method is then queued on a thread pool thread. If the delegate method, `ReceiveStream()` throws an exception, then the newly created `Async` thread is terminated, and another exception is generated in the caller thread. The diagram below further illustrates the situation:

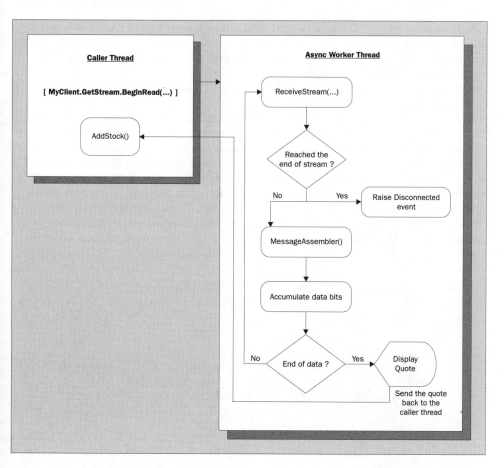

If the number returned from the EndRead() method is anything less than one, we know that the connection has been lost and we can raise the Disconnected event to take care of the appropriate work that needs to be done to handle that situation. However, if the number of bytes in the byte array is bigger than zero, we can start receiving the incoming data. At this point, we are going to need the assistance of a helper method to help us construct a string from the data that we retrieve from the server.

In fact, in .NET you can call almost any method asynchronously in much the same manner that we used the BeginRead() method. All you have to do is declare a delegate and call that delegate using the BeginInvoke() and the EndInvoke() methods. The intricacies of the asynchronous infrastructure are abstracted away from you and you don't have to worry about background threads and synchronization (not entirely, however).

OK, now let's move on to the next portion of the code in which you see a call to the MessageAssembler() method. Due to the asynchronous nature of the BeginRead() method, we really have no way of knowing for sure when and in what quantity the data will arrive from the server. It could arrive all at once, or it could arrive in a hundred smaller pieces, each being only one or two characters long. So, we have to perpetually read the data until we receive some sort of a signal indicating the end of the data for now. In this case, we will append a single character (#) to the end of our message which will act as a trigger agent for the MessageAssembler() method indicating the end of the incoming string, at which point the MessageAssembler class can stop waiting for more data and work with the data. In the meantime, we are going to need assistance from a very useful class available in the System.Text namespace to help us put together a whole string from the pieces of incoming byte arrays. That class is the StringBuilder class. This class provides a set of useful methods that make it ideal for string accumulation. In addition, tests have proven its performance to be significantly better than manual string concatenations when done in large iterations. Let's take a closer look at the MessageAssembler() method:

```
Private Sub MessageAssembler(ByVal Bytes() As Byte, _
                             ByVal offset As Integer, _
                             ByVal count As Integer)
    Dim ByteCount As Integer

    For ByteCount = 0 To count - 1
        If Bytes(ByteCount) = 35 Then 'Check for '#' to signal the end
            Dim Params() As Object = {StrBuilder.ToString}
            Me.Invoke(New InvokeDisplay(AddressOf Me.DisplayData), Params)
            StrBuilder = New StringBuilder()
        Else
            StrBuilder.Append(ChrW(Bytes(ByteCount)))
        End If
    Next
End Sub
```

As you can see, the MessageAssembler() method loops through the byte array of data and accumulates the data as pieces of a string using the instance of the StringBuilder class until it encounters the # character. Once it encounters that # character, signaling the end of the incoming string, it will stop and flush out the string by calling the ToString() method of the StringBuilder instance. We don't have to worry about manual conversion of bytes to strings at this point since the StringBuilder class takes care of that for us. It will then call the DisplayData() method to process the data:

```
Dim Params() As Object = {StrBuilder.ToString}
Me.Invoke(New InvokeDisplay(AddressOf Me.DisplayData), Params)
```

This is the second time we've encountered something similar to the code above, and you may be wondering what it is doing. Remember that this method is running in the background worker thread and is in the same thread that the UI form is. Although we can call the methods anywhere in the application, it is definitely not a good idea since that operation would not be thread-safe. Windows Forms are based on Win32 Single Threaded Apartments (STA) and thus are not thread safe, which means that a form can't safely switch back and forth between operating threads (including the background threads spawned by an asynchronous operation) once it has been instantiated. You must call the methods of a form on the same thread in which the form is residing. To alleviate this issue, the CLR supports the Invoke() method, which marshals calls between the threads.

If you doubt the above claim, you can always see for yourself by stepping through the code and looking at the Threads window and seeing the thread ID of the code that indicates the current thread in which the code is executing. By creating a delegate and calling it through the form's Invoke() method, it's executed in the form's thread and interaction with the Form's controls is safely executed. Without marshaling, you often find that the code runs just fine and the desired functionality is accomplished initially, but you can run into problems later on as this can cause instability in the application, with at times unpredictable behavior. This can get worse the more the application spawns threads. Therefore, don't talk to the GUI without marshaling the threads. In addition, the signature of the delegate must always match that of the Invoke() method, and therefore we have to create an object array and insert the string in it; this is the only way we can use the Invoke() method. We call on the DisplayData() method to display the data as we wish:

```
Private Sub DisplayData(ByVal stockInfo As String)
    If stockInfo = "-1" Then
        MessageBox.Show("Symbol not found!", "Invalid Symbol", _
                    MessageBoxButtons.OK, MessageBoxIcon.Error)
    Else
        AddStock(stockInfo)
    End If
End Sub
```

In the `DisplayData()` method, we simply check the string to see whether its value is -1. As we shall see later, the server has been configured to simply return a -1 string if the requested stock quote cannot be returned as we've submitted an invalid symbol. Of course, in our case, an invalid symbol is any symbol that does not happen to be in our tiny database table of stocks, `tbl_stocks` (which we'll see later). Otherwise, we can go ahead and pass the `stockInfo` variable to the `AddStock()` method, which will gracefully add it to the `lstQuotes` control on the form:

```
Private Sub AddStock(ByVal stockInfo As String)
  Dim StockParameter() As String = Split(stockInfo, ",")
  Dim Item As ListViewItem

  Item = New ListViewItem(StockParameter)

  If CDbl(StockParameter(2)) > 0 Then
    Item.ForeColor = Color.Green
  ElseIf CDbl(StockParameter(2)) < 0 Then
    Item.ForeColor = Color.Red
  End If

  lstQuotes.Items.Add(Item)
End Sub
```

We will be configuring the server to return the data values in a string with the individual values being separated by a comma:

```
Symbol, Price, Change, Bid, Ask, Volume
```

So, the very first thing we have to do is to separate the individual values from one another by using the `Split()` method. We then create a new instance of the `ListViewItem` class and pass in the newly created string array as its constructor parameter. Lastly, we want to be able to color-code the stock quotes in the `lstQuotes` control such that if the price of a stock is down, the entire quote is displayed in red, and if the stock price is up, it is displayed in green. To accomplish this, we just have to convert the second value of the string array, which contains the current stock price, into a `Double` and check its value. After setting the color, we can just add a new entry into the `lstQuotes` control.

We are nearly done with the client code; we just need to create a few smaller methods to finish off. First, we need to add code to the `click` event of `btnGetQuote`:

```
Private Sub btnGetQuote_Click(ByVal sender As System.Object, _
                              ByVal e As System.EventArgs) _
                              Handles btnGetQuote.Click
  Send(txtStock.Text.Trim + "#")
  txtStock.Text = ""
End Sub
```

This method simply gets the string value of the `txtStock` textbox, appends a `#` character to the end of it to indicate the end of this string, and passes it to the `Send()` method. Remember that we needed the `#` character in the `MessageAssembler()` method to tell us when the end of the string was reached.

Once the data is passed on to the `Send()` method, the `Send()` method creates a new instance of the `StreamWriter` class by passing the underlying `TcpClient` stream to it as its constructor and calling its `Write()` method, which sends the data across the socket in the form a stream. We also call the `Flush()` method to ensure that the data is sent immediately and is not sitting in buffer until some point in the future:

```
Private Sub Send(ByVal sendData As String)
    Dim writer As New StreamWriter(MyClient.GetStream)
    writer.Write(sendData)
    writer.Flush()
End Sub
```

We're almost done here, but we have to do some minor clean-up code. For the most part, the Windows Form class does most of the cleanup by calling on its own `Dispose()` method and that of its base, but since .NET has non-deterministic garbage collection, it would a good idea for us to manually close the `TcpClient` connection. We can write a small function to do that, which will be called from the `SocketClient_Closing()` method, which is invoked when the user closes the form:

```
Private Sub StockClient_Closing(ByVal sender As System.Object, _
                                ByVal e As System.EventArgs) _
                                Handles MyBase.Load
    closeConnection()
End Sub

Private Sub closeConnection()
    If Not MyClient Is Nothing Then
        MyClient.Close()
        MyClient = Nothing
    End If
End Sub
```

We also need to instantiate a copy of the `StockClient` form in the form's `Main()` method to kick start the application:

```
Public Shared Sub Main()
    Application.Run(New StockClient())
End Sub
```

Lastly, we need to call the `Application.Exit()` method on the `Click` event of the exit menu item to shut down the application:

```
Private Sub mnuExit_Click(ByVal sender As System.Object, _
                          ByVal e As System.EventArgs) _
```

```
                                    Handles mnuExit.Click
        Application.Exit()
    End Sub
```

We're done with the client portion of the application.

Creating the Server

OK, let's move on to creating the server application. Due to the multi-client nature of the target environment, we have to take a slightly different approach while creating the StockServer application. We want to be able to keep track of clients and know when they connect and disconnect. Client management would be far more effective with the use of a single class instance per client. Therefore, we are going to have to create a separate client class that will represent the clients that are connected to the server as you can see in the UML class diagram below:

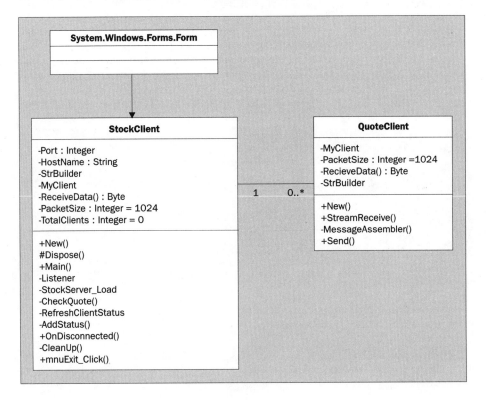

A new instance of the QuoteClient class is created for each new client that connects to the server and so the StockServer class and the QuoteClient class have a one-to-many relationship. The QuoteClient class is always instantiated in a newly spawned thread made to handle the new client that has just connected. The QuoteClient class takes in a TcpClient object, responsible for the new client, as its constructor. We will talk about the QuoteClient class a bit more later on. But first, let's see what the user interface is going to look like. The server application is a bit simpler than the client in terms of the UI. We are going to have a single ListBox control to display some information along with the standard File menu with only the Exit sub item. In addition to those controls, drag and drop a new StatusBar and change its Anchor property to Bottom, Right, such that you can place it in the lower right portion of the form. Be sure to change the name and the text property of the form to StockServer. Your form should now look something like the form below:

We will also need a class module that we will call QuoteClient.vb. This application is going to access a SQL Server database to get the stock quote information, and so we are going to need to make references to the necessary data namespaces in addition to the others shown below:

```
Imports System.Threading
Imports System.Net
Imports System.Net.Sockets
Imports System.Text
Imports System.Configuration
Imports System.Data
Imports System.Data.SqlClient
```

We are also going to need some Private variables that will be used throughout the application. You will see their use as we explore the code for this application:

```
Private ListenerThread As Thread
Private MyListener As TcpListener
Private Port As Integer
Private MyClient As TcpClient
Private TotalClients As Integer = 0
Private Const PacketSize As Integer = 1024
Private ReceiveData(PacketSize) As Byte
```

The server application is going to start running just as soon as it is opened and so we will start by entering some code in the StockServer_Load() method of the application. We will discuss the server's Listener() method, which is the core of the server itself, shortly; but first we start by spawning a new thread to run our Listener() method in the background:

```
Private Sub StockServer_Load(ByVal sender As System.Object, _
                             ByVal e As System.EventArgs) _
                             Handles MyBase.Load
   Dim HostSettings As IDictionary

   Try
      HostSettings = ConfigurationSettings.GetConfig("HostInfo")
      Port = CType(HostSettings("port"), Integer)
      ListenerThread = New Thread(AddressOf Listener)
      ListenerThread.Start()
      RefreshClientStatus()

   Catch ex As Exception
      AddStatus("An error has occurred. The server is not running." + _
                ex.ToString())
      CleanUp()

   Finally
      HostSettings = Nothing

   End Try
End Sub
```

Just as we did in the client application, we assign the port number from the configuration file into the Port variable, which we have already defined. We don't need the host name when creating server listeners since the server itself is the host. Since this application is really two autonomous parts running entirely independently of each other, please be sure to use to the same configuration file for both the client and the server as nothing is going to work if the port numbers of the two applications don't match precisely. If an error occurs, we notify the user by using the AddStatus() method and do some manual cleaning up by calling the CleanUp() method, both of which we will see later. But for now, let's look at the Listener() method:

```
Private Sub Listener()

   Try
      MyListener = New TcpListener(Port)
      MyListener.Start()
```

```
        Dim Message() As Object = _
                        {"Server started. Awaiting new connections..."}
        Me.Invoke(New InvokeStatus(AddressOf Me.AddStatus), Message)

        While (True)
            Dim NewClient As New QuoteClient(MyListener.AcceptTcpClient())
            AddHandler NewClient.Disconnected, AddressOf onDisconnected
            AddHandler NewClient.QuoteArrived, AddressOf CheckQuote

            Dim ConnectMessage() As Object = _
                            {"A new client just connected at " + _
                            Now.ToShortTimeString()}
            Me.Invoke(New InvokeStatus(AddressOf Me.AddStatus), _
                    ConnectMessage)
            TotalClients += 1
            RefreshClientStatus()
        End While

    Catch ex As Exception
        Dim Message() As Object = _
                        {"The server stopped due to an unexpected error" + _
                        vbCrLf + ex.ToString()}
        Me.Invoke(New InvokeStatus(AddressOf Me.AddStatus), Message)

    End Try
End Sub
```

This is a very important part of the server application since it basically represents the underlying engine of our server. As you can see, upon initialization of the port number, we called the `AcceptTcpClient()` method of the `TcpListener` class instance to accept incoming requests for connections. In essence, the `TcpListener` class is the server. It builds upon the `Socket` class to provide TCP services at a higher level of abstraction. However, the reason for spawning a new background thread to handle the `Listener()` method is the `AcceptClient()` method, which is a *synchronous* method that waits for connections while keeping the thread it's running on blocked, therefore we need to run it as a background thread. Once again, since this method is running in a background thread, we need to marshal between the current working thread and the thread in which the UI controls are running by using the `Invoke()` method of the form. We also start the *asynchronous* process of listening for incoming data, which in this case is going to be stock quote requests from the client. In much the same manner as we did in the client application, we will use the `StreamReceive()` method that is located in the `QuoteClient` class:

```
Public Sub StreamReceive(ByVal ar As IAsyncResult)
    Dim ByteCount As Integer

    Try
        SyncLock MyClient.GetStream
            ByteCount = MyClient.GetStream.EndRead(ar)
        End SyncLock
```

```
      If ByteCount < 1 Then
         RaiseEvent Disconnected(Me)
         Exit Sub
      End If

      MessageAssembler(ReceiveData, 0, ByteCount)
      SyncLock MyClient.GetStream
         MyClient.GetStream.BeginRead(ReceiveData, 0, PacketSize, _
                                 AddressOf StreamReceive, Nothing)
      End SyncLock

   Catch ex As Exception
      RaiseEvent Disconnected(Me)

   End Try
End Sub
```

The major difference between this and its sister method in the client application arises from the fact that we are now in a multithreaded, multi-user environment and that we can't just get the default stream and do whatever we want with it. There would be a very good chance of resource collisions, such that while we're reading data from it here, another thread in our server might attempt to send data to that same stream; and so we need to use synchronization. For simple synchronization, we are going to use the keyword SyncLock to lock the requested stream while we read from it. SyncLock is the most basic thread synchronization tool available. Don't forget to use good judgment when it comes to locking resources, as it can be detrimental to your application's performance if used in excess. For more sophisticated and custom tailored thread synchronizations, you can use some of the other classes available in the System.Threading namespace, such as Interlocked, which allows you to increment and decrement interlocks. Other than that, the ReceiveStream() method is more or less the same as the one in the client application.

The MessageAssembler() method also very closely resembles its counterpart defined in the client application. The only difference is that it calls the CheckQuote() method to connect to the database and retrieve the stock quote by raising the QuoteArrived event, which is dealt with in the Listener() method discussed previously .

```
Private Sub MessageAssembler(ByVal Bytes() As Byte, _
                        ByVal offset As Integer, _
                        ByVal count As Integer)
   Dim ByteCount As Integer

   For ByteCount = 0 To count - 1
      If Bytes(ByteCount) = 35 Then 'Check for '#' to signal the end
         RaiseEvent QuoteArrived(Me, StrBuilder.ToString)
         StrBuilder = New StringBuilder()
      Else
         StrBuilder.Append(ChrW(Bytes(ByteCount)))
      End If
   Next
End Sub
```

Before we move on to the CheckQuote() method, let's briefly discuss the data source from which the server retrieves its quote information.

We need to start by creating a SQL Server database called StockDB, which will contain a single table called tbl_stocks with a structure as outlined in the following table.

Database setup and population scripts will be available at the Wrox Press web site http://www.wrox.com along with all the code from the book.

Field	Description
Symbol	The actual stock symbol
Price	The last price of the stock
Change	The price change of the stock
Bid	The last bid price of the stock
Ask	The last bid price of the stock
Volume	The total traded volume of the stock in a trading session

That's all we need for the database so back to the code and the CheckQuote() method. The CheckQuote() method resides in the class module attached to the main form of the application and is called by the local event handler when the QuoteArrive() method is triggered. The role of this method is to make a connection to the database, query it to retrieve the quote information, and pass the data back to the client. You can use the SqlConnection control in Visual Studio .NET and follow the wizards to generate a connection string to the database, or you can simply instantiate the SqlConnection class, which resides in the System.Data.SqlClient namespace, and manually assign it a connection string, as shown here:

```
Private Sub CheckQuote(ByVal sender As QuoteClient, _
                       ByVal stockSymbol As String)

    ' Connection string using SQL Server authentication
    Dim SqlConn As New SqlConnection("Initial Catalog=StockDB;" + _
                    "Data Source=(local);User ID=sa;Password=")

    ' Alternative Connection string using Windows Integrated security
    ' Dim SqlConn As New SqlConnection("Initial Catalog=StockDB;" + _
    '                 "Data Source=(local);Integrated Security=SSPI")

    Dim SqlStr As String = _
                "SELECT symbol, price, change, bid, ask, volume " + _
                "FROM tbl_stocks WHERE symbol='" + stockSymbol + "'"
```

```vb
    Dim SqlCmd As SqlCommand = New SqlCommand(SqlStr, SqlConn)

    Try
      SqlCmd.Connection.Open()

      Dim sqlDataRd As SqlDataReader = SqlCmd.ExecuteReader()
      Dim FieldCount As Integer = 0
      Dim Records As Integer = 0
      Dim TempString As New StringBuilder()

      Do While sqlDataRd.Read()
        For FieldCount = 0 To 5

          TempString.Append(sqlDataRd.GetValue(FieldCount).ToString() _
                            + ",")
          Records += 1
        Next

      Loop
        If Records = 0 Then
          sender.send("-1#")
        Else
          TempString.Replace(",", "#", TempString.Length - 1, 1)
          sender.send(TempString.ToString())
        End If

    Catch sqlEx As SqlException
      Dim Message() As Object = {sqlEx.ToString()}
      Me.Invoke(New InvokeStatus(AddressOf Me.AddStatus), Message)

    Catch ex As Exception
      Dim Message() As Object = _
        {"Unable to retrieve quote information from the Database."}
      Me.Invoke(New InvokeStatus(AddressOf Me.AddStatus), Message)

    Finally
      ' Close the Connection
      If SqlConn.State <> ConnectionState.Closed Then
        SqlConn.Close()
      End If
    End Try
  End Sub
```

We also need a SQL query to return all six fields of the table for the individual stock the client has requested:

```vb
    Dim SqlStr As String = _
              "SELECT symbol, price, change, bid, ask, volume " + _
              "FROM tbl_stocks WHERE symbol='" + stockSymbol + "'"
```

Now that we have the necessary SQL string and connection, we can instantiate the `SqlCommand` and `SqlDataReader` objects to read the data from the database server.

> **If you use any database other than Microsoft SQL Server 7.0/2000, you can't use the `SqlConnection`, `SqlCommand`, or `SqlDataReader` objects since they have been specifically designed for use with the MS SQL Server. You should use the OleDB versions of those classes.**

Finally, we execute the query by creating a new `SqlDataReader` class instance, and setting it to the result of the `ExecuteReader()` method of the `SqlCommand` object. After that, we iterate through each of the columns of returned data and append the values into a `StringBuilder` object, with a comma in between each value. If `ExecuteReader()` does not return any rows of data, then we have to send a string with a value of -1 back to the user to notify them of the non-existence of the requested data. Otherwise, we replace the last comma in the string with a # (to indicate the end of string) and send it back to the client using the `Send()` method. Lastly, we must ensure that the database connection is closed once we're finished with it. As you can see, the code in the `Finally` clause checks to see if the connection to the database is still open. If so, it will close it.

The `Send()` method of the server application resides in the `QuoteClient` class and requires slightly different code from the same method in the client application. The main difference is that we now are going to send the message asynchronously back to the client:

```
Public Sub send(ByVal sendData As String)

    Dim Buffer() As Byte = _
                  System.Text.ASCIIEncoding.ASCII.GetBytes(sendData)
    SyncLock MyClient.GetStream
       MyClient.GetStream.BeginWrite(Buffer, 0, Buffer.Length, _
                                Nothing, Nothing)
    End SyncLock
End Sub
```

The `BeginWrite()` method is quite similar to the `BeginRead()` method in terms of interface. We first have to convert the string message to a byte array, which can be easily accomplished by using the ASCII class in the `System.Text` namespace. Once again, we have to lock the stream to ensure that other threads are not writing to it as well. That's all that is required to asynchronously write the data to the client.

Running the Applications

Build each project in its own instance of Visual Studio.Net and don't forget to include the configuration files that we created earlier in the same directory as the application executables.

OK, let's now run the compiled applications. We need to run the `StockServer.exe` first so that it will start listening for clients:

Now run an instance of the client application. As you probably recall, we had disabled all the UI controls on the form until the user successfully connected to the server. So, let's go ahead and click on the Connect item of the menu:

236

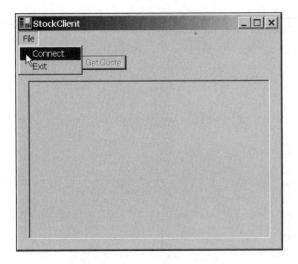

All the controls (except the **Connect** option of the menu) are now enabled and the
`ListView` control has been instantiated with all the right columns. Enter a valid stock
symbol from `tbl_stocks` table. Let's try `CSCO`, for example:

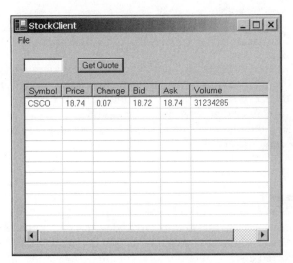

The Stock Server successfully returned a quote and, since the change amount is
positive, the entire row appears in the color green. Let's go ahead and create a few
other instances of the `StockClient` class and see if they all function correctly:

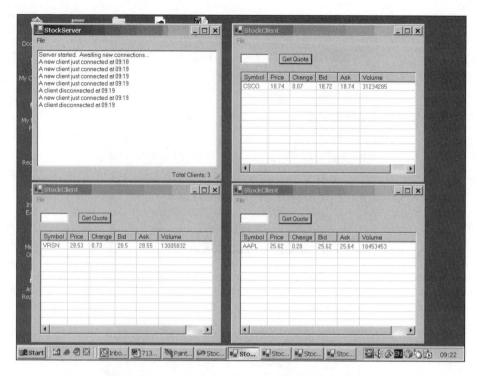

As you can see, the `StockClient` and the `StockServer` applications work very well with each other. The server keeps tracks of how many clients connect and disconnect and displays it in the `ListBox`. In addition, the multithreaded server is very easily able to handle numerous connections, as well as send and receive data in an asynchronous fashion. You can step through the code for both the client and the server application and get a better feel for the application workflow.

Summary

As we have demonstrated, it is straightforward to develop multithreaded network applications with Visual Studio.NET. Much of the plumbing and infrastructure has already been abstracted away in the form of a comprehensive and object-oriented set of classes. For even greater control over the network sockets, the `System.Net.Socket` offers plenty of rich functionality. We also experienced how simple it is to use .NET's intrinsic support for asynchronous operations that run in the background worker thread without much code.

We hope that you found this book both helpful and enjoyable. The extra features in .NET give the Visual Basic developer more power than they have ever had - threading being just one of them.

VB.NET

Threading

Handbook

Appendix

Support, Errata, and Code Download

We always value hearing from our readers, and we want to know what you think about this book and series: what you liked, what you didn't like, and what you think we can do better next time. You can send us your comments, either by returning the reply card in the back of the book, or by e-mailing us at feedback@wrox.com. Please be sure to mention the book title in your message.

How to Download the Sample Code for the Book

When you log on to the Wrox site, http://www.wrox.com/, simply locate the title through our Search facility or by using one of the title lists. Click on Download Code on the book's detail page.

The files that are available for download from our site have been archived using WinZip. When you have saved the attachments to a folder on your hard-drive, you will need to extract the files using WinZip, or a compatible tool. Inside the Zip file will be a folder structure and an HTML file that explains the structure and gives you further information – including links to e-mail support, and suggested further reading.

Errata

We've made every effort to ensure that there are no errors in the text or in the code. However, no one is perfect and mistakes can occur. If you find an error in this book, like a spelling mistake or a faulty piece of code, we would be very grateful for feedback. By sending in errata, you may save another reader hours of frustration, and of course, you will be helping us to provide even higher quality information. Simply e-mail the information to support@wrox.com; your information will be checked and if correct, posted to the errata page for that title.

To find errata on the web site, locate this book on the Wrox web site
(http://www.wrox.com/ACON1.asp?ISBN=1861007132), and click on the Book Errata link on
the book's detail page:

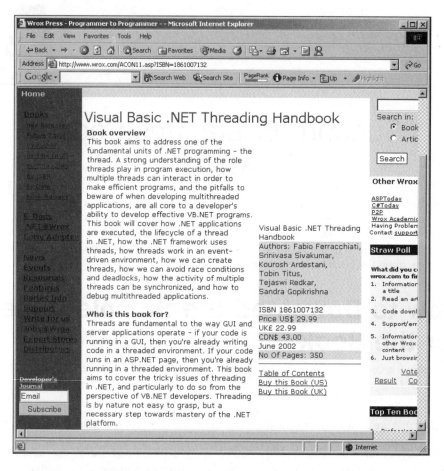

E-Mail Support

If you wish to query a problem in the book with an expert who knows the book in
detail then e-mail support@wrox.com, with the title of the book, and the last four
numbers of the ISBN in the subject field of the e-mail. A typical e-mail should include
the following:

❑   The name, last four digits of the ISBN (7132), and page number of the
    problem, in the Subject field

❑   Your name, contact information, and the problem, in the body of the message

We won't send you junk mail. We need the details to save your time and ours. When you send an e-mail message, it will go through the following chain of support:

❑ **Customer Support**

Your message is delivered to our customer support staff. They have files on most frequently asked questions and will answer anything general about the book or the web site immediately.

❑ **Editorial**

More in-depth queries are forwarded to the technical editor responsible for that book. They have experience with the programming language or particular product, and are able to answer detailed technical questions on the subject. Once an issue has been resolved, the editor can post the errata to the web site.

❑ **The Authors**

Finally, in the unlikely event that the editor cannot answer your problem, they will forward the request to the author. We do try to protect the author from any distractions to their writing (or programming); however, we are quite happy to forward specific requests to them. All Wrox authors help with the support on their books. They will e-mail the customer and the editor with their response, and again all readers should benefit

The Wrox support process can only offer support for issues that are directly pertinent to the content of our published title. Support for questions that fall outside the scope of normal book support, is provided via our P2P community lists – http://p2p.wrox.com/forum.

p2p.wrox.com

For author and peer discussion, join the P2P mailing lists. Our unique system provides Programmer to Programmer™ contact on mailing lists, forums, and newsgroups, all in addition to our one-to-one e-mail support system. Be confident that the many Wrox authors and other industry experts who are present on our mailing lists are examining any queries posted. At http://p2p.wrox.com/, you will find a number of different lists that will help you, not only while you read this book, but also as you develop your own applications.

To subscribe to a mailing list just follow these steps:

❑ Go to http://p2p.wrox.com/

❑ Choose the appropriate category from the left menu bar

❑ Click on the mailing list you wish to join

❑   Follow the instructions to subscribe and fill in your e-mail address and password

❑   Reply to the confirmation e-mail you receive

❑   Use the subscription manager to join more lists and set your mail preferences

VB.NET

Threading

Handbook

Index

Index

A Guide to the Index

The index is arranged hierarchically, in alphabetical order, with symbols preceding the letter A. Most second-level entries and many third-level entries also occur as first-level entries. This is to ensure that users will find the information they require however they choose to search for it.

Q

U

V

W